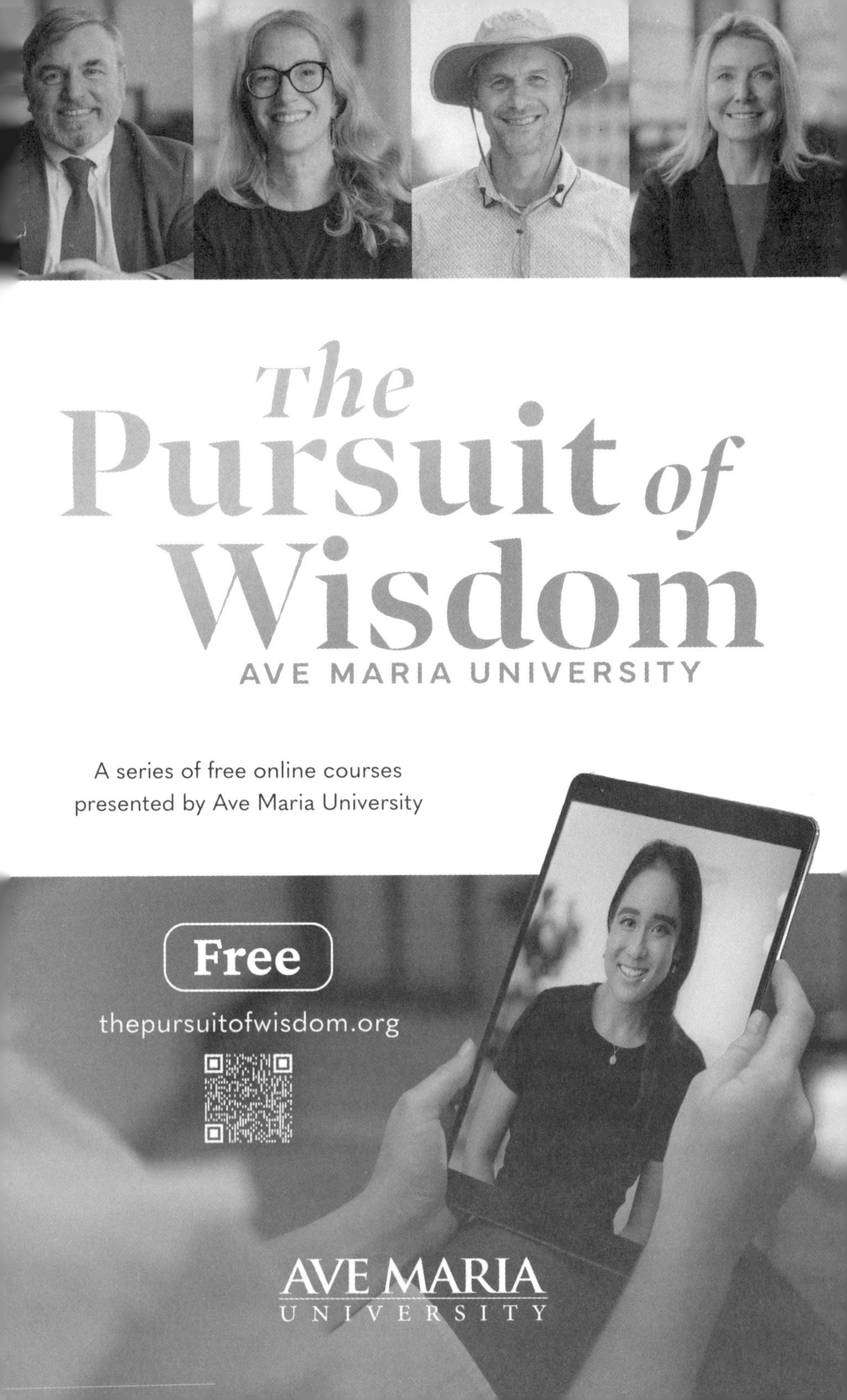
The Pursuit of Wisdom
AVE MARIA UNIVERSITY
A series of free online courses presented by Ave Maria University
Free
thepursuitofwisdom.org
AVE MARIA
UNIVERSITY

Praise for *A Lamp in the Darkness*

Anne Hendershott has once again written a brilliant book that accurately and vividly captures the true state of affairs within Catholic higher education. With that said, the good news is that she proceeds to articulate a genuine reason for hope that exists, as she highlights what a number of truly faithful Catholic colleges and universities are doing to be countercultural . . . to indeed be beacons of hope for students, parents, and other institutions who are searching for authentic Catholic education.

—***Tom Monaghan,*** Founder & Chancellor, Ave Maria University

"This is the most searing, and well-deserved, indictment of the current state of Catholic higher education in print. Hendershott speaks with authority when she notes that the Catholic temptation to be affirmed by secular elites frequently proves to be overwhelming and disastrous in the end. She is not a pessimist. She nicely chronicles those institutions that are true to Catholicism, detailing how some that have gone awry have been rejuvenated. Her cogent analysis, peppered with evidence, should be read by all Catholic parents considering a Catholic college or university for their children. She has done the Catholic community a wonderful favor by writing this book."

— ***Bill Donohue,*** President, Catholic League

"The pages that unfold in this master work on Catholic higher education manifest the keen and piercing intellect of its author, Dr. Anne Hendershott. The sheer complexity and volume of issues that led to the rise, the fall, and the slow recovery of Catholic universities and colleges, requires extraordinary mastery of the material. In the last analysis, Catholic orthodoxy will be victorious because truth is the lamp that cannot be extinguished."

— ***Dr. Charles P. Nemeth,*** Professor and Program Director of Criminal Justice, Franciscan University of Steubenville

"Anne Hendershott's *A Lamp In the Darkness* powerfully and insightfully describes and dissects the enormous, disturbing drift of the vast majority of professed Roman Catholic colleges and universities away from fidelity to Catholic doctrine and practice, looking at not only the 'what' but also the 'how' and the 'why' for the decline of faithfully Catholic higher education in the United States. But she also explores, in depth, the few, mostly relatively young, intrepid, faithfully Catholic colleges and universities that really are lamps in the darkness, supporting and serving their Church. This fascinating book is a must-read for all who care about truly Catholic higher education in the United States, and, frankly, it is also extremely instructive for those trying to advance and preserve orthodox Christian higher education outside the Roman Catholic Church."

— ***Dr. David Ayers,*** Professor of Sociology, Grove City College

"Anne Hendershott is a treasure to the Catholic Church in America. This lucidly argued book is Exhibit A: essential for Catholic educators everywhere and at every level."

— ***Sohrab Ahmari,*** Bestselling author,
From Fire, by Water and *The Unbroken Thread*

Dr. Anne Hendershott

A LAMP *in the* DARKNESS

How Faithful Catholic Colleges Are Helping to Save the Church

SOPHIA INSTITUTE PRESS
Manchester, New Hampshire

Cover by LUCAS Art & Design, Jenison, MI.

Cover image: Ave Maria University Students at Easter
Vigil Mass courtesy of Ave Maria University

Sophia Institute Press
Box 5284, Manchester, NH 03108
1-800-888-9344
www.SophiaInstitute.com

Sophia Institute Press is a registered trademark of Sophia Institute.

paperback ISBN 979-8-88911-380-5

ebook ISBN 979-8-88911-381-2

Library of Congress Control Number: 2024946126

First printing

Acknowledgments

I began this project in 2022, excited about the special role that Franciscan University of Steubenville continues to play in the New Evangelization of our Church, and grateful for the blessings I have received by being a small part of that revitalization of the Faith during my years at Franciscan. I have been encouraged by a number of individuals on campus and off who have inspired and supported me throughout my project to identify the ways in which faithful Catholic colleges and universities are helping to rebuild the Church.

A special thank you to Tom Monaghan, founder of Ave Maria University, whose humble faith and boundless enthusiasm for faithful Catholic higher education continues to inspire me. His life is a model of sacrifice and holiness as he provides a faithful witness to the transformative power of the gospel. I am most grateful for his encouragement and support for this project.

Thank you also to Mark Middendorf, president of Ave Maria University, for his enthusiastic response to our proposal and to Joseph Pearce for his brilliant ideas and assistance in crafting this book to final form. I am also grateful to Carl Olson, editor of *Catholic World Report,* and Eric Sammons, editor of *Crisis Magazine,* for their willingness to publish my ideas and theories in the early stages of this project. And, most importantly, thank you to the Franciscan University community for finding a way to allow me to become a contributor to the commitment Franciscan has made to the New Evangelization.

Finally, I am deeply grateful to David Willey, for all his hard work on this project and for bringing a great love for the Faith to it. David joined me early in the book's development and provided thoughtful insight and assistance during my preparation of this work. His contributions to chapters 2 and 5 in particular have been invaluable, in addition to his general involvement in researching and editing. I appreciate all his hard work.

Nor do men light a lamp and put it under a bushel, but on a stand, and it gives light to all in the house. Let your light so shine before men, that they may see your good works and give glory to your Father who is in heaven.

— Matthew 5:15–16

The rash traveler looks for his companions. He understands, then, that it is God's good pleasure that he be alone amid torments, and he goes on into the black immensity, bearing his heart before him like a torch!

— Leon Bloy, *Pilgrim of the Absolute*

Contents

Acknowledgments v
Introduction: Lamps in the Darkness 3
1. "A Smoldering Wick": How Most Catholic Universities Lost Their Way .27
2. Reclaiming a Catholic Mission 53
3. Letting the Fire Fall at Franciscan University of Steubenville 79
4. Led by the Spirit at Ave Maria University 97
5. Seeing Things as They Are: Liberal Arts at the Faithful Schools 119
6. "In the Light of the Spirit": The Struggle for Academic Freedom 145
7. The Sanctuary Lamp: The Culture of Worship at the Faithful Few. . . .173
8. Responding to the Secularizing Threats to the Faithful Few. 193
9. How Darkness Entered the Once-Faithful Colleges. 231
10. Keeping the Light of Christ at the Faithful Few 263
Sirach 51:13–30 305
About the Author 307

A Lamp in the Darkness

Introduction: Lamps in the Darkness

Why This Book?

Dr. Derry Connolly, the president of John Paul the Great Catholic University in San Diego, recalls a profound experience during a short visit he made in 2000 to Franciscan University of Steubenville. He was sitting in front of the Blessed Sacrament in the Portiuncula chapel on campus — a campus known for the dynamic orthodoxy of its student body — and he "felt the Lord place on my heart the request to build a university like Franciscan in San Diego." A few years later, he recalled his Franciscan experience as a moment that filled him with "joy and light."

It is not a surprise that Dr. Connolly's profound encounter with the Divine occurred in the Portiuncula, where Eucharistic Adoration is held all day and all night — for twenty-four hours each day — throughout the school year. He said he was grateful that God had touched his heart in this way, but he was also filled with the uncertainty of wondering how he could possibly do such a thing: "A university is too big and too expensive. And I don't know how to do it."[1]

[1] Conversation between Anne Hendershott and Derry Connelly on the campus of the University of San Diego, 2002.

To most of us who knew him at the time, it seemed impossible. But, as we would find out, God knew how to help him. In 2006, just a few years after his experience on that chilly November day in the Portiuncula, Connolly had located a building, gathered a cadre of dedicated Catholic professors who were experts in their crafts, and welcomed the first class of college students at John Paul the Great Catholic University.

Today, this school is a faithful Catholic university whose core purpose is to impact the culture for Christ by forming students as creators, leaders, and entrepreneurs in the creative arts and in business innovation, all while ensuring that they are steeped in the Catholic Faith and intellectual tradition. Since its founding, John Paul the Great has celebrated the achievements of more than seven hundred graduates, men and women who have gone on to impact culture in the entertainment industry of Hollywood and New York City, in the gaming world, in the corporate and tech worlds — and even in the religious life.

This book is about moments like the one Derry Connolly experienced at Franciscan. It is also the story of the colleges popularly known as the "*Newman Guide* schools," and the fight that these colleges have been engaged in to stay faithful to the mission of the Church. *The Newman Guide*, which has been published by the Cardinal Newman Society every year since 2007, provides detailed reports on universities and colleges that enable families to provide their children with an authentic Catholic education.[2] These schools, which we have collectively named "the faithful few," include:

2 Although we have been guided in our selection of the faithful few by the Cardinal Newman Society's *The Newman Guide*, a publication listing the faithful Catholic colleges and universities, we have done our own research and compiled our own list for our current book. Still, we are indebted to the Cardinal Newman Society for the guidance they have

Ave Maria University, Florida
Belmont Abbey College, North Carolina
Benedictine College, Kansas
The Catholic University of America, Washington, D.C. (CUA)
Christendom College, Virginia
Franciscan University of Steubenville, Ohio
John Paul the Great Catholic University, California
Thomas Aquinas College, California (TAC)
Thomas More College of Liberal Arts, New Hampshire
University of Dallas, Texas (UD)
University of Mary, North Dakota
University of St. Thomas, Texas
Walsh University, Ohio
Wyoming Catholic College, Wyoming.[3]

The following chapters will discuss how these faithful few *Newman Guide* institutions have resisted attacks and stayed true in their mission, their education, and their liturgies, to the magisterial teachings of the Church. These schools have made significant sacrifices to continue providing students with a faithful Catholic education that not only prepares them for careers but also prepares them to live lives of integrity, goodness, holiness, and authenticity. When any of these schools have fallen short — as some of them have — they have quickly recovered, because they have never lost sight of the salvific mission of authentic Catholic higher education. Many of these colleges, like Christendom, Thomas More, and TAC, were born from the ashes of

provided since 1993 in identifying the "exemplary Catholic educators and institutions committed to truth and the integral formation of their students." *The Newman Guide* reaches over 75,000 families online every year and has now served generations of families, helping them to make informed choices regarding faithful Catholic higher education.

3 There are other institutions on the *Newman Guide* list; however, in this book, we focus exclusively on American Catholic colleges and universities.

the secular revolution that gripped the Church following Vatican II and have become some of the most faithful Catholic colleges in the country. Others, like Belmont, Franciscan, CUA, and UD, were founded earlier, in the late nineteenth or early-to-mid twentieth centuries, but have each, in their own way, sought continuous renewal in faithfulness and mission-orientation. All of these schools continue to attract students who desire an authentically Catholic education, who come to them because they want to be a part of a faith-filled community that enriches their lives.

Franciscan University of Steubenville: An Exemplar of Renewal

Although this is not a book specifically about Franciscan, the renewal of orthodoxy on Catholic colleges and universities cannot be properly understood without acknowledging the important role played by that university. In a 2021 interview with Dr. Scott Hahn, a theology professor at Franciscan, Monsignor James P. Shea, the president of the University of Mary, North Dakota — one of the faithful Catholic universities profiled in these pages — spoke of the "ripple effect" of Franciscan University on his own campus: "What does St. Thomas say? *Bonum diffusivum sui* — the good is diffusive of itself. The ripples of the renewal of Catholic higher education, of which Steubenville is an exemplar, are felt all around. The students that we get to serve here at the University of Mary are recipients of that as well, and so I'm grateful.... May we be worthy of that legacy."[4]

Still, as the following pages will show, Franciscan University was not always the "passionately Catholic" place that it is today. It was not

[4] "Memories of Father Michael Scanlan with Scott Hahn and Monsignor Shea," Prime Matters, June 10, 2021, https://primematters.com/perspectives/memories-father-michael-scanlan-scott-hahn-and-monsignor-shea.

always a center of a dynamic orthodoxy that is "diffusive of itself." In fact, during the late 1960s and early 1970s, when it was still called the College of Steubenville, the struggling school was known as one of the premier party schools in the country, featuring a hook-up culture that involved heavy alcohol and drug use. Established in 1946 by Franciscans of the Third Order Regular (T.O.R.), the school had lost its way and was on the verge of collapse in the early 1970s. But in 1974, with the arrival of the university's dynamic new president, Father Michael Scanlan, the later renamed Franciscan University of Steubenville became a vibrant center of Catholic orthodoxy.

Recalling these early days in his autobiography, *Let the Fire Fall,* Father Scanlan wrote:

> The school was in trouble because academic concerns and money worries were taking everyone's attention. Spiritual matters had to take priority. Not only did we need to restore the college's Franciscan Catholic identity in all its historic splendor, but a vibrant dynamic Christian faith had to dominate and shape the environment.... To accomplish this, I said I would lead an effort to return the college to the spirit of the first Franciscans. Francis and his followers were charismatic, so I would cultivate a strong charismatic presence on campus.[5]

During his tenure as president, from 1974 to 2000, Father Mike, as he was affectionately known by the students, emphasized spiritual concerns and stressed the role of campus ministry and student communal life in the daily lives of the students. His first priority was establishing a spiritual culture on a campus where faith had all but

[5] Michael Scanlan, T.O.R., *Let the Fire Fall* (Ann Arbor, MI: Servant Books, 1986), 146.

disappeared. Father Mike always believed that academic excellence would come once the spiritual battles were won, and he was right about that; since then, Franciscan's commitment to academic excellence has grown strong.

The transformation effected by Father Mike inspired several leaders of the schools we will discuss in the following chapters, some of whom continue to look to him for inspiration today. In their interview, Monsignor Shea told Scott Hahn that he still looks to Father Mike for guidance: "I have the holy card from his funeral, and every now and then when I'm having a hard time, because the administration of a Catholic university is no easy task and probably nobody knew it better than him, I'll take it out and consider the contribution that he made to Catholic higher education. And not just the concrete contributions, but the manner in which he made them and the way in which he followed the Holy Spirit."[6]

The ripple effect continues. One person who was inspired by Father Mike was Tom Monaghan, who, in 1986, while still at the helm as president of Domino's Pizza, Inc., provided the following endorsement for the back cover of Father Scanlan's book *Let the Fire Fall*: "This book has given me inspiration and a road map for my life. Never in one book have I learned so much about my religion and how to live it. Now I will follow Father Scanlan's advice and get into the greatest book — the Bible." Monaghan's inspiration was just as concrete as Derry Connolly's was, and as Monsignor Shea's is today; he really did use the book as a "road map," creating Ave Maria Law School, and later Ave Maria University, as a way to honor God. The formation of these new, faithful Catholic colleges and universities were not vanity projects, but had instead a truly transcendent goal. Both vibrantly Catholic and faithful to the Magisterium, these

6 "Memories of Father Michael Scanlan."

schools exist, as Tom Monaghan often says, "to help as many people as possible get into heaven."

The Open Circle: The Fault Line in Catholic Higher Education

By the 1970s, the fallout of Vatican II had begun to hollow out much of what was distinctive about Catholic colleges and universities. Most had started downplaying their Catholic identity by becoming more ecumenical and accepting of theological differences in an effort to broaden their reach and out of a fear of marginalizing outsiders. This attitude continues today. In *The Future of Catholic Higher Education: The Open Circle* the Marianist Father James L. Heft, who heads the Institute for Advanced Catholic Studies at the secular University of Southern California, argues that the "open circle" is key to the survival and flourishing of Catholic colleges and universities. For Father Heft, "Catholic universities must welcome not only Catholic intellectuals, without whom it is impossible to have a Catholic university, but also as full and equal partners, faculty and staff of other faiths and even no religion who nonetheless support in various ways the mission of the university. A Catholic university should be an open circle."[7] As a recent work in the field, and a publication by a distinguished Catholic author, this book serves as an excellent framework within which the identity crisis of Catholic universities can be understood.

Heft opens his book by framing his own view as a medium between two extremes in the "post-Vatican II debate." At one extreme are university models described as the "marketplace of ideas" and at the other extreme are university models described as "the closed circle." He rejects the marketplace model, in which "all ideas are

[7] James L. Heft, S.M., *The Future of Catholic Higher Education: The Open Circle* (New York: Oxford University Press, 2021), 100.

examined and debated, and the institution takes no position itself" because "it is hard, if not impossible, to think without presuppositions." He contrasts this with the "closed circle model," which requires that schools maintain "full agreement on all significant aspects 'related to' the religious mission of their institution, only allow on campus speakers who represent their version of Catholic teaching, and locate their Catholicity primarily in moral teachings, fully reinforced by campus ministry and the theology department: no disagreement is permitted." For these schools, "fidelity to the Catholic tradition as interpreted by the magisterium represents the only reliable indicator of orthodoxy." He also criticizes these schools for being primarily or entirely composed of Catholics.[8]

Meanwhile, Heft's ideal American Catholic university is an "open circle" institution that will both "foster and engage critically a particular tradition, the Catholic intellectual tradition" while "seeking truth wherever it can be found, be it in the study of other religions or welcoming scholars from other religions as colleagues."[9]

Calling for a mixture of both Catholic and non-Catholic or even non-religious faculty, Heft writes that "Catholic universities need faculty who believe that a religious university makes a valuable contribution to the pluralism of American higher education." However, in practice, what a recognition of "valuable contribution" amounts to are faculty who have endorsed the classically liberal view of the Church as a voice among many, a contributor and sometimes an ally, but certainly not a teacher of modern culture. He extends his "open circle" idea further when talking of the attitude that is embraced at the institute where he currently works: "Independence for an institute for advanced studies is critically

[8] Ibid., 127.

[9] Ibid., 127–28.

important; without independence, it has no credibility. While every university has its propaganda, locating a Catholic research institute at a non-religiously affiliated research university offers both the appearance and the reality of more independence than would be the case if we had located [it] at a Catholic university."[10]

He later lists the "unique" Catholic contribution to a pluralistic culture as "the centrality of the person, the importance of community, and the search for wisdom," and calls on university leadership to "never tire of articulating the vision that makes Catholic colleges and universities a valuable and distinctive contribution to the pluralism of higher education in the United States."[11] However, Heft fails to recognize that there is nothing distinct or unique in the twenty-first century in an emphasis on the person, community, or "the search for wisdom." These talking points are as equally at home in a radically leftist institution as in a Catholic university. His emphasis on the Catholic university's "contribution to pluralism" shows an unfortunate lack of faith in any of the definitive truth claims made by the Church. However, Catholicism is decidedly non-pluralistic in the claims that it makes to the truth and in the beliefs it requires the faithful to accept.

Defending his use of "the Catholic intellectual tradition" instead of "Catholicism" as the criterion for Catholic universities (a topic he woefully delays discussing until the end of the book), Heft says he is trying to avoid the idea of a faith that is "only personal and private, or worse yet, superstitious and anti-intellectual."[12] However, doing this allows him to sidestep any emphasis on dogmatic orthodoxy, and so any concrete fidelity to the Church, in favor of an amorphous "tradition" which can be enriched and

[10] Ibid., 12.

[11] Ibid., 223.

[12] Ibid., 234.

developed by intellectual cross-pollination with non-Catholic cultures. Here, however, Father Heft would have been wise to pay greater attention to the late, great Don J. Briel, who wrote extensively on Catholic higher education and was the founder of the original and influential Catholic Studies program located in the University of St. Thomas, Minnesota. In his essay "The University Needs the Church," Briel wrote, "The Catholic intellectual tradition is ultimately inseparable from the deepest insights, convictions and assertions of the Catholic faith and it is in this sense that one must say that without the Church, the Catholic intellectual tradition is not only something relatively trivial, it is ultimately unintelligible."[13]

Heft, who only briefly references Don Briel before dismissing his concerns about the faithfulness of Catholic universities, would presumably assign him to the category of "sectarian" extremists, along with those who hold as a matter of faith that the Church is the guardian and defender of revealed truth. Indeed, unless we are to believe that Heft's critique of "closed circle" colleges is mere tilting at windmills, we can only assume that he has in mind places such as Ave, Franciscan, and John Paul. It is these schools which hold a firm institutional commitment to the living Catholic tradition guided by the Magisterium, and where most faculty are orthodox Catholics.

The fruits of the "open circle" model are clear, however, despite the hopeful Father Heft concluding his book on a note of optimism. It doesn't take long for Catholic universities who define their achievements in terms of their contribution to pluralism to end up downplaying their religious commitment and abandoning faithfulness to the Magisterium. Tragically, most once-Catholic universities

[13] Don J. Briel, *The University and the Church: Don J. Briel's Essays on Education*, ed. R. Jared Staudt (Providence, RI: Cluny Media, 2019), 91.

have capitulated to the enemy in the name of inclusion, adopting a curriculum and culture of atheism, modernism, and anti-gospel beliefs. Studies have shown that up to 85 percent of previously engaged Christian youth become disengaged with their faith as they transition into adulthood, renouncing years of formation from their parents.[14] Perhaps this explains the quote somewhat dubiously attributed to Ven. Fulton Sheen: "If you want your children to fight for their faith, send them to public school. If you want them to lose their faith, send them to Catholic school."[15]

A Road Map of This Book

This book tells the stories of those schools which have rejected the "open circle" model, believing instead that a faithful Catholic college needs to have faithful Catholic faculty members who are fully engaged in fulfilling the mission of the Catholic Church. This mission, as Ven. Fulton Sheen observed, involves the salvation of the soul of each child passing through the university, as well as a continued institutional faithfulness to the Church.

If it is to be of help to the Church and society, Pope St. John Paul II insisted that a faithful Catholic university "must have the courage to speak uncomfortable truths which do not please public opinion, but which are necessary to safeguard the authentic good of society."[16] That call to courage is a stumbling block for the "Catholic in name

14 Kelly Salomon, "CNS Launches Newman Guide Recognition for Schools, Graduate Programs," Cardinal Newman Society, June 19, 2023, https://cardinalnewmansociety.org/cns-launches-newman-guide-recognition-for-schools-graduate-programs/.

15 Father Horton, "Fulton Sheen and Catholic Schools," *Fauxtations: Because Sometimes the Internet Is Wrong*, November 11, 2014, https://fauxtations.wordpress.com/2014/11/11/fulton-sheen-and-catholic-schools/.

16 Pope John Paul II, apostolic constitution *Ex Corde Ecclesiae* (From the Heart of the Church) (August 15, 1990), no. 32.

only" colleges and universities that are afraid of speaking unpopular and uncomfortable truths about such matters as, to name just a few, the sanctity of marriage, sexuality, "reproductive rights" and abortion, sexual orientation, and most recently, gender identity.

The following pages will explore how the faithful few are bringing these sometimes uncomfortable truths into all areas of society. Each of these faithful schools was born, or born-again, from a crisis of truth and faith on Catholic campuses. Courageous leaders like Father Scanlan, Warren Carroll, Ronald McArthur, Tom Monaghan, Timothy T. O'Donnell, Derry Connolly, and Monsignor Shea have shown us that the fight for Catholic higher education can be won. These visionaries demonstrated their willingness to take on the burden and the joy of creating Catholic higher education in a manner that is worthy of Pope St. John Paul II's description of Catholic universities as born *ex corde ecclesiae*, "from the heart of the Church." Their stories are inspiring, and sometimes frustrating. They faced, and continue to face, attacks both from within and outside the walls of these faithful schools, as they continue their commitment to save the souls of the students entrusted to them. The stories in these pages will demonstrate that there is a fierce battle at today's Catholic universities; this battle for Catholic identity is being waged "against the principalities, against the powers, against the world rulers of this present darkness, against the spiritual hosts of wickedness in the heavenly places" (Eph. 6:12).

Chapter 1 provides some background to the current state of Catholic higher education and the decline in faithfulness among most colleges and universities. The story of how the "open circle" mentality, coinciding with a theological and social revolution, helped to secularize the vast majority of Catholic universities, has been told in greater detail elsewhere.[17] However, this chapter sketches the landscape to give an account both of the contentious history of mainstream Catholic higher education and some of the contributing factors that led these schools to lose their way.

Chapter 2 explores the role that vision and mission play in the culture of the faithful few. We discuss the evangelical character that informs the missions of these schools and the emphasis that each school places on the centrality of Jesus Christ. In the first third of the chapter, we take a close look at what Pope St. John Paul II has to say about mission in *Ex Corde Ecclesiae,* his 1990 apostolic constitution on the nature and duties of Catholic universities. Then, after a brief contrast to illustrate how most Catholic universities and colleges systematically weakened their mission statements, we walk through the statements of each of the faithful few. This chapter provides an essential foundation to the rest of the book, because a school's orientation and impetus to be faithful flow from its mission statement. The mission statement of each school becomes the standard by which we can judge whether or not it is faithfully executing its dual role as an institution of both faith and learning.

Chapters 3 and 4 provide concrete examples of how these missions have been lived out by taking a closer look at two schools in

[17] I provide a thorough account of the dire state of most modern institutions of Catholic higher education in my previous book: Anne Hendershott, *Status Envy: The Politics of Catholic Higher Education* (New York: Routledge, 2009). I am grateful for the permission to use some material from that book in chapters 1 and 2 of this volume (reproduced by permission of Taylor & Francis Group). See also James Tunstead Burtchaell, C.S.C., *The Dying of the Light: The Disengagement of Colleges and Universities from Their Christian Churches* (Grand Rapids, MI: Eerdmans, 1998). George Marsden charts a similar secularization story among non-Catholic universities in *The Soul of the American University: From Protestant Establishment to Established Nonbelief* (New York: Oxford University Press, 1994).

particular. In chapter 3, we tell the exciting story of how Father Mike Scanlan took Franciscan University from a failing party school that was about to be shuttered to one of the most well-known schools in the *Newman Guide* and a leader in faithful Catholic circles. Next, in chapter 4, we recount the inspiring story of Tom Monaghan, the billionaire who used his fortune to build Ave Maria University, a deeply faithful and visionary school just north of the everglades in Florida. These chapters show the importance of charismatic leadership, as well as foregrounding the need for courage in the face of overwhelming opposition. Most importantly, however, these chapters reveal how much can be accomplished when men of faith put their trust wholly in God's providence. Both of these men were highly improbable leaders of Catholic universities, yet their faithful yes to God has transformed the lives of tens of thousands of students and brought countless souls to Christ. These chapters also provide complementary examples of how faithful schools develop under very different circumstances. One was started with a strong vision and plan in mind, while the other had to undergo a great revival to restore its identity as a Catholic university. Telling these stories in conjunction illustrates different paths that leaders can take toward creating strong, faithful institutions. Readers will no doubt notice that Franciscan and Ave Maria are featured prominently, both in these dedicated chapters and across the rest of our book. This is less to elevate them above the other faithful few and more simply a choice we made; we are connected personally with these two schools and have chosen to write most about what we know best.

Chapter 5 discusses the liberal arts in the faithful few. The first section of the chapter considers the liberal arts in the classical mode as the "essential form of education for a free people,"[18] and then how

[18] Patrick Deneen, *Why Liberalism Failed* (New Haven, CT: Yale University Press, 2018), 13.

Christianity fulfilled the classical model by placing an encounter with Christ at the heart of the liberal education. The second part of the chapter dives into the specific approach to the liberal arts as taken by three schools: Thomas Aquinas College, Thomas More College, and the University of Dallas. Each school demonstrates a particular approach to a Catholic liberal education, ranging from an exclusively Great Books liberal arts curriculum to a liberal arts core combined with a range of majors and graduate programs. Yet each school models a faithful liberal arts vision rooted in tradition.

Chapter 6 looks closely at how the faithful few have navigated the topic of academic freedom. There is almost no thornier subject for a school, as it lives out its dual institutional vocations as university and as Catholic, than how to understand academic freedom. To address this problem, we turn again to *Ex Corde Ecclesiae,* as well as to canon law and the writings of theologians on this topic. The chapter also provides specific examples from the faithful schools to help clarify how a Catholic institution ought to approach academic freedom. Ultimately, we argue, academic freedom can only be properly understood in relation to divine revelation, which provides the justification as well as the constraints for fully exercising this freedom. As part of this discussion, the role of tenure on the campuses of the faithful schools is explored, as questions around the role of tenure go hand in hand with those of academic freedom.

Chapter 7 turns to the important topic of liturgy and the culture of worship on the campuses of the faithful few. Each of these schools understands that a university should form the whole person, because faith and reason are the "two wings on which the human spirit rises to the contemplation of truth."[19] These schools,

[19] John Paul II, encyclical letter *Fides et Ratio* (Faith and Reason) (September 14, 1998), Prologue.

following in the tradition of Cardinal John Henry Newman, know that they must nourish faith outside as well as inside the classroom, and so they provide ample opportunities for spiritual formation and access to the sacraments. This chapter also identifies some of these opportunities with testimonies from students who shared how deeply influenced they were by the liturgical life at these faithful schools. The chapter opens and closes with a discussion of Christendom's new Christ the King Chapel, as it is a magnificent tribute from the college to the glory of God.

In chapters 8 and 9, discussion turns from foundational topics like liturgy and curricula to take a closer look at the pressures these schools face on a daily basis. Chapter 8 identifies some of the attacks on the faithful few. As the chapter reveals, attacks mostly come from small, organized groups of alumni aggressively lobbying the colleges. These attacks most frequently are driven by a desire to liberalize school Lesbian, Gay, Bisexual, Transgender (LGBT) policies, though they have also involved the issues of abortion, academic freedom, and the pressure to downplay Catholic identity. It is important to reveal the pressure points these schools face, in the hope that "forewarned is forearmed" and that these stories might provide insight into those areas of Catholic institutions which are frequently threatened.

Chapter 9 looks at some schools where these attacks have been successful. This chapter profiles some of the formerly faithful colleges that used to be listed on the *Newman Guide* but, in the past fifteen years, have succumbed to the pressure to compromise. In many ways, this is the saddest chapter in the book. However, it is also one of hope. We tell these stories partly as a reminder that secularization is never inevitable, however frequently it is cast under the name of "progress" or "zeitgeist." These delisted schools had concrete reasons why, and particular moments when, they compromised their identity as Catholic institutions of higher education. Whether the individuals who made these decisions made them in genuine antagonism to Catholic teaching, or simply from moments of cowardice or timidity, these particular schools are a reminder of what is at stake in the fight to keep schools faithful to their missions. Hopefully this chapter provides a moment to pause and consider the nature of this struggle — before concluding with a more optimistic outlook for the future of faithful Catholic higher education and the important role it plays in the flourishing of our Church.

To be sure, the final chapter offers conclusions from the preceding chapters and takes stock of the current situation in Catholic higher education. It describes the difference between the faithful schools and their liberalized Catholic counterparts in terms of the practice of the Faith. Though the faithful few are distinct from one another, they are unified in that all of their actions are guided by Catholic doctrine. Conversely, most Catholic colleges maintain the name *Catholic* while keeping their Catholic commitments as abstract as possible. Ultimately, like so many divisions in Christianity, the divisions in this book can be reduced to the Incarnation. The faithful few genuinely seek to live incarnationally by letting Christ shape every part of campus life, while the schools that have departed this modus operandi have done so by limiting the ways He shapes campus life. Of course, it is impossible to touch on every element of a university, or a group of universities, as it relates to Catholic identity, and we do not attempt such a task. However, in the last section of chapter 10, I identify some foundational "rocks" that the faithful few should build upon to continue strengthening their Catholic identities.

There are two important features of the *Newman Guide* schools, as these characteristics set the schools apart from their counterparts. These two features are first, the institutional fidelity that maintains the mission of each school, and second, the liturgical character which lies at the heart of each school.

Institutional Fidelity at the Faithful Few

The late Monsignor George A. Kelly, one of the founders of the Fellowship of Catholic Scholars and a professor at St. John's University in New York City, devoted several essays to lamenting the widespread loss of the "institutional commitment to the teaching authority, or magisterium of the Church." Kelly warned that "the alienation of a college from the religious body that gave it birth necessarily facilitates the alienation of those whom it trains. At the very minimum, the doctrines and pieties of the Church are no longer controlling.... Authentic Catholic faith may be taught correctly in such an institution but no longer as uniquely true; it can just as easily be poorly taught, dissented from, or rejected outright."[20]

It is precisely an adherence to Kelly's concept of the "unique truthfulness" of Catholicism, handed down through the Church's apostolic tradition, that sets the *Newman Guide* schools apart from other Catholic institutions of higher education. The purpose of this book is not to set these schools on a pedestal or to claim that they are without their problems. As future chapters reveal, many of these schools have struggled with besetting difficulties, the temptation to compromise, and even scandals. What makes these schools different is their commitment to Catholic moral teaching and doctrine at the institutional level. This is the standard to which they hold themselves and to which they are held by others; when they slip up, they are critiqued from this vantage point.

When Pope St. John Paul II released *Ex Corde Ecclesiae* in 1990, he renewed the call for Catholic colleges to be faithful to their

[20] Msgr. George A. Kelly, "The Catholic College: Death, Judgment, Resurrection," *Crisis*, March 1, 1987, https://www.crisismagazine.com/1987/the-catholic-college-death-judgment-resurrection.

Catholic mission and accountable to their local bishops.[21] Fiercely resisted by most Catholic college presidents and faculty members, most of whom viewed *Ex Corde Ecclesiae* as a threat to their academic freedom, it took over a decade for Catholic colleges and universities to even consider implementing it. It remains ignored on most Catholic campuses — except for those of the faithful few.

Most colleges and universities have refused to give support to the Church and have ignored every aspect of *Ex Corde Ecclesiae*. Only the faithful few Catholic colleges and universities profiled in this book embraced the papal document, implementing it to shape all aspects of student life, spiritual life, and the curriculum on their campuses. Rejecting the status concerns of the secularized Catholic colleges, the faithful few are focused on eternal salvation and committed to revitalizing the Church. *Ex Corde Ecclesiae* identified this focus as integral to the work of the university: "The mission that the Church, with great hope, entrusts to Catholic Universities holds a cultural and religious meaning of vital importance because it concerns the very future of humanity."[22] For Pope St. John Paul II, "a Catholic University is without any doubt one of the best instruments that the Church offers to our age which is searching for certainty and wisdom. Having the mission of bringing the Good News to everyone, the Church should never fail to interest herself in this Institution."[23]

In some ways, it was the failure of the majority of the formerly faithful Catholic colleges that inspired the success of the faithful

21 In contrast, Father Heft, sees the current lack of ecclesial accountability as a favorable development for universities, writing, "Happily, according to *Ex Corde Ecclesiae*, bishops have no direct authority over nonpontifically chartered Catholic universities" (*Future of Catholic Higher Education*, 131).

22 *Ex Corde Ecclesiae*, no. 63.

23 Ibid., nos. 27–28.

few. These schools set themselves apart with an institutional fidelity of the university that recognizes and adheres to the teaching authority of the Church in matters of faith and morals. Pope St. John Paul II understood how important the faithful Catholic university remains to the life and the mission of the universal Church, writing of its "special bond with the Holy See by reason of the service to unity which it is called to render to the whole Church."[24] Don Briel provides a cogent explanation of this bond, and of the mutually enriching relationship held between the Church and the university, in his essay, "The Role of Faculty in Mission and Identity." He says that the Catholic intellectual tradition is the "incarnational expression of the mind of the Catholic community, the Church, and is expressed in the ongoing pursuit of the exploration and development of Catholic thought and culture." He goes on to insist that the particularly "ecclesial character" of this intellectual tradition can only be maintained through "an ongoing communion of the university and the Church."[25] Here we see a much richer understanding of a "Catholic intellectual tradition" than that espoused by Father Heft. The opposition set up between the living Magisterium and the intellectual heritage, which we see in Heft, is gone. Instead, their unity, based on the reconciliation between faith and reason, is presented as essential for forming the next generation of Catholic young people in the intellectual and spiritual culture of the Church. A truly faithful Catholic university offers an indispensable contribution to the Church by preparing men and women who, inspired by Christian principles and encouraged to live their Christian vocation in a mature and responsible manner, will be able to help the Church respond to the problems and needs of this age.

[24] Ibid., no. 39.

[25] Briel, *The University and the Church*, 150.

Liturgical Character at the Heart of the School

Just as liturgy is central to the life of the Church, it is central to the life of the faithful few colleges and universities. In *Ex Corde Ecclesiae,* the pope reminds us that "the university community should give a practical demonstration of its faith in its daily activity." This demonstration will take a variety of liturgical and sacramental forms, but finds its greatest fulfillment in "the Eucharist as the most perfect act of community worship" (no. 39). Worship is at the heart of Catholic pedagogy, and it is essential that universities ground their education in public professions of faith, drawing on the rich variety of sacramental and pious practices in the Catholic spiritual tradition. The schools profiled in this book are each inspired by the liturgical spirit that John Paul describes, and they are working so that each of their students may "be prepared for active participation in the life of the Church" (*Ex Corde Ecclesiae,* no. 41). This is stressed by Father Jonathan St. André, T.O.R, a 1996 graduate and now vice president of Franciscan Life at Franciscan University of Steubenville:

> Franciscan University is a place where we work to honor and guard the faith. How can the seed of faith grow if the soil is not carefully guarded and tended? We all take seriously our role in caring for the faith of our students. This doesn't mean coddling them. They may need to be challenged, but it is always done in a spirit of helping them to grow.... We do this by helping them to flourish here in body, mind, and spirit... whether we are worshipping the Lord in Holy Mass, serving the Lord through campus outreach, or walking to class, all of us have been created by the Father in the image of the Son according to the Spirit. This influences everything.... We belong to God and reverence and honor each other accordingly.[26]

[26] Conversation between Anne Hendershott and Father Jonathan St. André, 2023.

At Franciscan and similar schools, the liturgy is approached as more than just an academic discipline or something to study theoretically; rather, it is viewed as the way to holiness and communion with God. Anyone who has attended the daily Masses on Franciscan's campus understands that the liturgy is the place of maximum encounter with God. At the noonday Mass — one of four daily Masses — the pews are often filled to the capacity of Christ the King Chapel, and the presence of the Holy Spirit is palpable as students, faculty, and staff engage with the salvific events of Christ on the cross. The community bonds in a liturgical experience that strengthens their faith and reinforces their commitment to living their faith in their day-to-day lives on campus. Students who attend daily Mass understand what it means to be part of a Catholic community here on earth as preparation for our heavenly life with God. In some important ways, this community bonding experience through the liturgy helps to insulate Franciscan students from the alienating culture that permeates so many secular campuses.

Lamps in the Darkness

The title for this book, *Lamp in the Darkness,* was chosen because it communicates what, or rather *who,* lies at the heart of the mission of every Catholic university: the light of Jesus Christ. Pope St. John Paul II said that every university must balance the search for truth with the certainty that truth has been revealed in the person of Jesus.[27] This dynamic, which defines the history of Catholic higher education, is exemplified by the faithful few in everything they do, from worship to student life policies, and from curricula to school leadership.

St. Paul writes to the Corinthians, "For it is the God who said, 'Let light shine out of darkness,' who has shone in our hearts to give

[27] *Ex Corde Ecclesiae,* no. 1.

the light of the knowledge of the glory of God in the face of Christ" (2 Cor. 4:6). The apostle is stressing how knowledge of the glory is not merely an intellectual endeavor but is supposed to touch the deepest part of the person. This approach to education, with its emphasis on its effect on the heart, was picked up by the great educator Cardinal Newman in his episcopal motto, *Cor Ad Cor Loquitur* (Heart speaks unto heart), and is signaled in the opening line of *Ex Corde Ecclesiae*: "From the heart of the Church."

The education offered by the faithful few creates this transformative influence specifically because it centers on an encounter with the person of Jesus. Both as an institution and in the lives of each member of the university community, the mission is first and foremost to keep the burning flame of truth close to the source of light, Christ Himself. "Again Jesus spoke to them, saying, 'I am the light of the world; he who follows me will not walk in darkness, but will have the light of life' " (John 8:12). The image of light is a key motif in this book because it simultaneously captures the educational endeavor and its Christian cadence. Socrates famously viewed education "not as the filling of a vessel, but as the turning of the eye of the soul towards the light."[28] With the Incarnation, that light took flesh, and He is still present in His Church today.

The book proposes that Catholic universities must present a living institutional witness to Christ and His gospel, and I will tell the story of how some of these schools have maintained that witness. Evangelization is an integral part of the mission of the faithful few. Pope St. John Paul II reminds us in *Ex Corde Ecclesiae* that "the primary mission of the Church is to preach the Gospel in such a way that a relationship between faith and life is established in each

[28] Benjamin Jowett, introduction to *The Dialogues of Plato*, vol. 3 (Oxford: Oxford University Press, 1892), cci.

individual and in the socio-cultural context in which we live" (no. 51). The faithful Catholic universities and colleges are in harmony with the evangelizing mission of the Church in that they provide for their students and other constituents a greater awareness of the authentic message of Christ and of the salvific mission of the Church. These colleges have refused to be guided by the status striving Catholic colleges, which no longer seem to support the Church's mission of saving souls. They have kept the flame of Catholic higher education alive, even as this light has flickered out in many other schools across the nation. The true goal of the faithful Catholic university, as Tom Monaghan identified it, is to save souls. The faithful few Catholic colleges and universities presented here are authentically working toward that goal.

Chapter 1

"A Smoldering Wick": How Most Catholic Universities Lost Their Way

As the college term drew to a close in the spring of 2017, Anthony Esolen, the most prominent and prolific professor at Providence College, packed up and got ready to leave the school where he had spent nearly thirty years. He would renounce his tenure at the century-old college, give up his well-earned sabbatical, and accept a teaching position at Thomas More College of Liberal Arts, a tiny Catholic college with only ninety students in Merrimack, New Hampshire. Esolen's choice to leave one Catholic school for another had nothing to do with a desire for greater status or a higher salary. Rather, Esolen was attracted to the curriculum and the Catholic culture at Thomas More, as well as to its commitment to a classical Catholic education that values the theology of Thomas Aquinas more than diversity studies. He was drawn to Thomas More College, he told a *National Catholic Register* reporter, because "students are meant to be surrounded by beauty and sanity," and he admired how "the education at Thomas More focuses on the whole human being." He said he was leaving Providence because he wanted to be "part of delivering a curriculum that was based on the Truth." He wanted to bring to students at his new school what he had always sought to give

Providence undergraduates: "a love for art and poetry and the best of human wisdom and the trust that such things can bring us into the precinct of the divine.... Being around people filled with the faith strengthens me in my own faith."[29]

Professor Esolen captured the essence of what faithful Catholic higher education is all about when he spoke of the importance of creating a community of people who are "filled with the faith." There are others of us in academia who, like Professor Esolen, have given up tenure and higher salaries at prestigious universities to teach on small but faithful Catholic campuses. We've sold our homes, sometimes at a loss, and uprooted our families in a search of an academic home where we could be reminded each day of God's great gift of faith. I made a similar decision to abandon a tenured position after fifteen years as a sociology professor at a southern Californian Catholic university that had lost its way. I opted instead to join the faithful faculty at the "dynamically orthodox" Franciscan University of Steubenville in 2013. Although it meant leaving behind a larger and more prestigious university, I have never doubted that it was the right decision.

A faith-filled community is important to both students and faculty, but it is not easy to find a community like that. The dearth of faithful Catholic colleges and universities is the reason that faithful Catholic families have long relied on *The Newman Guide,* published by the Cardinal Newman Society, as mentioned in the introduction to this book, to help them find the kind of faith-filled environment they want for their college-age children.[30] Founded in 1998, the

[29] Peter Jesserer Smith, "Anthony Esolen in His Own Words: 'Why I Left Providence College for Thomas More,'" *National Catholic Register,* May 4, 2017, https://www.ncregister.com/blog/anthony-esolen-in-his-own-words-why-i-left-providence-college-for-thomas-more.

[30] First published in 2007, the *Newman Guide* is reissued every year and is fully accessible online at the Cardinal Newman Society's website: https://cardinalnewmansociety.org/the-newman-guide/.

original goal of the Cardinal Newman Society was to bring attention to what the founders saw as the scandalous behavior of honoring pro-abortion politicians and celebrities on Catholic campuses. Many Catholic colleges and universities go beyond awarding honorary degrees and speaking opportunities to those who flout Catholic teachings on life and marriage, seeming to seek out those who have done everything they can to destroy the Church.

In the early years of its existence, in its efforts to bring attention to this problem, the Cardinal Newman Society used to organize protests, including facilitating letter-writing campaigns to Catholic bishops and Catholic college presidents in an effort to address the "culture of death" that it identified on these secularizing Catholic college campuses. In those early days, it released major reports from the frontlines of colleges, like its 2004 special report, "The Culture of Death on Catholic Campuses: A Five-Year Review." It documented nearly two hundred incidents of speakers and honorees invited to Catholic campuses who vocally opposed Catholic teachings on abortion, euthanasia, and contraception.[31]

A few years later, the Newman Society released another report, this time focused on student life, which pointed to a degraded culture surrounding "dating and mating" on many Catholic college campuses.[32] The data pointed to important religious differentials in student dating behavior. While a student's affiliation as a conservative Protestant reduced the odds of engaging in casual sex in college, holding a Catholic affiliation actually increased the odds of engaging in such

[31] "The Culture of Death at Catholic Colleges in the U.S." Zenit, July 19, 2004, https://www.ewtn.com/catholicism/library/culture-of-death-at-catholic-colleges-in-us-9719.

[32] Anne Hendershott and Nicholas Dunn, "The 'Hook-Up' Culture on Catholic Campuses," Cardinal Newman Society, June 1, 2011, https://cardinalnewmansociety.org/hook-culture-catholic-campuses-review-literature/.

behavior on most mainstream Catholic campuses. Indeed, students who identified themselves as Catholics (but did not engage in a culture of authentically Catholic life) displayed roughly a 72 percent increase in the odds of engaging in casual sexual relationships compared to those women with no religious affiliation at all. Conversely, authentic religious involvement did in fact reduce the odds of engaging in sexual behavior at college; this pattern was driven by the kinds of religious service attendance available at the faithful Catholic colleges. These findings suggest that "co-religionist networks may be particularly important during the college years, when individuals have increased dating and sexual opportunities, yet little or no supervision." The data also indicated that "being Catholic" in and of itself, yields few protective effects from engaging in casual sexual behavior. In fact, Catholic women who are not frequent church attendees are more likely than their unaffiliated counterparts to engage in casual sexual behavior during their college years. One of the studies referenced in this report indicated that, "Unlike students on evangelical or conservative Protestant campuses, students on most Catholic campuses do not constitute what the authors called a 'moral community.' When Catholic students enter most mainstream Catholic colleges, it appears that they do not enter with the same level of religious commitment or knowledge of their faith as their Protestant counterparts." This poor socialization often continued when they arrived on Catholic campuses and were confronted with religious studies professors rather than theologians who teach about faith and morals. Many religious studies professors on mainstream Catholic campuses are committed to providing that critical "open circle" perspective of the Catholic Faith, rather than instruction on morality and what the Faith teaches about, for example, love and marriage.[33]

[33] Ibid.

Although the Newman Society no longer performs the kind of "watchdog" function it used to provide for families, it continues to publish *The Newman Guide* as an excellent resource for families attempting to find a faithful Catholic college or university for their children. Relying on research on the curriculum, the faculty, and student life culture, *The Newman Guide* identifies which Catholic campuses deserve to be included in the short list of fewer than two dozen faithful Catholic colleges and universities out of the more than two hundred that call themselves Catholic. Only a decade ago, Providence College was prominently featured on this list of faithful Catholic colleges. But, as Professor Esolen pointed out, in a misguided attempt to achieve higher status by embracing the secular gods of multiculturalism and diversity — including radical feminism, racial divisiveness, and support for LGBT causes — Providence College no longer merits inclusion in the *Newman Guide*. It has been dropped from the list.

Esolen's departure from Providence, a college administered by Dominican friars that had, until recently, been highly regarded as a bastion of faithful Catholic education, represents only the most recent example of a phenomenon under way for nearly fifty years: the abandonment by Catholic colleges and universities of their religious identities. It is a development with ramifications not only for Catholicism but also for the broader institution of higher education. It was the Catholic tradition that created the idea of the Western university, with its devotion to the good, the true, and the beautiful, and a commitment to reason's capacity to help us discover all three. Today, rather than embracing the good, the true, and the beautiful, too many Catholic universities, like Providence, have adopted the same curricular fads as their secular peers, hosting departments of gender studies, black studies, ethnic studies, and gay and lesbian studies. Campus leaders claim that their

Catholic campus commitment to social justice differentiates them from non-Catholic colleges, but they neglect to mention that their definition of social justice is so broad that campuses like the University of San Diego and Santa Clara University now hold drag shows and gay and lesbian dances for the LGBT undergraduate community. Some Catholic-in-name-only colleges and universities provide community service-learning opportunities for course credit to undergraduate students who want to work as interns or volunteers at Planned Parenthood and other abortion providers. According to a Newman Society report, Nazareth College's campus ministry promoted internship and service-learning opportunities for students to serve as "clinic escorts" to women seeking abortion services at Planned Parenthood. Georgetown University's website even goes so far as to refer students to local abortion providers.[34]

The culture of death on Catholic campuses is even worse at the graduate level. In some Catholic nursing programs, like the one at the University of San Diego, nurses enrolled in the graduate programs are given the option to complete clinical work providing abortion services at local abortion providers. Several Catholic law schools — including Georgetown and Fordham University — host chapters of the pro-abortion Law Students for Reproductive Justice (LSRJ, recently renamed "If/When/How: Lawyering for Reproductive Justice").[35] This pro-abortion organization has been helping Catholic law schools train and mobilize students to foster legal expertise in and support for "reproductive justice." Collaborating with the pro-abortion organization Catholics for Choice, the law student advocacy group aims to produce a new generation of lawyers who will lobby on behalf of a "reproductive justice" that

[34] "Culture of Death at Catholic Colleges."

[35] If/When/How: Lawyering for Reproductive Justice, https://ifwhenhow.org/.

claims access to full reproductive rights — including, of course, the right to an abortion. Catholics for Choice is an important partner for the Catholic university law schools that host chapters. In fact, the national LSRJ was so grateful to Catholics for Choice in 2014 that they awarded it their Allied Organization Award. This was done in recognition of its help in creating their "Keeping Faith in the Conversation" event toolkit, which was designed to help chapters on Catholic campuses to invite speakers who could encourage what they have called "the intersection of faith and abortion rights." With campus chapters at DePaul, Fordham, Georgetown, Loyola of Los Angeles, Loyola of Chicago, Santa Clara, Seattle, St. Louis, Detroit Mercy, the University of San Diego, and the University of San Francisco, the pro-abortion advocacy group has helped to create a new generation of Catholic law school graduates who are ready, willing, and able to defend a woman's "right" to choose abortion. While some of these chapters, like the one at Georgetown, have said that they are not officially "affiliated with the University," the abortion advocacy activities have been held on the Georgetown campus at the Tower Green and in various rooms in McDonough Hall, the main Law School building. When asked about the University of San Diego's support for a pro-abortion club on campus, Dr. Timothy L. O'Malley, vice president of university relations at the University of San Diego, justified the presence of the "reproductive rights" club on the Catholic campus by telling a reporter for TFP Student Action, "The fostering of legal expertise in all aspects of the law is consistent with the educational objectives of the USD School of Law."[36]

[36] John Ritchie, "Pro-abortion Group Enjoys Full Recognition at the Catholic University of San Diego," TFP Student Action, August 7, 2013, https://tfpstudentaction.org/petitions/pro-abortion-group-enjoys-full-recognition-at-the-catholic-university-of-san-diego.

The growing culture of death entrenched on many campuses indicates the presence of a protracted culture war on many of the once-faithful Catholic campuses, thanks to progressive Catholics drifting from obedience to some of the most important teachings of the Church. The campus culture wars reflect the greater culture war between those who assert that there are no truths, only "readings," and those who still believe that truths have been revealed and require constant rereading and application. It is a war between those, on one hand, who believe that the Church is a site of oppression for women, gay men, and lesbians and those who, on the other hand, are faithful to the Church's teachings on abortion and sexual morality. But, most important, it is a war between those who are committed to the negation of the authority of Scripture and the hierarchy of the Church, and those who are leading and are dedicated to a renaissance of the Catholic intellect and a renewed appreciation for the continued contributions of the Catholic Church.

In his authoritative work *The Rise and Triumph of the Modern Self*, Grove City College professor Carl Trueman goes even further. He argues that, in most universities, traditional educational philosophy has been radically overhauled and replaced with a postmodern notion of the self that prioritizes self-expression over formation. Schools elevate "inward-directed therapeutic categories over traditional outward-directed educational philosophies" and provide their students with "safe spaces" for self-discovery instead of classrooms where they will be taught truth.[37] Many formerly faithful Catholic campuses have been unable to resist this revolution in thought and identity; they have backed away from the authoritative teaching of the Church and have begun to favor more

[37] Carl Trueman, *The Rise and Triumph of the Modern Self: Cultural Amnesia, Expressive Individualism, and the Road to Sexual Revolution* (Wheaton, IL: Crossway, 2020), 49.

amorphous commitments to sentiments of social justice and the liberal notion of freedom.

The following chapters will profile the schools that have resisted this revolution. Even as the situation has deteriorated at other Catholic universities, these schools have remained beacons of light that inspire figures like Anthony Esolen to give up everything to join their ranks. Before I tell their stories however, it is important to understand the maelstrom of rebellion and heterodoxy that gave birth to the revival.

Land O' Lakes and Beyond: A History of Institutional Rebellion

Many Catholic commentators point to the 1960s and specifically to a gathering of Catholic college leaders in Land O'Lakes, Wisconsin, as the moment most Catholic colleges and universities began abandoning their Catholic identity. It was here that the first official statement was made distancing key Catholic higher education institutions from the authority of the hierarchical Church. However, the root of the Land O'Lakes insubordination lies almost eighty years prior to that document's publication. Starting in the late 1800s, secular academic leaders from elite Protestant schools derided the Catholic curricular focus on philosophy, theology, Greek, and Latin; understandably, some Catholic leaders were chagrined by this. In an article in *The Atlantic* in 1896, Harvard president Charles W. Eliot mockingly compared the Catholic university curriculum with "the most backward educational system of religious fundamentalists."[38] Other secular schools would echo Eliot's criticisms over the years. Eventually, the embarrassment became too much for Catholic college leaders, and they too began to join in the criticisms of their own

[38] Burtchaell, *Dying of the Light*, 569.

schools. Notably, in 1956, Monsignor John Tracy Ellis, a faculty member at Catholic University in Washington, published an essay accusing faculty on Catholic campuses of "perpetuating mediocrity" by devoting too much emphasis to students' moral development instead of their scholarship and intellectual excellence.[39]

The essay appeared at the dawn of an era of monumental social change that would usher in a new religious pluralism, the sexual revolution, the civil rights movement, and the questioning of the authority of traditional institutions like the Church. Within six months, as historian Philip Gleason recounts, more than 3,500 reprints of Eliot's essay had been distributed: "It had been commented on in the Catholic press, noted by *Newsweek*, read aloud in the refectories of many religious communities, and discussed at meetings of Catholic educators." Monsignor Ellis became a Catholic celebrity — and Catholic higher education has yet to recover.[40]

As Catholic teachings began to become an embarrassment for status-seeking Catholic college leaders, 1962 brought the opening of the Second Vatican Council. The implementation of the council would come to cause a revolution in Catholic parish life and liturgy, as well as in Catholic higher education. Described as an "epoch-making act of liberalization" within the Church, it came at a time when many were already beginning to believe that Catholic doctrine was a site of contested knowledge.[41] As Yale University sociologist Michele Dillon points out, "The strong consensus among sociologists, historians and theologians is that Vatican II redefined the Church from a rigidly

[39] John Tracy Ellis, "American Catholics and the Intellectual Life," *Thought* 30 (Autumn, 1955): 351–388.

[40] Philip Gleason, *Contending with Modernity: Catholic Higher Education in the Twentieth Century* (New York: Oxford University Press, 1995), 290.

[41] Philip Jenkins, *The New Anti-Catholicism: The Last Acceptable Prejudice* (New York: Oxford University Press, 2003), 49.

hierarchical authoritarian, imperialist, anti-modern institution to one that has become more relevant to and engaged in the modern world."[42] For progressive Catholics like Professor Dillon, the documents of Vatican II stressed that decision-making within the Church was not just the purview of the clergy but rather belonged to the entire People of God. For orthodox Catholics, however, the reforms of Vatican II opened a door to the dismissal of the authority of the Church itself.

Ellis's bitter essay in 1956, combined with the upheaval caused by Vatican II, set in motion a series of Catholic conferences and discussions that culminated on July 20, 1967, when Notre Dame president Theodore M. Hesburgh gathered that small group of Catholic academic leaders — including ten Jesuit priests — in Land O'Lakes, Wisconsin, to declare independence from Church authority. Viewed nostalgically by progressive professors as a bold proclamation of autonomy for Catholic colleges and universities, the statement was better described by Professor Esolen as a "suicide pact" for Catholic higher education.[43] Immediately following Land O'Lakes, Catholic colleges removed most priests and nuns from their governing boards, and some secularized their mission statements. Some Catholic colleges went so far as to remove crucifixes from classrooms and saint statues from their grounds. Manhattanville College of the Sacred Heart and Webster College publicly declared themselves "no longer Catholic." Manhattanville prompted deleted the "Catholic part" of its name; Webster College's President Sister Jacqueline Grennan renounced her religious vows and withdrew from her religious order to

[42] Michele Dillon, *Catholic Identity: Balancing Reason, Faith, and Power* (New York: Cambridge University Press, 1999), 10.

[43] Anthony Esolen, "When Will They Ever Learn?" *The Catholic Thing*, March 30, 2017, https://www.thecatholicthing.org/2017/03/30/when-will-they-ever-learn/.

become a lay leader. She justified this action by claiming that she could lead the now-secular institution "without the embarrassment of being subject to religious obedience."[44] When President Grennan died in 2012, the *National Catholic Reporter* published a fawning obituary lauding the former Sister of Loretto's "pioneer spirit" in recognizing Webster's "potential growth as a secular institution."[45]

For progressive Catholic faculty and administrators, the path to upward mobility for their schools strayed far from the Church. "The best and only traditional authority in the university is intellectual competence," claimed Father Hesburgh, who served as Notre Dame's president from 1952 until 1987. He continues, in *The Challenge and Promise of the Catholic University*: "A great Catholic university must begin by being a great university that is also Catholic."[46] Father Hesburgh's stature in the academy and beyond gave his musings moral and intellectual authority. The recipient of more than 150 honorary degrees, Hesburgh, who died in 2015 at the age of 95, also became the first higher-education professional to receive the Congressional Gold Medal; it was given to him in 2000. He was the first priest elected to Harvard's Board of Directors and would in fact go on to serve as the president of the board for two years. He made a career of distancing himself from Church authority and sometimes from Church teachings. Such was the case during the years he served as a trustee — and later, chairman of the board — for the Rockefeller Foundation, a frequent funder of causes that are counter to Catholic doctrine, including population control and abortion.

44 Gleason, *Contending with Modernity*, 317.

45 Maureen Fiedler, "Loretto Pioneer Jacqueline Grennan Wexler Dies," *National Catholic Reporter*, January 25, 2012, https://www.ncronline.org/blogs/ncr-today/loretto-pioneer-jacqueline-grennan-wexler-dies.

46 Theodore M. Hesburgh, *The Challenge and Promise of a Catholic University* (South Bend, IN: University of Notre Dame Press, 1994), 1–2.

Jesuit institutions led other Catholic colleges in the quest for higher status, seeking parity with their secular peers by abandoning the traditional mode of Catholic higher education. Until the 1960s, the Society of Jesus was seen as the main defender of the Faith, though by then most Jesuits had lost touch with faithful Catholics in the pews — the ones who raised the money that had helped to build their colleges and universities. With their faithfulness and zeal in propagating the Faith, Jesuits in the past had provided the Church with thirty-eight canonized saints and 243 martyrs, put to death for their loyalty to the Church. But, in the 1960s, the order began waging war on Church authority and teachings.[47] "Almost overnight the pope's light infantry became a battalion in which every man decided for himself which war he was fighting," wrote Paul Shaughnessy, a Jesuit priest, in a 2002 *Weekly Standard* article entitled "Are the Jesuits Catholic?" With the chaos of the 1960s, an institutional nightmare ensued: "Confusion and cowardice at the top; despair, rage and disillusionment in the ranks.... American Jesuits went from 8,400 members in 1965 to fewer than 2,500 today."[48] But the real crisis, as Shaughnessy saw it, was "not one of size but of allegiance." The Jesuits and the Church continue today to be engaged in a battle for control over what Catholicism should stand for.

In 2013, a canon lawsuit, filed with the Vatican, charged that Georgetown, a Jesuit university and the first Catholic university in the country, should be denied the right to call itself Catholic. The canon law petition was filed by the late William Peter Blatty, author of the best-selling novel, *The Exorcist,* and it placed the identity of

[47] On the decline of Jesuit higher education, see Hendershott, *Status Envy,* chaps. 3–4.

[48] Paul Shaughnessy, "Are the Jesuits Catholic?" *Weekly Standard,* June 3, 2002, 27.

Georgetown at the center of a major battle.[49] Concluding that his alma mater "takes pride in insulting the Church and offending the faithful," Blatty wrote an open letter to the Vatican which pronounced Georgetown a "Potemkin Village ... the Borgia university, reflecting more the spirit of Alexander VI, than of Archbishop John Carroll, John Henry Cardinal Newman, or Pope John Paul II." Proclaiming Georgetown "dishonest," Blatty told an interviewer that to present a Catholic façade at alumni dinners and fundraisers, "the university will make sure there is a Jesuit in a collar at every table like the floral arrangement."[50]

Before his death, Blatty said he hoped that his two-hundred-page petition, documenting what he called "23 years of scandals and dissidence" at Georgetown, would demonstrate to Pope Francis that his once-beloved alma mater had become the "leader of a pack" of Catholic colleges failing to live up to their Catholic identity. Sadly, this hope failed to materialize. On April 4, 2014, Archbishop Angelo Zani, secretary of the Vatican's Congregation for Catholic Education, sent Blatty a cordial letter reassuring him that the congregation was "taking the issue seriously" and was "cooperating with the Society of Jesus in this regard." Blatty died two years later and, although Manuel A. Miranda, the counsel on his petition, promised that the case would continue, it seems to have died as well. This has happened despite the fact that more than two thousand Georgetown alumni, students, and parents

49 Patrick Reilly, "'Exorcist' Author's Canon Law Case Against Georgetown Continues," *Cardinal Newman Society*, January 16, 2017, https://cardinalnewmansociety.org/exorcist-authors-canon-law-case-against-georgetown-continues/.

50 Anne Hendershott, "Taking the Catholic Out of Universities," *City Journal*, Autumn 2017, https://www.city-journal.org/article/taking-the-catholic-out-of-catholic-universities. I am grateful for *City Journal*'s permission to use material from that article in this chapter.

pledged to pursue the Vatican for correction of what they called "the university's serious abuses of Catholic identity."[51]

We must acknowledge that the apparent "threat" of losing federal funds for higher education also played a role in the secularization of Catholic colleges and universities. In a 1987 essay in the *New York Times,* Father Hesburgh cautioned that unless Catholic colleges and universities were completely independent of Church control, the Supreme Court would rule that they should be deprived of the growing flood of government money to higher education. This was never true, but, as secular sources of funding increased, Catholic colleges became less dependent on financial support from alumni and the faithful Catholics in the pews who had helped to build those Catholic colleges and universities. There was much less willingness to accommodate faithful Catholic donors when the federal government was willing and able to shower the schools with taxpayer money. As this money was given without any expectation that the Catholic identity would be maintained, it continues today to motivate Catholic universities and colleges to shed their Catholic identity. Saint Louis University, the second-oldest Jesuit university in the United States, found itself facing a lawsuit in 2009 when plaintiffs claimed that the $8 million in state tax-increment financing that the university had received for its new sports arena violated Missouri's constitutional ban on public funding for religious institutions. In response, seeking to defend its ability to receive government funds, the university reaffirmed publicly that it is "not controlled by the Catholic Church or by its Catholic beliefs.... The school does

51 Michelle Boorstein, "Vatican Responds to Georgetown Petition by 'Exorcist' author William Peter Blatty," *Washington Post,* May 13, 2014, https://www.washingtonpost.com/local/vatican-responds-to-georgetown-petition-by-exorcist-author-blatty/2014/05/13/22f780de-daa3-11e3-bda1-9b46b2066796_story.html.

not require employees or students to aspire to Jesuit ideals."[52] In the end, the Supreme Court awarded the funds to the university and concluded that Saint Louis University "is not a religious institution simply because it is affiliated with the Jesuits or the Roman Catholic Church.... A university's motivation or aspirations to follow certain teachings does not indicate that it is controlled by a religious creed.... SLU's mission is education, not indoctrination, and its focus is on development of students, not on the propagation of the Jesuits' faith."[53] In a brief opposing the university's position, the American Civil Liberties Union wrote: "It is surprising that the University would sell its heritage for $8 million."[54]

Catholic college leaders are more than happy to dust off their religious identity when it serves their purposes. For example, despite their proudly proclaimed commitments to social justice, most Catholic colleges have blocked attempts by employees to unionize. When adjunct professors at Manhattan College voted for the right to unionize in 2011, college administrators argued that the college was exempt from National Labor Relations Board (NLRB) jurisdiction because it was a church-operated institution. The NLRB ruled however that the "public representations of Manhattan College clearly demonstrate that it is not providing a religious educational environment." While the college frequently cited its Lasallian tradition in public documents, the NLRB concluded that those references were made in "purely secular terms." Noting that Manhattan College's admissions brochure includes no references to the Catholic Church or

[52] Christopher Tritto, "Missouri Supreme Court Decisions Gives St. Louis University $8 million," *St. Louis Business Journal*, April 19, 2007.

[53] "Saint Louis University v. Masonic Temple Association of St. Louis," Supreme Court of Missouri, April 2007, Justia, https://law.justia.com/cases/missouri/supreme-court/2007/sc-88075-1.html.

[54] Quoted in Tim Townsend, "Did SLU Sell Its Jesuit Soul for a Sports Arena," *St. Louis Post-Dispatch*, April 21, 2007.

to Catholicism, the NLRB issued a twenty-six-page report arguing that the college cannot claim a religious affiliation as justification for preventing employee unionization.[55]

Likewise, on January 6, 2015, the NLRB issued a "Certificate of Representation" allowing adjunct professors and lecturers at St. Mary's College in Moraga, California, to join the Service Employees International Union (SEIU). A month earlier, adjunct faculty at St. Michael's College in Vermont voted in favor of joining the SEIU and later, in 2015, the NLRB ordered officials to reconsider labor disputes involving employees at St. Xavier University in Chicago, at Duquesne, and at Seattle University. Leaders at these universities had attempted to thwart unionization, claiming that such efforts posed a threat to their schools' religious character. In 2016, when Loyola University of Chicago mounted a battle against unionization, it went so far as to claim that the union would be in direct contradiction to Loyola's religious identity and mission. Loyola's interim president, John Pelissero, told the faculty that the SEIU was "not consistent with our deeply rooted Catholic intellectual tradition."[56] That was a hard case to make at Loyola, however, which has been encouraging students for decades to participate in activities antithetical to Catholic teachings, including internships at the Chicago Abortion Fund and Planned Parenthood. Loyola's Law School hosted a chapter of LSRJ, and through its chapter of OUTLaw — an advocacy group for LGBT issues on law school campuses — it lobbied for same-sex "marriage." For the past decade, Loyola had invited undergraduate students to perform at the university's Annual Drag Show as part of the LGBTQIA Heritage Month on campus. In such an environment,

[55] Hendershott, "Taking the Catholic Out of Universities."

[56] Hendershott, "Taking the Catholic Out of Universities."

unionization could hardly be considered the actual threat to the university's Catholic identity.

In the face of such cultural shifts, *Ex Corde Ecclesiae* had earlier attempted to combat the slide toward secularism by calling for Catholic colleges to be accountable to the local presiding bishop. A key component of the papal document was a controversial requirement that all theologians obtain a *mandatum,* or certificate, from the local bishop attesting that their teaching is consistent with official Church doctrine.[57] The American bishops formulated this requirement in the following way: "Catholics who teach the theological disciplines in a Catholic university are required to have a mandatum granted by competent ecclesiastical authority."[58] More than three decades later, most of the nation's Catholic colleges and universities have continued to resist *Ex Corde Ecclesiae,* with faculty and administrators seeing it as a threat to their academic freedom and independent governance. After the document was released, Notre Dame's faculty senate voted unanimously to ignore it. In the Jesuit publication *America,* Notre Dame's then-president Father Edward Malloy co-authored an angry response with Father Donald Monan, then-chancellor of Boston College, warning of "havoc" if *Ex Corde Ecclesiae* were implemented. Calling the papal document "positively dangerous" to Catholic institutions, Fathers Monan and Malloy wrote that they would have preferred a "document that they would be proud to display to sister institutions of higher education," revealing that their concerns were heavily influenced by concern for their

[57] *Ex Corde Ecclesiae,* Norms, art. 4, sec. 3.

[58] *The Application for Ex Corde Ecclesiae for the United States,* Particular Norms, art. 4, sec. 4e, USCCB, https://www.usccb.org/committees/catholic-education/application-ex-corde-ecclesiae-united-states.

status.[59] In other words, these leaders of prestigious Catholic colleges were — and continue to be — embarrassed by any suggestion that their schools are "different" or "lesser" than the prestigious secular schools — what they call their "sister schools."

In an especially hyperbolic article, one theologian likened the approval of *Ex Corde Ecclesiae* to a "Doomsday Clock" for Catholic higher education. Drawing on a Cold War metaphor referring to the Bulletin of Atomic Scientists' use of the image of a doomsday clock to indicate how close the world was to mass nuclear annihilation, Jon Nilson, a theology professor at Loyola University in Chicago, warned of a similar annihilation for Catholic higher education.[60] Father Raymond Collins, dean of the Religious Studies Department at the Catholic University of America, advised faculty members to "selectively dissent" from *Ex Corde Ecclesiae* by refusing to implement the parts they disagreed with. In a 1999 letter to the *National Catholic Reporter*, Collins wrote that he hoped that Catholic University would become a model of selective dissent by this advised method of piecemeal implementation of *Ex Corde Ecclesiae*. Father Collins, who finally retired from Catholic University in 2005, knew that outright confrontation with church authorities would bring negative attention, but he also knew that Catholic University's theology department would gain higher status by refusing to comply.

In a speech to United States Catholic college presidents in 2008, Pope Benedict XVI warned that any appeal to the principle of academic freedom to justify positions that contradict the Faith and teaching of the Church betrayed a university's Catholic identity and mission. Yet a congratulatory headline in the *Chronicle of Higher*

59 Edward Molloy and Donald Monan, "New Norms for Catholic Higher Education: Unworkable and Dangerous," *America*, November 14, 1998, 3–4.

60 Jon Nilson, "The Impending Death of Catholic Higher Education," *America*, May 28, 2001.

Education proclaimed that "Pope Benedict Thanks Educators and Addresses Academic Freedom in Talk." Putting a positive spin on it, Mary Lyons, then-president of the University of San Diego, declared the pope's speech "affirming and generous" and pronounced the controversies surrounding *Ex Corde Ecclesiae* as "so 90s."[61]

For those few faithful faculty members on nominally Catholic campuses who have spent the past three decades fighting for the implementation of *Ex Corde Ecclesiae,* it must appear that the war is over, and that their side has been defeated. The contentious battles that once surrounded the release of that apostolic constitution have ended, as most college presidents refused to implement it and most bishops were reluctant to require it. Even the faithful at these universities seem, by now, to have given up hope and abandoned the fight. By 2003, University of Notre Dame professor of law Gerard Bradley, a longtime proponent of the implementation of *Ex Corde Ecclesiae,* had pronounced the document "dead."[62]

The Battles Continue Today

A recent illustration of the loss of Catholic identity at the collegiate level came to the once-venerable University of Notre Dame in the spring of 2023, when yet another pro-abortion speaker was invited to campaign for the unlimited right to abortion. To the discouragement of faithful Notre Dame faculty, many of whom had welcomed *Ex Corde Ecclesiae* as a way to renew the fading Catholicity of their campus, there has already been a parade of pro-choice politicians honored by

[61] Richard Byrne, "Pope Benedict Thanks Educators and Addresses Academic Freedom at Catholic U," *Chronicle of Higher Education* 54 (April 18, 2008), https://www.chronicle.com/article/pope-benedict-thanks-educators-and-addresses-academic-freedom-in-talk-at-catholic-u-707/.

[62] Gerard V. Bradley, "Looking Ahead at Catholic Higher Education," *Fellowship of Catholic Scholars Quarterly* 26 (Winter 2003): 14–19.

their university — including President Barack Obama, who was given an honorary degree in 2009 by Notre Dame's then-president Father John Jenkins, despite the fact that Obama was the most pro-abortion president in American history, until President Joe Biden. The award of the Laetare Medal — the most prestigious award given by Notre Dame — was also bestowed on then-Vice President Joseph Biden in 2016, even though he had encouraged an expansion of abortion at the state and federal level as a senator and, as vice president, had promoted both abortion and same-sex "marriage."[63] The Laetare Medal is an award given by Notre Dame in recognition of outstanding service to the Catholic Church and society, and the award is supposed to be granted to an American Catholic "whose genius has ennobled the arts and sciences, illustrated the ideals of the Church, and enriched the heritage of humanity."[64] Biden's record on abortion and same-sex "marriage" should have disqualified him as someone who had provided "outstanding service to the Church and society," as the Laetare Medal honor has traditionally been described.

However, while the honors awarded to Biden and Obama created a scandal for the faithful, nothing could have prepared them for the speaker that was provided with access to Notre Dame students in order to promote and actually celebrate abortion on March 20, 2023. Ash Williams, a self-described "transgender man," devoted her entire Notre Dame presentation for students to describing the "goodness" of abortion. Declaring that "abortion is a type of birth," Williams, who calls herself an "abortion doula," claims to draw upon the experiences in her "Black, trans, abortion-having life" to question supposedly

[63] Dennis Brown, "Biden and Boehner to Jointly Receive Laetare Medal," Notre Dame News, March 5, 2016, https://news.nd.edu/news/2016-laetare-medal/.

[64] "About" (the Laetare Medal), University of Notre Dame, accessed August 12, 2024, https://laetare.nd.edu/about/.

oppressive norms against abortion. As an "abortion doula" Williams claims to provide physical, emotional, or financial help to people seeking to end a pregnancy, suggesting that the reason we don't understand an abortion as a type of birth "is because it has become so disenfranchised."[65] Williams, who shared with Notre Dame students that she had undergone two abortions, has a tattoo on her left forearm of a surgical instrument used for manual vacuum aspiration abortion. In an interview with a reporter for National Public Radio, Williams confided that she "loves the [vacuum suction] procedure because it's one and done. It's quick." Glib about her own abortions, and the abortions of the women she helps, she joked that she tells her abortion stories "as often as a broken record."[66]

According to news reports covering the scandal of inviting Williams to be an honored speaker, Notre Dame student response to the pro-abortion doula was "mixed," with faithful students saddened by the pro-abortion symposium on their campus, and others grateful for the opportunity to hear Williams's testimony. In an interview published in *The Irish Rover*, the independent Notre Dame student newspaper, a Notre Dame student described the lecture by Ash Williams as "incoherent, nonsensical." Suggesting that Williams "took seeming pleasure in contradicting the views that the university professes to believe in," this student decried the fact that, although Notre Dame's policy allows for opposing views to be presented, "it stipulates that the Catholic position is to be articulated by the department."[67] Unfortunately, but unsurprisingly, a pro-life

[65] Ellie Knapp, "Reproductive Justice, Trans Care, Abortion Care Webinar," *Irish Rover,* March 23, 2023, https://irishrover.net/2023/03/reproductive-justice-trans-care-abortion-care-webinar/.

[66] Destinee Adams, "What It's Like Being an Abortion Doula in a State with Restrictive Abortion Laws," NPR, October 19, 2022, https://www.npr.org/2022/10/19/1123778633/abortion-doula-north-carolina.

[67] Knapp, "Reproductive Justice, Trans Care, Abortion Care Webinar."

position was not presented. Williams's appearance was sponsored by multiple departments: Gender Studies, Anthropology, Sociology, History, English, Political Science, and Film, Television and Theatre—as well as the Office of the Dean of the College of Arts and Letters and the Reilly Center for Science, Technology and Values. Not one of these offices or departments provided a pro-life response. Even the Center for Social Concerns — a Notre Dame institute dedicated to applying Catholic social teaching — provided sponsorship and support for the pro-abortion event.

In the past, the Cardinal Newman Society attempted to encourage bishops to intervene in such cases. This was undertaken by sending a letter to each of the U.S. bishops, urging them to consider diocesan policies banning inappropriate speakers and honorees at Catholic institutions. Most of the bishops — and nearly all the senior leaders on non-*Newman Guide* campuses — ignored the letter and the reports. Father Heft, then the provost at the University of Dayton, dismissed the letter, claiming in an interview for the *Baltimore Sun* that "it is not entirely clear who should be barred from honors."[68]

During his tenure as provost, Father Heft said he "interviewed hundreds of candidates for faculty positions. I never asked any of them if they were Catholic; I did not need to." Claiming that he could discern from speaking with them whether they would support the Catholic identity of the University of Dayton, Father Heft asserted that those of other faiths, or even atheists and agnostics, could contribute to the open circle by helping it to "engage more comprehensively [with] the great questions that humanity faces." These non-Catholic scholars "keep the circle more honest and raise questions and contribute insights that, enclosed within themselves,

[68] Janice D. Arcy, "Cardinal Says New Policy Led to Loyola Boycott," *Baltimore Sun,* May 20, 2005, https://www.baltimoresun.com/bal-te.md.keeler20may20-story.html.

Catholic scholars may be unlikely to do." Father Heft rejected the kinds of faithful Catholic colleges and universities presented in the following chapters, describing them as "closed circles" which "oppose modern culture." He believes that "an integral part of being Catholic is seeking truth wherever it can be found, be it in the study of other religions or welcoming scholars from other religions as colleagues."[69]

Father Heft's original "open circle" school, the University of Dayton, has truly opened that circle. A few years ago, Dayton hired an LGBTQ+ student service coordinator to provide programming and workshops for that community on campus. Dayton offers single occupancy restrooms for transgender students and encourages faculty members, staff members, and students to post Ally+ rainbow stickers on doors of offices and classrooms throughout the campus to indicate "safe spaces" for gay and lesbian students.[70] According to the University of Dayton website, the rainbow stickers promise that "transphobic and heterosexist comments and actions will not be tolerated" in that space, leaving one to assume that "heterosexist comments" include any defense of the Church's position on the sanctity of marriage. The University of Dayton is not the only once-upon-a-time faithful Catholic university that now offers gay and lesbian support clubs and single occupancy restrooms for transgender students. A majority of the two hundred mainstream Catholic colleges offer LGBT support groups. Some, including many of the Jesuit universities, as well as the University of San Diego, have been holding gay dances and an annual drag show for the past several years.

Despite the many battles that have been lost on these campuses, the war for the heart and soul of Catholic higher education

[69] Heft, *Future of Catholic Higher Education*, 128, 130.

[70] "The Ally+ Workshop: A New Way to Ally," University of Dayton, https://udayton.edu/studev/health_wellness/brook/lgbtq/ally.php.

continues. There are glimmers of hope even on the campuses where the Faith has seemed so lost. Less than a decade after Notre Dame awarded the Laetare Medal to then-Vice President Biden, the 2021 attempt to provide an honorary degree to now-President Biden met tremendous resistance from Notre Dame students and alumni; more than 4,300 members of the Notre Dame community signed a petition asking the university's President Jenkins not to invite or honor Biden at the commencement ceremonies held on the Notre Dame campus. Citing Biden's pro-abortion and anti-religious liberty agenda as the reason to decline proffering those honors to Biden, the powers-that-be at the university replaced him, having a member of Notre Dame's own board of trustees give the commencement address.[71]

It is a positive sign, indicating the possibility of recovery, that such a large contingent of Notre Dame's students and alumni recognized how inappropriate it was to award an honorary degree to someone with views antithetical to settled Catholic doctrine on life and the sanctity of marriage. But, in the meantime, the battles continue. And they are being waged by some unlikely conscripts: the Domino's Pizza magnate who donated millions of dollars to create a university on the edge of the beautiful Florida Everglades to help as many people as possible find their way to Heaven; a Harvard-educated priest from Park Avenue in New York City who took on the task of rescuing a failing Catholic college in Steubenville, Ohio — and almost single-handedly created the model that other faithful Catholic colleges follow; an entrepreneur from San Diego who wanted to find a way to train students to bring God into the

[71] James Crump, "Joe Biden Skips Notre Dame Speech Amid Petition Criticizing His Abortion Views," *Newsweek*, May 24, 2021, https://www.newsweek.com/president-joe-biden-notre-dame-university-abortion-commencement-speech-1594160.

entertainment world in Southern California; and a bishop from Cheyenne, Wyoming, who wanted to form students through the classical liberal arts tradition and the spiritual heritage of the Catholic Church in the mountain wilderness — often on horseback.

The following chapters will introduce these inspired founders and those who followed them in the battle for the soul of Catholic higher education. These chapters will look closely at their challenges as well as their triumphs — and will look more deeply at the once-faithful colleges which have decided to give up the fight, leading to a protracted Catholic campus culture war. We can learn from their stories how best to continue the battle, which still goes on between those formerly faithful Catholic colleges and universities and the faithful few — between those who have embraced secular influences in order to maintain status, and those who are seeking a radical transformation that will end the culture of death and bring renewed faith to America.

Chapter 2

Reclaiming a Catholic Mission

In a recent video in Christendom College's series *Principles,* college president Timothy O'Donnell makes a claim which many in both the Catholic and secular educational world would find outrageous, even anathema.[72] He states boldly that Christendom College was founded with an explicitly practical goal: namely, the forming of its students to restore the kingdom of Christ (Christendom) in the temporal order. This claim runs counter to those who argue for liberal education's "neutral value" and who insist that teaching should provide a non-confessional pursuit of the truth. It will also embarrass those Catholic universities who have spent decades burying the lamp of their Catholic identity under bushels of secular virtue signaling.

In support of his view, O'Donnell quoted a lengthy passage from Newman's *Idea of a University* where the saint draws an analogy between a general training his soldiers for battle and the Church educating students in university. The passage is worth quoting in full:

> Just as a commander wishes to have tall and well-formed and vigorous soldiers, not from any abstract devotion to

72 "The Purpose of the Catholic University," *Principles: From Christendom College,* video, 2:17, https://www.getprinciples.com/the-purpose-of-the-catholic-university/.

> the military standard of height or age, but for the purposes of war, and no one thinks it anything but natural and praiseworthy in him to be contemplating, not abstract qualities, but his own living and breathing men; so, in like manner, when the Church founds a University, she is not cherishing talent, genius, or knowledge, for their own sake, but for the sake of her children, with a view to their spiritual welfare and their religious influence and usefulness, with the object of training them to fill their respective posts in life better, and of making them more intelligent, capable, active members of society.[73]

Christendom was founded on just such a conviction, says O'Donnell. The school's motto, *Instaurare omnia in Christo,* translates "To restore all things in Christ."

When, as a recent convert, Warren Carroll founded the school in 1977, he had already studied and taught at some of America's elite institutions and had become thoroughly disenchanted with the state of education in the country. Even within the Church, caught as it was in the throes of the post-conciliar decline, Carroll could not find a robust Catholic educational institution. As a scholar of history, Warren had become convinced that the Church must rediscover her evangelical call to convert all of human society. Christendom would accomplish its motto of restoring *all things* by "forming men and women to contribute to the Christian renovation of the temporal order. This mission gives Christendom College its name."[74]

[73] John Henry Cardinal Newman, preface to *The Idea of a University* (London: Longmans, Green, 1907), xi-xii, available at Newman Reader, https://www.newmanreader.org/works/idea/preface.html.

[74] Thomas L. McFadden, Jr., *Restoring All Things in Christ: A History of the Founding of Christendom College* (Front Royal, VA: Christendom College, 2012), 5.

This same founding vision is very much alive today. We spoke to one of Carroll's early hires, Dr. Robert Rice, who described the fervor with which Christendom has maintained its apostolic founding vision. As the vice president of Academic Affairs for the vitally formative years of 1983 to 2002, Rice quoted the introduction to the oath of fidelity to the Magisterium taken by all faculty at Christendom. It begins: "In view of the institutionally Catholic character of Christendom College, and in view of the principle that the truth of the Gospel illumines and is integrated with the entire curriculum at Christendom College. . . ." This evangelical vision is by no means an anomaly in the history of Catholic higher education. However, by the 1970s, it was quickly being lost as Catholic universities all around the country retreated from their ecclesial identity. It was this collapse that inspired Carroll to start Christendom, as part of his contribution to the building up of the kingdom.

Though marked by large-scale apostasy, the period when Carroll chose to found Christendom, following the end of Vatican II in 1965, was also a particularly vibrant one in certain sectors of Catholic education. In quick succession, the first generation of universities faithful to a Catholic mission and inspired by Vatican II's call for an educated laity started appearing across America. Thomas Aquinas College in California was founded in 1971, the same year that Benedictine Abbey merged with its sister institution to found Benedictine College; Franciscan University was revived by Scanlan in 1974, while the New Hampshire college, Thomas More, started in 1978.

Inspired by the military analogy articulated by Newman, these schools set the explicit goal of forming students as soldiers in the *Ecclesia Militans*—the Church Militant. It is this radical orientation toward the Christian mission which sets them apart from colleges and universities across the board and even from other nominally Catholic schools. They have put themselves forward as places of authentic

Catholic education. For starters, even to be included in the *Newman Guide* requires a lengthy application process. Beginning with that and advancing each step of the way, these schools illustrate a desire first and foremost to be faithfully Catholic — and to be understood as such.

The near-simultaneous founding and flourishing of these various schools reveals the movement and work of the Holy Spirit, who is at work guiding these missions. This spiritual movement received its confirmation, so to speak, in the publication of *Ex Corde Ecclesia*, a document I have already introduced. At this point, I want to highlight its emphasis on the twin pillars of a Catholic university's mission: a rigorous educational standard married with a transcendent spiritual vision.[75] With this standard, it not only served as a confirmation of the path pursued by the first generation of *Newman Guide* schools but also ended up becoming a catalyst for the second generation. It was after its 1990 publication that a new wave of colleges was founded. These included Ave Maria University and John Paul the Great Catholic University, both in 2003, and Wyoming Catholic College in 2005. To properly understand what makes the mission statements of these various schools unique, it is good to begin by briefly identifying key themes from *Ex Corde Ecclesiae* as a source of both confirmation and inspiration for these schools.

Ex Corde Ecclesiae: The University as a Fundamentally Catholic Institution

The opening sentence of this apostolic constitution immediately points to the intimate relationship between the Church and the university:

[75] Those who feel the tension between these two elements (high educational standards and the rule of Faith) do well to remember that all the Church's doctrines exist in a fecund tension: faith and reason, spirit and matter, law and spirit, love and death. And, in fact, the mystery that sits at the center of our Faith (namely, the Trinity) stands as the model for all tensions.

"Born from the heart of the Church, a Catholic University is located in that course of tradition which may be traced back to the very origin of the University as an institution" (no. 1). Not only is the university ideologically related to the Church, but it finds its birth literally, and as a matter of historical fact, from within the Church.

The pope describes his apostolic constitution "as a sort of 'magna carta,'" which will draw on the long, fruitful "experience of the Church" in relation to universities while also looking to a promising future that will be reached through "courageous creativity and rigorous fidelity" (no. 8). By calling it a magna carta, John Paul is signaling that the document is not a radical imposition from above, as some of his detractors took it to be.[76] Rather, he is articulating an understanding of the university as it existed historically for almost a thousand years, going back to the medieval colleges of Paris, Bologna, and Oxford. It is this history and trajectory that the pope masterfully condenses into a unified vision and set of principles that can guide Catholic colleges going into the twenty-first century. These principles will help modern Catholic universities "to fulfil their indispensable mission in the new advent of grace" (no. 11).

Ex Corde Ecclesiae and Mission

John Paul describes the primary mission of a Catholic university as "a continuous quest for truth through research." He adds secondarily that the Catholic university is tasked with "the preservation and

[76] John Paul's choice of analogy is significant. The Magna Carta was the foundational document of the English constitution and is the principal basis of all future English common law. Signed by the English King John I and his barons in 1213, it famously served as a guarantor of rights from the monarch to his subject. However, the Magna Carta is not a theoretical expression of abstract rights. In fact, the document was simply an official recognition by the king of the rights already enjoyed by a free, Christian people, and through common consent and writing, a protection of those rights.

communication of knowledge for the good of society."[77] Catholic universities have a unique mission because of their ability to further the message of the Church in the world, and because they are places where contemporary problems are considered and addressed.

Calling for a renewal of universities in terms of both their collegial and their Catholic identities, John Paul issues a blow to the very heart of secular liberalism: "By its Catholic character, a University is made more capable of conducting an *impartial* search for truth, a search that is neither subordinated to nor conditioned by particular interests of any kind" (no. 7). Here, he delivers a devastating rejection of the status-striving pretensions of those Catholic universities that water down their Catholicity under the guise of "impartiality." John Paul instead claims that it is precisely a university's Catholicity which *guards* the honest and rigorous pursuit of truth, "without fear but rather with enthusiasm" born of the conviction that "truth is [its] real ally" (no. 4).

The pope speaks of a dual fidelity, of the institution and the person, which is necessary to protect the impartial search for the truth. First, there is the "*institutional* fidelity of the University to the Christian message," which recognizes and submits to the completeness of that message in the Church's magisterial teaching on faith and morals. Second, the Catholics within the university are also bound by their faith to maintain "a personal fidelity to the Church with all that this implies," and the non-Catholics must respect this character of Catholicism, while their religious liberty is preserved (no. 27).

Next, John Paul gives four characteristics that outline the identity of a Catholic university and inform its mission. The first

[77] *Ex Corde Ecclesiae,* no. 30. Earlier, in numbers 15–19, John Paul delved into the concerns which guide a Catholic "research" methodology, identifying four characteristics: "(a) the search for an *integration of knowledge,* (b) a *dialogue between faith and reason,* (c) an *ethical concern,* and (d) a *theological perspective.*"

characteristic is recognizing and acting on its duty to serve both the Church and society. This service involves an engagement with "serious contemporary problems" and requires that it bring the developed "Christian anthropology, founded on the person of Christ," to bear upon the issues that are relevant to the modern world (nos. 32–33).

Catholic universities, the pope continues, also ought to exercise a pastoral ministry by educating the whole man, and not merely his intellect. In other words, their second essential characteristic is that they should provide opportunities for the individual student to achieve an "integration of faith with life" (*sicque vitam cum fide componendi*). The reason for this is that conversion of heart is always the fundamental mission of the Church for each Catholic, and so this mission also stands at the center of the Catholic university (no. 38).

Third, Catholic universities are to stand in active dialogue with modern society.[78] Acting as an electrical conductor, the Catholic university is positioned to be a vital point of connection between the universal Church and the particular culture in which the university is located. In fact, says John Paul, more than other institutions, Catholic universities hold "a primary and privileged place for a *fruitful dialogue between the Gospel and culture*" (no. 43). He insists that Catholic universities have a particular role to play in engaging with modern culture, and he warns of the negative consequences that will follow if the university does not sincerely engage with its local culture: "A faith that places itself on the margin of what is human, of what is therefore culture, would be a faith unfaithful to the fullness of what the Word of God manifests and reveals, a decapitated faith, worse still, a faith in the process of self-annihilation" (no. 44).

[78] It is of note that, within the various elements of modern culture, John Paul calls for a Catholic study of the role and effect of modern technology and mass media upon society (no. 45).

The fourth and final characteristic he identifies is that they must live out and impart an active evangelization. Though it should be unsurprising that a Catholic institution stands perennially under the call to spread the good news of the gospel, there are many in the Church today who are uncomfortable with the notion that an academic institution has an evangelical purpose. However, the pope is insistent on this point. The Catholic university, flowing from its very nature and informing "all the basic academic activities," is a witness to and defender of Jesus Christ and His gospel (no. 49). It is a pivotal player in bringing about the kingdom of God on earth. This call to evangelization should be read in light of the other characteristics identified by the pope, meaning that the university is an evangelizer of cultures (ascending vertically) and not merely of individuals (extending horizontally). That is to say, a Catholic university doesn't only, or even primarily, spread the gospel to new peoples and nations. It also has the duty to evangelize hierarchically, transforming individuals and cultures into more just and more Christ-like modes of being.

John Paul states that great fruits will come from those schools that commit themselves as charismatic, institutional witnesses and that remain faithful to their mission as Catholic universities: "They give me a well-founded hope for a new flowering of Christian culture in the rich and varied context of our changing times, which certainly face serious challenges but which also bear so much promise under the action of the Spirit of truth and of love" (no. 2).[79] It is this promise — grounded in the authority of the divine

[79] Warren Carroll spoke in similar terms when he described the hope that inspired him to found Christendom College: "Christendom College is educating and preparing young men and women who will bring what our great and holy Pope John Paul II calls 'the new springtime of the church.' In the face of scandals and despair, believe in that springtime! It's coming, and nothing can stop it!" Quoted in Timothy D. O'Donnell, "Eulogy for Dr. Warren Hasty Carroll, RIP," July 26, 2011, Christendom

"Spirit of truth and of love" — which the faithful few Catholic universities are seeking to deliver.

The Subversive Shift: 1960s to the Present

The several decades before the publication of *Ex Corde Ecclesiae* witnessed a decisive shift away from this traditional educational vision toward one more akin to Protestant and secular counterparts. In my previous book *Status Envy: The Politics of Catholic Higher Education*, there is a chapter which documents in great detail the mission statements of over two hundred Catholic universities — well beyond those of the faithful few. Starting in the 1960s, leadership on these campuses started making "a conscious, and in some cases, well-documented effort to create ambiguity when describing the Catholic identity of their schools."[80] (In the later chapters of this book, I recount similarly subversive attempts, in an effort to undermine Catholic identity, to vitiate the mission statements of some *Newman Guide* and former *Newman Guide* schools.)

As noted in chapter 1, the subsequent widespread rejection by many Catholic universities of *Ex Corde Ecclesiae* and the evangelical

---

College, https://www.christendom.edu/wp-content/uploads/2016/02/Eulogy_for_Warren-Carroll_7-26-11.pdf. Carroll was an admirer of the pontiff, and the pope, in return, was aware of Warren Carroll and Christendom College and thought highly of its work.

80 Hendershott, *Status Envy*, 47. This trend was described by Ronald McArthur and Marcus Berquist as "doctrinal rather than economic" in their 1969 *Proposal for the Fulfillment of Catholic Higher Education*, the founding document of Thomas Aquinas College (see discussion later in this chapter). They saw an attack on "the very idea of a college that educates under the light of the Faith." *A Proposal for the Fulfillment of Catholic Liberal Education: The Founding and Governing Document of Thomas Aquinas* College (1969), 6, https://www.thomasaquinas.edu/sites/default/files/2021-06/BlueBook-2020-email.pdf. While this text is officially an institutional document without authors, the introduction makes clear that it is the work of McArthur and Berquist, with later revisions by John W. Neumayr.

mission it described was a result of that deliberate shift that took place in the 1960s.[81] It began with Jesuit schools. Most of their twenty-eight Catholic colleges and universities have described themselves as "Jesuit institutions" rather than as Catholic colleges and universities. They began by changing the "goal of the transformation" of their students from "conversion" to "social justice," shifting the emphasis from the spiritual kingdom to the physical kingdom. Malachi Martin, in his insightful text *The Jesuits: The Society of Jesus and the Betrayal of the Roman Catholic Church,* explains how this change affected the whole Jesuit order. "Material well-being" became the aim of their evangelical efforts, and, instead of sin, "the enemy was now economic, political, and social."[82] Caught up in the social and religious confusion which was rampant in the second half of the twentieth century, the Jesuits made a bid to remain relevant by siding with the activist movements. *Status Envy* reveals how each of the Jesuit universities quietly replaced their former mission statements, which originally had the goal to bring students "to the knowledge of the truth of salvation and the Kingdom of God," with missions that gave students a "commitment to social justice."[83]

In 2014, the Jesuits made a conscious and quite public decision to further define down the Catholic identity on their campuses. A feature article in *The Atlantic* identified a "major rebranding" when Rockhurst University in Kansas City, Missouri, removed the word *Jesuit* from its university tagline; similarly, Regis University in Denver, Colorado, launched a new brand campaign deleting both the words *Jesuit* and *Catholic* from the school's definition and its brand platform. "We hide the word 'Catholic' from prospective students," a

81 Hendershott, *Status Envy,* 58.

82 Malachi Martin, *The Jesuits: The Society of Jesus and the Betrayal of the Roman Catholic Church* (New York: Touchstone Books, 1987), 479.

83 Hendershott, *Status Envy,* 58–59.

Regis spokesperson, Traci McBee, who worked in development, told an *Atlantic* reporter: "We focus on the Jesuit piece rather than the Catholic piece. We're able to transform a little quicker because we are not waiting for the archbishop to give us permission. We don't have to ask the Pope when we want to make changes."[84] Affirming openly what most of us have known for decades, McBee was just acknowledging that most nominally Catholic colleges—with most Jesuit colleges and universities leading the pack—are embarrassed by their connection to the Catholic Church.

A consequence of this mission shift was that the day-to-day functioning of these universities eventually grew farther and farther distant from the work of an active, properly enculturated Catholic identity. An indication of this change can be seen in the prominence of the word "rooted," which is prevalent across many of the mission statements of Catholic universities: "Rather than referring to the Catholic identity, colleges are increasingly describing themselves as being 'rooted' in the Catholic tradition or in the tradition of their founders."[85] This word and its synonyms are often used to indicate a soft, ambiguous relationship to the Church, where Catholicity is viewed primarily as an (intangible) tradition and not as a (tangible) living Magisterium. However, as was noted in the introduction, "Without the Church, the Catholic intellectual tradition is not only something relatively trivial, it is ultimately unintelligible."[86]

The problem of muddying or obscuring Catholic identity became especially apparent as the trend to prioritize social justice spread and became institutionalized "beyond the twenty-eight

[84] Autumn Jones, "The New Brand of Jesuit Universities," *Atlantic*, December 30, 2014, https://www.theatlantic.com/education/archive/2014/12/the-new-brand-of-jesuit-universities/384103/.

[85] Hendershott, *Status Envy*, 50.

[86] Briel, *The University and the Church*, 91.

Jesuits campuses to the majority of Catholic colleges and universities."[87] As the spiritual vision that had given these schools their distinctive shape withered, a counterfeit ideology, laden with enough jargon to make it appear similar, sprang up in its place. This ideology used gospel language to call for a better society and, in this way, seemed to answer what John Paul II had called for in "cultural dialogue" that brought the Faith to the center of what is human.[88] However, for John Paul, an essential premise to this social action was the knowledge "that human culture is open to Revelation and *transcendence*."[89] But it was exactly this openness to transcendence, and especially the revelation of a transcendent God through the Church, that Catholic universities became embarrassed by. As a result, "Catholic education [became] no more distinctive than a secular education."[90]

None of this suggests that a commitment to social justice is bad. Not only is the opposite true, but the Catholic university is a "primary and privileged place" in which to consider the pressing social needs of society, and to respond to them by deploying a robust Christian anthropological vision.[91] The problem arises when the university cuts itself off, in the name of "academic freedom" or "inclusivity," from the living trunk of the Church, relativizing her tradition to the status of one voice among many. Catholic universities cannot hope to pass on faith from a tradition. They must *enculturate* the students into a living and fruitful way of life, or else condemn the student's faith to "the process of self-annihilation."[92] If

87 Hendershott, *Status Envy*, 62.
88 *Ex Corde Ecclesiae*, nos. 43–44.
89 Ibid., no. 43, emphasis added.
90 Hendershott, *Status Envy*, 64.
91 *Ex Corde Ecclesiae*, no. 43.
92 *Ex Corde Ecclesiae*, no. 44.

the Catholic university seeks to remain relevant by always adopting the most current social justice cause, it will inevitably condemn itself to true irrelevance. It will constantly be in a state of *reaction,* and students will quickly lose interest when they realize there are other and more efficient modes of changing the world. The only way to maintain the relevance of the Church is to show the student the perennial truth of how she transcends all of the fluxes that contaminate our social order. The Church alone is the reliable reference point from which those fluxes might be understood.

Of course, it is a paradox of faith that the Church not only transcends this world but is also immanent to it. She is not only the reference point by which social injustices can be judged; she is also a pilgrim walking through the very heart of these struggles. This vision of the Church — at once both far and near — undergirds any proper mission statement. Emphasizing one characteristic to the detriment of the other will leave the Church either cold and unfriendly, like a distant star, or so close to our problems that she is unable to offer any wisdom. Through a deliberate acquiescence to secular culture, most Catholic universities today have fallen into the latter category.

The mission statements of the faithful few, however, reflect a correction to this error. Drawing on the authentic vision of higher education of which *Ex Corde Ecclesiae* is the charter, their mission statements exemplify a commitment to the wholeness of what the Catholic university is.

The First Wave: An Evangelical Mission

Amid the chaos that enveloped Catholic education following Vatican II, a movement of the Spirit led to a revival in some Catholic universities. This caused the first wave of the *Newman Guide* schools, in which several colleges were either reformed or newly founded in the late 1960s and into the 1970s. At the time, there was little external guidance for these founders. However, their universities were grounded in a fervent faithfulness and evangelical zeal inspired by the fact that mainstream Catholic universities were retreating from explicit creedal commitments; they knew that somebody had to hold the standard, and they stepped forward to pick it up.

Franciscan University of Steubenville, Ohio

As discussed in the introduction, Franciscan University experienced its renewal under the hands of Father Scanlan, who took the helm of the school in 1974. As a reflection of its mission orientation, and of the school's renewal as oriented both by Catholicism and the liberal arts, it was renamed from the College of Steubenville to Franciscan University of Steubenville in 1986. Several years later, in 1989, its full-time theology faculty were the first to take the new oath of fidelity to the Magisterium.[93] This came in the same year that the Sacred Congregation for the Doctrine of the Faith had issued a directive requiring all teachers of theology at Catholic institutions to take this oath.

Franciscan's mission statement is a model for Catholic universities of what is expected according to the standards of *Ex Corde Ecclesiae*: a "continuous quest for truth" that accompanies "institutional fidelity to the Church;" an examination of contemporary problems through the lens of Christian anthropology; active pastoral ministry; cultural dialogue; and an outgoing attitude focused on evangelization.

Franciscan University's mission is set out in its bylaws, according to the 1988 revisions, and it is broken down into two parts.[94] The

[93] "The Oath of Fidelity," Franciscan University of Steubenville, https://academics.franciscan.edu/oath-of-fidelity/.

[94] "The Mission, Visions, and Charisms of Franciscan University of Steubenville," Franciscan University of Steubenville, https://franciscan.edu/mission-charisms/.

first part sets out its educational aims, which are to "further the higher education of men and women through programs of liberal, professional and pre-professional studies." Its second paragraph states that the university is "publicly identified as a Catholic and a Franciscan institution," which entails both a "full submission to the teaching authority of the Catholic Church" and a "primacy of theological studies" within the university's educational program.

The mission states that its second, though not secondary, aim, is "to promote the moral, spiritual, and religious values of its students," according to the values of its Catholic and Franciscan identity. To this end, the university follows five general policies: intellectual and faith community, dynamic orthodoxy, evangelization, good stewardship, and Christian maturity. "Dynamic orthodoxy" signals the university's commitment to the active teaching Magisterium of the Church, as it interprets her rich ecclesial tradition. "Christian maturity" references the all-important exchange between faith and life which is present at the university, while the policy on "evangelization" guides the students in learning and communicating a Christian anthropology to the secular world.

Thomas Aquinas College, California

Thomas Aquinas College (TAC) in California established its mission in a much earlier, more contested time. Responding to the Land O'Lakes statement from 1967, founders Ronald McArthur and Marcus Berquist produced "a founding and governing document" for the planned school in 1969, titled *A Proposal for the Fulfillment of Catholic Liberal Arts Education*.[95] Weighing in at fifty-six pages, this document surely deserves a place in the history of Catholic higher education as a lonely light defending the Catholic educational vision at a time when such a view had been

[95] See note 80 above.

sidelined by most in Catholic higher education. Written more than twenty years before *Ex Corde Ecclesiae,* it serves as evidence of John Paul II's "Magna Carta" thesis. Its stated aims of a Catholic university closely match the vision articulated later by the pope.

Essential to TAC's understanding of the university is its emphasis on the importance of institutional fidelity to the Church. The document insists upon the "the central role the teaching Church" must play in a Catholic institution that cultivates the intellectual life.[96] TAC provides an articulate defense for the university's dependence on that teaching authority of the Church. Every person, community, and institution depends on customs, as well as reason, to guide its action. Though reason can be used to refine, interpret, and sometimes reject specific customs, the need for guidance from customs is ubiquitous to the working of the mind. In a similar manner, the Catholic intellectual is to be guided by the Magisterium, as the founding president of TAC, Ronald McArthur, stated: "In so judging theological doctrines, the Church establishes an intellectual custom which is opposed to the fluctuations, weaknesses, and perversities of human custom; it is based upon God's word and the inspiration of the Holy Spirit, and it can never deceive. In following the teaching of the Church here as elsewhere we are more certain of being in the path of truth than we are of any purely human truth we can ever hold."[97]

96 *Proposal for the Fulfillment of Catholic Liberal Education,* 11.

97 Ronald P. McArthur, "The Formation of the Catholic Mind," Thomas Aquinas College, accessed August 12, 2024, https://www.thomasaquinas.edu/a-liberating-education/about/seminal-documents/formation-catholic-mind. He concludes his essay with a stark warning to those Catholics who had abandoned their faithfulness to the Church as a teaching institution: "If, on the other hand, we knowingly reject the guidance of the Church, we, Catholics who have been graced with so many gifts, will be worse than those who have never been given them, and who wander about without ever finding the right path."

This provides support for the claim made by John Paul, that "by its Catholic character, a University is made more capable of conducting an impartial search for truth, a search that is neither subordinated to nor conditioned by particular interests of any kind."[98]

Christendom College, Virginia

Christendom College is a small liberal arts school in Northern Virginia. Overlooking the Shenandoah River, Christendom was also born from the 1960s and 1970s crisis of Catholic identity. Its mission statement opens firmly: "Christendom College is a Catholic coeducational college institutionally committed to the Magisterium of the Roman Catholic Church."

One emphasis within its statement is on the continuous quest for the truth, which the university seeks to impart to its students. Christendom identifies the central purpose of its education as a holistic formation of the person "for a life spent in the pursuit of truth and wisdom." There is a strong alignment with the specific calling of students that John Paul identifies in *Ex Corde Ecclesiae* when he writes that, as a fruit of their education, "they are challenged to continue the search for truth and for meaning throughout their lives."[99] This theme is again picked up under the heading "Service to Church and Society," where John Paul identifies the Catholic university as having a unique role in forming the individual student for a lifelong appreciation of their vocation, having been made "able to assume positions of responsibility in the Church."[100]

[98] *Ex Corde Ecclesiae,* no. 7. As the TAC founding document puts it, "Rather, the Christian student, because of his faith, can be liberally educated in the most perfect and complete way." *Proposal for the Fulfillment of Catholic Liberal Education,* 45.

[99] *Ex Corde Ecclesiae,* no. 23.

[100] Ibid., no. 31.

Christendom's website describes its mission in the following words: "The particular mission of Christendom College, both at the undergraduate and graduate levels, is 'to restore all things in Christ,' by forming men and women to contribute to the Christian renovation of the temporal order. This mission gives Christendom College its name." This expression echoes the words of her founder, Warren Carroll, and the vision driving his work to establish the college. In a report from 1977, the school's first year, Carroll wrote, "Our college takes its name from the word which embodies the Christian social and political ideal: a society … in which Christ the King reigns." According to Carroll, the living out of this ideal "is the heart of our mission."[101]

This mission feeds the whole university system and provides its education with clear direction. In a memo written in the early 1980s, Carroll spoke of the "*apostolic* character of that education" which was "Christendom College's original purpose and mission."[102] Apostolic drive is not an accidental characteristic of this education; rather, it is its guiding light.

Thomas More College of Liberal Arts, New Hampshire

Several of the other *Newman Guide* schools are also deliberately small institutions which each provides its own unique vision for a Catholic liberal arts education. For example, Thomas More College of Liberal Arts (TMC) locates its mission in the great conversation of authors seeking wisdom, identifying the components of its education as great books, discursive dialogue, and sacramental and liturgical life. TMC sees Catholic education as "integral to the mission of the Church in Her proclamation of the Good News." It describes its education as

101 Laura Gossin, *One Man Perched on A Rock: A Biography of Warren Carroll* (Front Royal, VA: Christendom College Press, 2018), 189.

102 Ibid., 222.

one of "Catholic humanism" that thrives on the connection between "faith, reason, and culture."[103]

The Second Wave: Following the Call of *Ex Corde Ecclesiae*

A second wave of faithful universities were founded after 1990. These schools had the ability to form their mission and identity while drawing directly upon *Ex Corde Ecclesiae*. This influence is seen most explicitly in the mission of Ave Maria, but the evangelical spirit of the apostolic constitution can be seen running through each school's mission.

Ave Maria University, Florida

Ave Maria explicitly evokes *Ex Corde Ecclesiae* in its mission statement, as well as its school motto (established in 1998 and 2003, respectively). Describing its educational purpose of "teaching, researching, and learning" from within the "abiding tradition of Catholic thought," Ave Maria roots its work in faithfulness to "Christ and His Church."[104] To fully reflect its ongoing commitment of faithfulness to the institutional body of the Church, the administration added a sentence to its mission after the university relocated to Florida, recognizing the local Diocese of Venice as the guardian and promoter of the university's Catholic identity.[105]

103 "Mission," Thomas More College, https://thomasmorecollege.edu/about/mission/.

104 "Mission," Ave Maria University, https://www.avemaria.edu/about/mission/#readmission.

105 The relationship between a diocese and a university is primarily spelled out in the general norms of *Ex Corde Ecclesiae*, article 5, which is titled, "The Catholic University within the Church." It calls for a "close communion" to be "especially" present between a university and its diocese. Section 2 emphasizes that it is a responsibility of the bishop to "promote the welfare

The mission specifically identifies the role of "a liberal arts curriculum," ordered to the advancement of human culture, in educating its students. Drawing from *Ex Corde Ecclesiae*, it also acknowledges its responsibility as a university for the promotion of dialogue between faith and reason, the formation of men and women in the intellectual and moral virtues of the Catholic Faith, and the development of professional and preprofessional programs in response to local and societal needs.

In this powerful statement, Ave Maria University is recapitulating, almost verbatim, the characteristics of a university mission according to *Ex Corde Ecclesiae*. All of its endeavors find their motivation and purpose in a response to "the call of Vatican II for greater lay witness in contemporary society." Ave Maria places the call, or vocation (from the Latin *vocare*, "to call"), to evangelization at the center of its education.

Wyoming Catholic College, Wyoming; John Paul the Great University, California

Wyoming Catholic College, founded in 2005 and located in central Wyoming, has perhaps the most unique educational mission of any of the *Newman Guide* schools. It identifies a trifecta of "primary sources" — the liberal arts, the Catholic Church, and the wilderness — as the foundation of its education.[106] Believing that an immersion in these primary sources is key to formation of the

of the Catholic universities in his diocese" and to be actively involved if any problem regarding the Catholicity of the university's identity is to arise. Though this guidance leaves a high degree of flexibility for how each university relates to its bishop, Ave Maria chooses what might be described as a "maximalist" approach that recognizes the living authority of the Church in the local diocesan authority.

[106] "Mission," Wyoming Catholic College, https://wyomingcatholic.edu/about/mission/.

mind, spirit, and body, Wyoming includes as part of its curriculum a course of outdoor activities, "answering the call to read God's first book, i.e., creation."[107]

John Paul the Great Catholic College, located in Southern California just outside San Diego, is primarily a technical rather than a liberal arts college, though it does provide a rigorous liberal arts core. Its primary mission is "to impact the culture for Christ" by forming Catholic creators and entrepreneurs, though its technical education is provided alongside classes which steep students "in Catholic Intellectual Tradition."[108]

The Catholic "Legacy" Schools

University of Dallas, Texas; Belmont Abbey, North Carolina; Benedictine College, Kansas; The Catholic University of America, Washington, D.C.

While a significant portion of the *Newman Guide* schools are recent arrivals on the scene, others are historic Catholic colleges that have the impressive legacy of being faithful to a Catholic mission amid the mainstream turmoil of the 1960s and 1970s. The youngest of these, University of Mary, was founded in 1959, while the eldest, Belmont Abbey College, was founded by Benedictine monks in 1876. However, despite not being founded during the revival movement that gave birth to Franciscan, Christendom, and Thomas Aquinas College, each one of these schools has been faithful to John Paul's call for "continuous renewal" in their dual identities as "Catholic" and as a "university."[109]

[107] Interview with Jon Tonkowich, Wyoming Catholic's vice president of Student Affairs, June 16, 2022.

[108] "Vision and Mission," John Paul the Great Catholic University, https://jpcatholic.edu/about/vision.php.

[109] *Ex Corde Ecclesiae,* no. 7.

The University of Dallas (UD), which describes itself as "the Catholic university for independent thinkers," has a strong mission of providing a Catholic, liberal arts education. Identifying "wisdom, truth and virtue" as ends of its education, UD emphasizes its rigorous education that takes students deep into the classical and Western tradition of liberal arts, while preserving a Catholic lens. "The university is dedicated to the recovery of the Christian intellectual tradition, and to the renewal of Catholic theology in fidelity to the Church and in constructive dialogue with the modern world."[110]

Meanwhile, Belmont Abbey College in North Carolina describes itself as "a Benedictine institution," and it states its aim of glorifying God in all things, with its mission "especially revealed in the development of the whole person, guided by the liberal arts, as a responsible steward of the true, the beautiful, and the good."[111] Benedictine College in Kansas describes itself as a "Catholic, Benedictine, liberal arts" school that forms a community on the twin pillars of "faith and scholarship." In its mission statement, the school draws on the commitments of a Benedictine culture and spirituality, represented in the order's vocation to prayer and work (*ora et labora*). The mission statement also describes its firm adherence to "those beliefs and natural principles that form the framework of the Judeo-Christian tradition," as well as "those specific matters of faith of the Roman Catholic tradition, as revealed in the person of Jesus Christ and handed down in the teachings of the Church."[112]

110 "Mission," University of Dallas, https://udallas.smartcatalogiq.com/en/2023-2024/academic-catalog/about-the-university/mission/.

111 "Mission and Vision," Belmont Abbey College, https://belmontabbeycollege.edu/about-us/mission-vision/.

112 "Mission," Benedictine College, https://www.benedictine.edu/about/core/index.

Catholic University of America is the only papally chartered university in the *Newman Guide,* and this pedigree is profiled in its mission. The statement describes the university as "the national university of the Catholic Church in the United States."[113] As such, it leans into the tension of an education that balances the dual identities of American and Catholic, proudly stating that it is "a comprehensive Catholic and American institution of higher learning."[114]

Founded in 1959 and located on the Missouri River just outside Bismarck, North Dakota, the University of Mary (UM) is one of the larger schools profiled in our book, with a population of almost four thousand students. It is sponsored by the Benedictine Sisters of the Annunciation, and the school is a legacy of a Benedictine presence in the Dakotas that stretches back to the 1870s.[115] Its mission statement describes the school's purpose as serving "the religious, academic, and cultural needs of the people in this region and beyond," in language that anticipates *Ex Corde Ecclesiae*'s vision of universities standing in a fruitful relationship with local cultures and communities. In unambiguous terms, UM asserts the university's intellectual and spiritual heritage and identity: "It is Christian, it is Catholic, and it is Benedictine."[116]

University of St. Thomas, Texas; Walsh University, Ohio

The mission statement of the University of St. Thomas, in Houston, Texas, commits the university to the "Catholic intellectual tradition

[113] "At a Glance," Catholic University of America, https://www.catholic.edu/about-us/at-a-glance/index.html#mission.

[114] Ibid.

[115] "Benedictine Sisters of Annunciation Monastery," University of Mary, https://www.umary.edu/about/history-mary/benedictine-sisters-annunciation-monastery.

[116] "Mission & Identity," University of Mary, https://www.umary.edu/about/mission-identity.

and the dialogue between faith and reason."[117] Though it describes itself as a "Catholic university in the heart of Houston," the phrase "Catholic intellectual tradition" is decidedly ambiguous. While this mission statement certainly does not promote anything contrary to a Catholic identity in its mission, its vague language makes it vulnerable to the risk of "mission drift."

In Canton, Ohio, Walsh University's mission statement describes it as a "Catholic, liberal arts and sciences institution." Of the statements discussed so far, it uses the most anemic language, providing what it calls a "values-based education" that derives from an "international perspective in the Judeo-Christian tradition."[118] Choices of words such as "values-based" and "perspective" provide Walsh with a flexibility within which to calibrate its allegiance to Catholic doctrine. It does, however, encourage students to behave in accordance with reason and to be "guided by the example and teachings of Jesus Christ."

Conclusion: Christ-Centered Missions

All but two of the school mission statements (Wyoming Catholic and University of Dallas) explicitly invoke the name of Jesus Christ in either their mission statement or vision statement. Whether they are as bold as Belmont Abbey, which leads its vision with finding "its center in Jesus Christ," or more subtle, like the University of Mary's mention of "faithfulness to the Gospel of Jesus Christ" in the description of its Christian identity, these schools recognize the importance of an explicit recognition of the kingship of Christ as a guide for their work. This stands in stark contrast to the secularized

117 "Mission and Vision," University of St. Thomas, https://www.stthom.edu/About/Mission-and-Vision.aqf.

118 "Vision, Mission, and Identity," Walsh University, https://www.walsh.edu/mission.html.

Catholic schools, like the University of San Diego, whose mission statement was edited to omit "any references to God, Christ, or faith — all included in the mission statements of the past."[119] On May 5, 2023, the University of San Diego's mission statement was revised yet again to proclaim its support for the secular values of "inclusivity and sustainability."[120]

It is worth noting that Catholicity and inclusivity genuinely coexist in the faithful schools not in spite of but *because of* their strong Catholic mission statements. These schools do not exclude participation in the university community because of differing faith or creed but instead sincerely welcome those outside the Faith. However, all participation is modulated by the strong mission and dedication to truth in line with the Magisterium.

Belmont's mission indicates that it "welcomes the talents of everyone, from any background and tradition, who is committed to fostering that development and contributing *to the mission* of the college."[121] The University of St. Mary's statement proclaims, "We warmly welcome students and faculty of many faiths and convictions," but stipulates that "our common discourse ever takes place in a spirit of authentic respect for Catholic teaching and practice."[122] Thomas More College of Liberal Arts states in its mission that it provides "a *Catholic* education for students of *all faiths*, united in the quest for what is true, good, and beautiful."[123] The University of

[119] Hendershott, *Status Envy*, 51.

[120] "Mission, Vision, and Values," University of San Diego, https://www.sandiego.edu/about/mission-vision-values.php.

[121] "Mission and Vision," Belmont Abbey College, https://belmontabbeycollege.edu/about-us/mission-vision/#placement, emphasis added.

[122] "Mission & Identity," University of Mary, https://www.umary.edu/about/mission-identity.

[123] "Mission," Thomas More College of Liberal Arts, https://thomasmorecollege.edu/about/mission/, emphasis added.

Dallas describes itself as "open to faculty and students of all denominations, and it supports their academic and religious freedom" while as an institution it "acknowledges its commitment to the Catholic Church and its teaching."[124] John Paul the Great University mentions in its core values that it "appreciate[s] the diversity among our community with respect to age, intellectual talents, financial resources, creed and ethnic background[s]," yet locates this appreciation within its central mission to "impact culture for Christ" by forming its graduates "to boldly proclaim His Gospel in culture impacting fields."[125]

Clearly then, these universities understand that each of their missions, consecrated as it is to a Catholic education, does not exclude freedom of expression, but also that such freedom is to be exercised *from within* the mission, as an outgrowth of a properly Christian freedom. As Christ Himself says, "If the Son makes you free, you will be free indeed" (John 8:36). These universities know and promote the freedom that Christ speaks of here.

[124] "Vision and Mission," University of Dallas, https://udallas.edu/about/mission.php.

[125] "Vision & Mission," John Paul the Great Catholic University, https://jpcatholic.edu/about/vision.php.

Chapter 3

Letting the Fire Fall at Franciscan University of Steubenville

It is difficult to describe the impact of Franciscan University's beloved former father-president Michael Scanlan on the Franciscan University community without lapsing into what many might view as hyperbole. Just mentioning the late-Father Mike Scanlan's name on campus to those who knew him opens a floodgate of emotion. For most, gratitude for Father Mike's gift to the university characterized our conversations, but for others, there was a real sadness and regret for what one longtime faculty member called "all we've lost" now that he is no longer walking among them on Franciscan's campus. In fact, some of the retired faculty and staff who were interviewed for this book became emotional when they recalled Father Mike's influence on the school and on their own lives; a few of them could hardly get through a short conversation about him without having to stop and compose themselves in order to continue. To say that Father Mike left a lasting impression on Franciscan University is an understatement.

Franciscan professor Scott Hahn, who currently holds the Father Michael Scanlan Chair of Biblical Theology, spoke shortly after Father Mike's death on January 7, 2017, describing him as "one of the pillars of the temple that revitalized the Catholic Church after the

Second Vatican Council.... Father Mike had this charism that, when you met him and left him, your life was never the same."[126]

His legacy reached far beyond the campus. Catholic author George Weigel described Father Mike as "a dynamo of evangelical energy who knew that the renewal of Catholic higher education was a critical component of the New Evangelization. His personal witness, exuberant manner of life, and ability to communicate the Gospel in a joyful way made major contributions not only to Franciscan University, but to the entire Catholic Church in the United States — indeed, to the world Church."[127]

Like all of us who understand what Father Scanlan accomplished in revitalizing a desolate Ohio campus, bereft of a Catholic identity and destined for the dustbin of Catholic history, Weigel knew that Father Mike was no ordinary man. In some ways, he was a revolutionary with a radical openness to the wisdom of the Holy Spirit. He was Harvard-educated and brilliant, but most importantly, Father Mike was first a humble and obedient son of God, willing to do anything God asked him to do. And, like Derry Connolly on that day in the Portiuncula, Father Mike was convinced that God wanted him to rebuild that decaying Ohio campus.

It is not an exaggeration to say that faithful Catholic higher education may have simply disappeared by any meaningful measure had it not been for the inspired efforts of a handful of dedicated Catholic educators, and prominent among these is Father Michael Scanlan. It is true that the once vibrantly Catholic schools such as Georgetown and Notre Dame would have continued to offer an elite secular education with the thin veneer of Catholicity that they offer today. However, it is likely that, in an attempt to broaden their appeal to

[126] Joseph Pronechen, "Father Michael Scanlan (1931–2017): When You Met Him, Your Life Changed," *National Catholic Register*, January 7, 2017.

[127] Pronechen, "Father Michael Scanlan."

more potential students, most of the 230 Potemkin village Catholic schools with their façade of faithfulness and piety would likely have given up the pretense of a Catholic identity altogether. Father Mike knew, even in 1974, that these Catholic-in-name-only schools were flouting Church doctrine on marriage, sexuality, and abortion. Long before the celebrations of Gay Pride month had taken root on most Catholic college campuses, including Notre Dame, there was already an attempt to disregard Catholic teachings on faith and morals. It was not a coincidence that Sandra Fluke, the angry pro-choice law student who made national headlines in 2012 for demanding in a congressional hearing that the government mandate free contraception to students and staff on her campus, was a pro-choice Georgetown University student on a campus that was housing an openly pro-abortion club called "Hoyas for Choice." And although much of the anti-Catholic rhetoric we experience today on most mainstream Catholic campuses was hidden from the public back in 1974, Father Scanlan had the wisdom to know exactly what was coming. He knew that it was only a matter of time before all Catholic higher education would be completely co-opted by the secular culture, and he was determined to stop it.

As part of their presidential search in 1974, the Franciscan University Board of Trustees interviewed three finalists for the position. Two of the candidates handed the board proposals for shuttering the failing university. Father Mike was the only one of the three who was not only adamant that he would keep the school open, but who also refused to be part of the new, secularizing trend in Catholic higher education. He would go on to dedicate the university to Christ the King and draw upon the vibrant Catholic covenant communities in Steubenville to help him renew and revitalize the spirituality of the campus community.

Just as God often chooses unlikely people to do the most extraordinary things, so it seems that God made an unlikely choice in Father Michael Scanlan. While most of us look first at academic qualifications and experience for a job like this, the truth is that God looks at the heart and at our willingness to do good and to put our trust in Him. What He asks for is an openness and a willing spirit to obediently follow His plan for us. As God declared to Samuel, "The LORD sees not as man sees; man looks on the outward appearance, but the LORD looks on the heart" (1 Sam. 16:7). In the kingdom of God, and in the world of Catholic higher education, the person best suited to help a troubled university find its way back may be someone unlooked for or ignored.

Just so, Father Mike had no real preparation to be a university president. He was raised by his mother after his parents divorced when he was just three years old. She later remarried, and the family lived at an exclusive Park Avenue address in New York City. Michael's stepfather was openly hostile to the Catholic Faith, perhaps because of Michael's mother's sadness over her irregular marriage. Nevertheless, Michael was given the opportunity to attend Coindre Hall, a Catholic boarding school led by the Brothers of the Sacred Heart in Huntington, Long Island. It was during the five years he spent at there that Michael fell in love with what he called "sacred things." In his autobiography, *Let the Fire Fall*, Father Mike fondly recalls his favorite teacher there, Brother Bertin, who "combined the highest standards for personal conduct and academic performance with an irresistible loving nature. He was the first man who ever hugged me, and he hugged me often. At the same time, he would correct me for the slightest infraction of the rules. He was especially perturbed when I failed to do my best."[128]

[128] Scanlan, *Let the Fire Fall*, 12.

Graduating at the top of his grammar school class, he won a scholarship to prep school, before going on to Williams College and then completing a law degree at Harvard Law School. As it happened, Coindre Hall was the only formal Catholic education Michael received until he entered the seminary more than twelve years later. Few would have predicted that he would go on to be the leader of a Catholic university that, under his leadership, would become one of the leading faithful Catholic colleges in the country.

God knows, and Michael Scanlan understood, just how tenuous faith can be during the college years when it is not nurtured. He experienced his own crisis of faith during his undergraduate years at Williams College. On the night before his twentieth birthday, on December 1, 1950, feeling lost and confused by what he was learning in his philosophy classes at Williams, he began to question the existence of God:

> I bundled up in warm clothing the next morning, took a notebook and pen and went off into the woods near the campus. I told God my predicament as well as I could. I was too much the confused student to really cry out to God. I knew that he understood my problem better than I did — that is if he existed. So I simply said something like this: "I know you don't want me to be so confused, so lost, so uncertain about everything. Especially about you. If you are there, will you let me know?"[129]

At first, there was nothing particularly prayerful about Michael's long day in the woods. It was hard for him to pray to an abstract God whose existence he doubted. But then, as he recalls, at 9:30 that night, still

[129] Ibid., 16.

in the cold and darkness of the woods, he "suddenly became a believer.... I was very quickly and very unexpectedly filled with faith. I believed in Jesus Christ, the Son of God. I believed that he founded a Church, one that I could trust and give my whole life to. I grasped the truth of the Christian faith again.... The truth was the gospel of Jesus Christ, the rock I could build my life on."[130]

It appears that it was that same rock of the gospel that Father Mike used to rebuild Franciscan University in 1974. When he arrived, the school was clearly failing. Looking back on the state of the university in those first days, he recalled:

> Dorm life was full of promiscuity and predatory sex.... An epidemic of vandalism was turning the campus into a heap of rubble.... Alcohol, drugs, sex, and destructive anger were symptomatic of pervasive loneliness and isolation in student life.... Many were using alcohol and drugs to medicate their depression. Many of the one-night stands and promiscuous relationships were desperate and doomed attempts to find some kind of love and human concern. The year before I came, ten students tried to kill themselves on the Steubenville campus.[131]

The spiritual life of the campus was, he remembered, "virtually non-existent."

In an attempt to try to make the students happy, the dean of students life and his associates sent two petitions to the new President Scanlan. The first was a request for an open, co-ed dorm policy and no curfews; the second petition requested that the college cancel Sunday morning Mass in the chapel, retaining only the afternoon

[130] Ibid., 17–19.
[131] Ibid., 155.

liturgies for students who wanted to go. Few of the students were practicing Catholics, and attendance at Sunday Mass was poor because most stayed in bed on Sunday morning to sleep off their previous night's partying. The dean thought it was a waste of resources to offer the Mass to students who no longer cared about it.

Father Mike denied both petitions and responded to the request to cancel Sunday morning Mass with a surprising announcement: "I am taking over the Sunday liturgy myself. Mass is going to be about one and a half hours long. We're going to need the extra time for singing, praise, intercession, and preaching."[132] Also rejecting the co-ed dorm policy, Father Mike announced the creation of the household system, a program that would become perhaps the most distinctive thing about Franciscan in those early days: "Starting next fall, the dorms are going to be organized into households. Every student will belong to a small group. This group will have a leader. The students in the group will meet regularly for sharing, personal support, discussion of values and goals, and I hope, prayer. By fall everyone will be in them. There will be no exceptions."[133] The household advisors were local laypeople affiliated with the Steubenville Catholic charismatic group known as the Covenant Community. Father Mike credited the household system at Franciscan for the success in elevating dorm life and enhancing the quality of life for all students.

Households are still an important part of campus life today, though they are no longer compulsory. They are often named after biblical themes or after individual saints as role models of a devout life. For example, there is a household called the Apprentices of St. Joseph (ASJ) which encourages its male members to be "lowly apprentices" for Christ, modeling themselves after St. Joseph's virtues

[132] Ibid., 156

[133] Ibid., 157.

of humility, fortitude, chastity, faith, hope, and charity. In their identity statement, members ask St. Joseph to "accept us as his lowly apprentices, that he may teach us the ways of manhood in all things, as he taught Our Lord." Another household, called the Servants of the Savior (SOS), is best known on campus for asking its members to wear distinctive one-piece jumpsuits on one day each week to remind themselves that they are in solidarity with those who serve the Lord. Looking like holy handymen on campus, the SOS jumpsuits provide each member with a constant reminder of their mission to "serve our Lord through serving those around us, as we lay ourselves down at the feet of our neighbors as if each one was the Lord Himself." The female household Daughters of Divine Mercy (DDM) is committed to reminding the world of the merciful love of God toward every human being. Some of the households sell freshly baked bread to raise money for mission trips and charity. One of the male households makes and sells beer bread, while the discernment household for women, Mary, Spouse of the Spirit, sells fasting bread through the Lenten season.

The household system remains the greatest legacy of Father Mike's revitalization efforts because it is a visible and still vibrant presence of Christ in student residential life. When compared with the depravity of modern fraternities and sororities, the utterly unique aspects of the household system become obviously appreciable. Elements of faith and religious ritual are intricately woven into inductions, commitments, activities, and the fabric of daily life. According to Gabriel Salamida, a 2017 Franciscan University graduate and currently Franciscan's coordinator of households on campus, the households continue to reflect Father Mike's vision. A theology major and the coordinator of his own household as an undergraduate, Salamida wanted to mentor students, "to walk with them, pray with them, and to support them."[134] He sees his role as a teacher and a mentor for both the students in the households as well as household leaders, known as coordinators, whom he helps to train and inspire. When we spoke with him, Salamida talked about the importance of the retreats that he plans for the household coordinators each summer, as they give him the opportunity to get to know the coordinators and impress upon them the importance of the spiritual aspects of their position.

About two-thirds of all Franciscan students are affiliated with a household, and Salamida believes it is the most important aspect of student life at Franciscan. When he spoke of their role on campus, he said that "households are the key element that sets us apart.... They make up our social DNA." He said that there is "none of the drama" that you might see in groups like fraternities or sororities on secular campuses. And, he added, "it is rare for a student to dis-affiliate once they have chosen a household.... It almost never happens because they see how much the household brings to their spiritual life — and to their everyday life on campus." Father Mike would be gratified to hear that, especially as he originally intended for the households to directly address the loneliness and alienation prevalent within the student body in 1974. He believed that providing a way for students to find meaning in their lives on campus would enable them to feel connected to each other and to the school. Gabriel Salamida believes that the households are still functioning in this way today.

Once he made inroads into elevating the spiritual life on Steubenville's campus, Father Mike turned his attention to addressing problems in the academic sphere. There were faculty members who were not on board with the new spiritual mission, and Father Mike knew it was time to clean house. He knew the damage that even a single faculty member could do if he or she were hostile to the school's Catholic

[134] Phone interview by Anne Hendershott of Gabriel Salamida, June 17, 2021.

mission. As a result, 1974 and 1975 saw a lot of turnover. For Father Mike, it was important that every faculty member understand the unique Catholic mission of the renewed Franciscan University of Steubenville. Quite simply, those who were not in agreement with that mission could not continue to teach there.

There was still much work to do, but the remaining faculty, together with Father Mike, were committed to the work of improving the school's academics. While business and education majors were strong, few students were majoring in the humanities, and theology was not even offered as a major. Although the school did require two courses in theology in 1974, many on the faculty wanted to reduce that requirement. In fact there was so little commitment to theology that there was not a single full-time theology professor on the entire campus. Father Mike immediately recruited Father Daniel Sinisi, a professor of moral theology at St. Francis Seminary, and charged him with creating a new theology department. Other key faculty who joined included Father Francis Martin, Father Tom Weinandy, Father Jon Bertolucci, and Dr. Alan Schreck, a much loved and highly respected theologian who is still teaching theology at Franciscan University today. Father Mike recognized the talent he was bringing to campus, remembering in his autobiography: "Alan Schreck had been a brilliant student and renewal leader at Notre Dame before studying for his doctorate at St. Michael's in Toronto."[135] Less than a decade after Father Mike became president and began his revitalization campaign on campus, theology became the most popular major in the university. By 1985, there were twice as many theology majors at Steubenville than at either Catholic University or Notre Dame.[136] This trend continues to be true today, as Franciscan University of

[135] Scanlan, *Let the Fire Fall,* 168.

[136] Ibid.

Steubenville is the only university in the country where theology and philosophy are the most popular majors on campus.

As Franciscan has grown, it has continued to expand its course offerings into every corner of academic and preprofessional studies, teaching each discipline under the light of perennial Catholic principles. In addition to the popularity of the theology and philosophy majors, criminal justice is the university's newest major and is on target to become one of the most popular. It is likely that Father Mike would be proud of that major, especially given the current climate of distrust surrounding law enforcement. Rooted in Franciscan's Catholic heritage and commitment to orthodoxy, the criminal justice major has as its center the Catholic legal tradition and moral philosophy. This teaching is essential for forming justice personnel who are as ever mindful of the sacred as they are of the essence of law, the nature of right and justice, and the value and dignity of every human person. Through the analysis of crime, justice, and social control, in a multiplicity of applied settings, Franciscan's criminal justice students develop a definition of justice that is guided by Catholic teachings and its unrivaled moral philosophy.

Meanwhile, nursing continues to be a popular major at Franciscan and is a good example of Father Mike's effort to build a Christian vision into academic work wherever possible. Father Mike wanted every nursing student to enroll in a course in spiritual healing as well as to learn about death and dying from a Christian point of view. Forming this holistic sense of the person was essential. As Father Mike said:

> We are striving to integrate all that we do at Steubenville into a unifying vision. Human life is splitting apart today. Church is separated from state. Communities of people who once shared a common life divide, divide and divide

> again. Sacred knowledge and secular learning have nothing to do with each other. Even secular knowledge has shattered into specialties and subspecialities and sub-subspecialities, with specialists unable to explain to outsiders what they are doing and why they are doing it.[137]

Underpinning all this academic revitalization, Father Mike knew that the renewal of the campus could only come when he was allowed to make spiritual revitalization the highest priority. He knew that spiritual concerns had to be given priority ahead of either financial concerns or academic elitism. Most people who run institutions are not willing to do that. This faithfulness to a Catholic vision, exemplified by Father Mike, is what separates the successful faithful Catholic colleges and universities from the ones that put status concerns ahead of renewal.

While the household system was the most important component of Franciscan's spiritual renewal, Father Mike was not content to stop there. Those who knew him well said that he would pray every morning before the Blessed Sacrament until he "knew" with certainty what God wanted him to do that day. Father Mike wrote in his autobiography that the most important role he had was as "the keeper of the vision.... God supplies the vision and I proclaim it; initiate its implementation in constantly new areas; reinforce it; correct, admonish, pastor, and encourage based on it, and sell it to benefactors, faculty candidates and potential students. I also pray a lot and I try to hear what the Lord wants next for the university." For Father Mike, running the school was a lot like "tending a garden — the flowers are planted there, bursting with potential, but also facing dangers that would snuff them out. My job is to protect and nurture them while the Lord does His work. When the

[137] Ibid., 169.

students are tended properly, they blossom. For my part, I watch in awe; praising God."[138]

Indeed, Franciscan's faithfulness had always been Father Mike's primary concern. In the late 1980s, long before the implementation of *Ex Corde Ecclesiae* on Catholic campuses, he wanted Franciscan's theology and philosophy faculty to join their colleagues teaching at seminaries, who had already begun taking the oath of fidelity in the late 1980s, as required by canon 833. And so, in 1989, Franciscan University gained prominence by becoming the first Catholic university in the United States whose theology faculty, priests, and campus ministers publicly pledged fidelity to the local bishop and to the universal Church. In an interview with Tim Drake of the *National Catholic Register*, Alan Schreck said, "We wanted to make a public statement that we are proudly in submission to the Church."[139] This public statement continues in the presence of the incoming freshman class at a Mass each fall, when the presiding bishop administers the oath of fidelity to all theology and philosophy professors on campus.

Although the mandatum protects students from heretical theology and philosophy professors on faithful campuses, it does not address the content of student courses in the other humanities, in the social sciences, or in the natural sciences. This is why it is so important that the academic administration take an active role in monitoring exactly what occurs in the classroom on a campus that is striving to be faithful. It is also why the job of the president of a faithful Catholic college has an extra layer of difficulty when

[138] Ibid., 172.

[139] Tim Drake, "Mandatum Part VII: Taking an Oath: Franciscan University of Steubenville," *National Catholic Register*, June 2003, available at Catholic Education Resource Center, https://www.catholiceducation.org/en/education/philosophy-of-education/mandatum-part-vii-taking-an-oath-franciscan-university-of-steubenville.html.

compared to most other higher education presidential job descriptions. As I will address in detail later in this book, it is not a coincidence that very few of the faithful *Newman Guide* colleges and universities award tenure to their professors — and even among these limited numbers, Franciscan awards tenure comparatively infrequently. Tenure for a faculty member essentially provides a job for life unless the faculty member engages in such egregious and purposeful conduct that is contrary to the mission of the university as to warrant his or her dismissal.

Revitalizing the Charismatic Authority at Franciscan University of Steubenville

Management theory on transformational leadership predicts that truly transformational leaders are able to alter the self-concept of each follower by linking the identity of the follower into the collective identity of the organization. This is exactly what Father Mike started in 1974 when he began transforming Franciscan from a failing school that had forgotten its mission into the faithful university that it is today. Transformational leaders like Father Mike forge this link between the individual and the organization by emphasizing the intrinsic rewards held by the mission, while deemphasizing the extrinsic rewards. Throughout the process, transformational leaders express high expectations for followers and help them to gain a sense of confidence and self-efficacy. The goal is that followers will start to view their work as an expression of themselves, as the follower is now linked by their own concept of self to the organizational identity.

People who knew Father Mike often referred to him as a "charismatic leader." The original meaning of this word, *charisma,* has relevance in helping to explain the remarkable renewal that Father Mike accomplished. In early Christianity, *charisma* had a very specific meaning, with the Greek root suggesting "divine favor." Key to the power of charisma was renunciation. Some leadership theorists now use the term "charismatic leadership" as synonymous with transformational leadership, which can be true as long as the term *charismatic* is not viewed in purely secular terms, as the prominent German sociologist Max Weber viewed it. Weber recast charismatic authority as the exceptional powers or qualities of certain individuals. But as sociologist Philip Rieff wrote in *Charisma: The Gift of Grace and How It Has Been Taken From Us*, the early uses of the word *charisma* denote a divine origin or a special gift given by God by which certain individuals possess the capacity to remind others of the moral life.[140] Rieff points out that true charisma is tied to the notion of the covenant with God, a covenant that required its followers to resist their lower instincts and to instead obey certain laws and submit themselves to particular prohibitions. In true Christian understanding, charisma is not a rare possession but rather a virtue that is open to all who restrict their self-destructive impulses and instead obey the divine commands that make possible a genuine culture and human inwardness.

From this perspective, the true charismatic leader is one who can convey that, just as there is remarkable good in the world, so there is also evil in the world and in oneself. As R. R. Reno points out, true charisma, in the Christian sense, "describes the gift of what Rieff calls a 'high and holy terror,' which installs the power of divine command so deeply in the soul that we can bear the thought of 'evil in oneself and in the world.' "[141] Rieff points out, as the Catholic leaders of the past used to do, that holy terror is properly the fear of oneself, a fear of the evil within which is drawn to the world's

[140] Philip Rieff, *Charisma: The Gift of Grace and How it Has Been Taken Away from Us* (New York: Pantheon Books, 2007), 6.

[141] R. R. Reno, "Philip Rieff's *Charisma*," *First Things*, April 25, 2007, https://www.firstthings.com/web-exclusives/2007/04/philip-rieffs-charisma.

evil — as well as being the fear of punishment. An understanding of the gift of charisma is key to understanding Father Michael Scanlan's ability to revitalize and renew the failing campus.

Following the model of transformational leadership and charismatic authority that characterized Father Mike's tenure at Franciscan, in 2019 the board of trustees chose Father Dave Pivonka, T.O.R., to lead the university as president. For many on campus and off, Father Pivonka was an inspired choice, perhaps the only choice the board could possibly have made, because of his close association with Father Mike's legacy. Having graduated from Franciscan in 1989, Father Pivonka played a key role in the household system, serving as director of household support from 1996 until 1998. In 1998, he went on to serve as Father Mike's assistant in the president's office. He also served as a professor of theology, director of the university's youth conferences, and director of Franciscan's Austrian study abroad program. In 2003, Father Pivonka was appointed to be the vice president for mission and planning at the university; he served in that capacity from 2003 until 2005. Perhaps even more important, Father Pivonka has combined his academic administrative experience with the kind of evangelistic outreach that Father Mike valued so highly. Prior to his assuming the presidency in 2019, he spent several years as the leader of Franciscan Pathways, an evangelistic initiative of his Franciscan province focused on conversion, spiritual formation, and the Holy Spirit in the lives of Catholics. In that role, he produced a very popular ministry video series on the Holy Spirit called *The Wild Goose*.[142]

Father Pivonka has shown himself committed to Franciscan's mission of providing higher education "from the heart of the

[142] The series is available at Wild Goose TV, https://wildgoose.tv.

Church." Commenting on the choice of Father Pivonka by the board of trustees, David DeWolf, vice-chair of the board, told a Catholic News Agency reporter that the board searched for a president

> who was led by the Holy Spirit, a champion for dynamic orthodoxy and an exceptionally strong executive who understands and values the unique culture and demands of academia and the importance of a strong collaboration between the president and the faculty.... After significant prayer and a robust interview process, it quickly became clear that Father Dave Pivonka possesses all of these qualities.[143]

It is equally clear that the challenges to the mission of faithful Catholic higher education cannot be met through political solutions and a renewed search for better policies. Rather, Father Mike knew that the kinds of problems he faced on that failing campus in 1974, and that Franciscan faced again in 2018 and 2019, emerged from a growing relativism and a loss of meaning. The problems emerged from a lack of will and an unwillingness to confront challenges to the faith-filled culture that guided decision-making under Father Mike's tenure and is guiding it again. Father Pivonka has resurrected a creedal campus ethos and a theology that has already allowed for the reconstruction of a Spirit-infused campus culture. In his newest book, *Living Metanoia: Finding Freedom and Fulfillment in Christ,* he has provided Franciscan with a road map for the future. The word *repent* in Greek is *metanoia,* but as Father Pivonka points out, the original Greek word means much more than just feeling sorry. It means to

[143] "Pivonka Appointed Franciscan University President," *Catholic News Agency,* May 22, 2019, https://www.catholicnewsagency.com/news/41348/pivonka-appointed-franciscan-university-president.

change, to turn, to think differently. It is "not a one-time event but a process."[144]

In 2024, Father Pivonka announced the strategic plan for the future of the university. Entitled "Be Light," the plan calls on the university to "continue the fight for what is right and to be authentically, fearlessly Catholic: courageously standing against the tide of secularism and chaos and committed to the magisterium in everything we do." To accomplish this, the strategic plan calls on Franciscan faculty and staff to "educate, evangelize and form students to engage fully with the world and make a transformative impact," so that they can become "sources of light in board rooms, emergency rooms, classrooms, and courtrooms."[145]

The future of a faithful Franciscan University is promising, but the torch of the Holy Spirit can burn out if it is not continually renewed. If the Faith becomes lukewarm, if Franciscan forgets the lessons of the past, or if future leaders, dissident faculty, or activist students and alumni who are hostile to the faithful mission conspire to extinguish it, its bright light could be extinguished. The challenges and threats are real, and some of these threats will be described in upcoming chapters. Still, for those who are praying for Franciscan University's faithful and continued revitalization, there is much to be thankful for.

[144] Father Dave Pivonka, T.O.R., *Living Metanoia: Finding Freedom and Fulfillment in Christ* (Huntington, IN: Our Sunday Visitor, 2021).

[145] "Strategic Plan Summary," Franciscan University, https://franciscan.edu/be-light/.

Chapter 4

Led by the Spirit at Ave Maria University

When people asked Father Michael Scanlan how Franciscan University differed from other Catholic schools, he told them to look at the mission statements of the more than two hundred Catholic schools: "Notre Dame says it's in the Catholic tradition while Franciscan presents the mind of the Church as it is today, as interpreted by the Magisterium."[146] And although Franciscan University's mission statement remains strong today, describing itself on its website and in all promotional materials as "passionately Catholic," Ave Maria University has the clearest and boldest mission statement in the country. One of the newest and most faithful universities, Ave Maria's mission assures students and their families that the university is "founded in fidelity to Christ and His Church" and promises that "Faith informs the life of the community and takes expression in all its programs."[147]

This bold mission statement at Ave Maria University is not a surprise to those of us who know the story of the founding of this faithful university in a newly created Catholic college town in southwest Florida, near Naples. The school's promise to prospective

[146] Robert McClory, "Steubenville: Echo of Old, or Glimpse of the Future?" *National Catholic Reporter*, March 1, 1996.

[147] "Mission," Ave Maria University, https://www.avemaria.edu/about/mission.

students "to accomplish the distinguishing task of the Catholic university" as identified by *Ex Corde Ecclesiae* comes from the inspiration of her founder, Tom Monaghan. Ave Maria University was born from Monaghan's dream to "unite existentially by intellectual effort two orders of reality that too frequently tend to be placed in opposition as though they were antithetical: the search for truth, and the certainty of already knowing the fount of all truth."[148]

Ave Maria's mission statement, as well as the mission statements of the rest of the faithful few profiled in this book, stands in contrast to the ambiguous mission statements of most nominally Catholic colleges and universities. Ave Maria clearly states its commitment "to the advancement of human culture, the promotion of dialogue between faith and reason, and to the formation of men and women in the intellectual and moral virtues of the Catholic faith."[149] Meanwhile, other "Catholic" schools have moved entirely away from defining themselves as Catholic, while still others have taken a more selective approach to describing their Catholic identity by claiming to value only those aspects of their Catholic heritage they find appropriate.

As we have discussed before, a systematic review of the mission and values statements of more than 230 Catholic colleges and universities confirms Father Scanlan's observations and reveals that most of them have carefully constructed their institutions' descriptions to downplay their ties to Catholic teachings on faith and morals.[150] As noted earlier, some of these so-called Catholic schools have actually deleted the word *Catholic* from their own websites, catalogues, and bulletins, while others have taken a more selective — and ambiguous — approach by describing their Catholicism

[148] *Ex Corde Ecclesiae*, no. 1.

[149] "Mission," Ave Maria University.

[150] Hendershott, *Status Envy*, 47–68.

in terms of "Catholic roots" or "Catholic heritage," claiming to value the aspects of the Catholic tradition they find more palatable, like social justice or inclusivity. Several even seem to apologize for their own Catholic heritage. For example, the statement promoted by the University of St. Joseph in West Hartford, Connecticut, claims that it promises to look "critically" at the Catholic Church — in "an ecumenical manner." It describes itself as "founded by the Sisters of Mercy in the Roman Catholic tradition" and "grounded in its heritage as a Catholic institution, expressing the Catholic tradition in an ecumenical and critical manner." Pledging to prepare students as "global citizens," St. Joseph's mission and values statement claims that the university is "committed to fostering the growth of an inclusive community that welcomes differences among community members and benefits from them."[151]

Father Richard Neuhaus, the late editor of *First Things*, recalled a colleague telling him that when a school is haggling over its mission statement in order to broaden its appeal to non-Catholics or those without faith, or even those who are hostile to the teachings of Catholicism, "it is a sure sign that it has already lost its way."[152] And while that may be too strong a statement, the truth is that decision-makers on Catholic campuses have made a conscious and, in some cases, a well-documented effort to create ambiguity when describing the Catholic identity of their schools. This was the kind of mission uncertainty that led Tom Monaghan to found Ave Maria University as a faithful university in the bona fide Catholic tradition. His goal was that it should reflect the mission to which he has dedicated his

[151] "USJ History, Mission and Goals," University of St. Joseph, Connecticut, https://www.usj.edu/about/usj-history/.

[152] Richard John Neuhaus, "A University of a Particular Kind," *First Things*, April 2007, 32.

own life: "helping as many people as possible get into heaven."[153] It was clear to Monaghan that the best way to save souls was to help students and their families to reject the once-Catholic colleges and universities that have lost their way, and to turn instead to building and supporting an orthodox Catholic university devoted to teaching the truth of the Gospel as it comes to us through the Magisterium of the Catholic Church.

Tom Monaghan's Formation and Transformation

Born during the Great Depression and suddenly fatherless at age four, Tom Monaghan was raised in a Catholic orphanage, then in a foster home, and even for a while in a juvenile detention facility in Michigan, as his widowed mother could not financially support her two children. From the start, Monaghan was an unlikely candidate to become the billionaire businessman and Catholic philanthropist who founded Ave Maria University. Lacking direction after his high school graduation, he joined the Marines, a move that he believes changed his life. It was during his time in the Marine Corps that he came to the realization that, in order to have a good life, he had to find meaning in his life. Having been raised as a Catholic by Felician nuns in the orphanage, the young Marine was "providentially guided" to identify five priorities that would govern the rest of his life: spiritual, social, mental, physical, and financial. Of the five, Monaghan knew that the spiritual priority was the most important. He told his biographer, Joseph Pearce: "Someday, I'm going to die. As I've been taught through my Catholic faith, I am going to spend eternity in heaven or hell, depending on how I lived my life." The Catholic nuns who had taken care of him in the orphanage for more than six years

[153] Burton Bollag, "Who is Catholic?" *Chronicle of Higher Education* 50 (April 9, 2004), 31.

had told him many times, echoing the words of Christ, "What does it profit a man if he gains the whole world but loses his soul?"[154]

The clarification of these priorities and the demands they put on his life provided a kind of road map for the twenty-two-year-old marine. As Pearce writes, "He had been embattled the whole of his young life, and occasionally battered, but never did he become embittered.... He retained trust in his fellow man in spite of the frequent betrayal of that trust from his earliest years."[155]

That trusting nature continues today, and it helps to explain why so many others have, in turn, trusted completely in him. Monaghan has often said, "Nobody can succeed in business without the help of friends."[156] The trust and optimism that has characterized his life is most likely the key to his success, as it inspired a willingness to be open to opportunities and an openness to taking chances, coupled with the confidence that things will eventually turn out the way they are supposed to. It is really just a form of having faith in God and a belief that God is in charge. As long as we are living in accord with God's plan for us, we may suffer setbacks and failures, but we will always be living the way we should be living.

Still, having survived a childhood reminiscent of a Dickens novel, replete with evil men who tried to prey on him, few would have predicted that Tom Monaghan would turn a nine-hundred-dollar investment on December 9, 1960—in a tiny pizza shop in Ypsilanti, Michigan—into the billion-dollar Domino's Pizza empire. And even fewer would have guessed that, in the fall of 1983, he would become the owner of the wildly successful Detroit Tigers, the dream team that won the World Series the following year. But as we

[154] Joseph Pearce, *Monaghan: A Life* (Charlotte, NC: TAN Books, 2016), 47–48.

[155] Ibid., 52.

[156] Ibid., 52.

know from reading his biography, Tom Monaghan always knew he would be successful, and he worked harder than anyone could ever imagine to make his worldly success a reality, achieving a place on the list of the wealthiest Americans by the mid-1980s. He fulfilled each and every one of his boyhood dreams: purchasing his own Sikorsky S-76 helicopter, a Gulfstream jet, and a fleet of more than two hundred cars, including Duesenbergs, Ferraris, a Bugatti Royale, and even the Packard that was used to transport Franklin Delano Roosevelt to his inauguration. He spent $35 million purchasing and building an island resort, and he became the world's leading collector of the works of Frank Lloyd Wright. An article in the *New Yorker* reported that he spent $1.6 million on a Frank Lloyd Wright dining room suite.[157]

But just as he had experienced the providential insight as a young Marine that he needed to get his "five priorities" in order, Monaghan experienced yet another revelation — this time, a more painful one — when he realized that he was becoming prideful. In an interview with Joseph Pearce, he recalled how he was reading C. S. Lewis's book *Mere Christianity,* and became aware of his own pride. He realized that pride was "the essential vice, the utmost evil.... It was through Pride that the devil became the devil; Pride leads to every other vice; it is the complete anti-God state of mind." Monaghan realized that he had become prideful. He knew that he "wanted to impress other people with his worldly goods and accomplishments." He said that he "realized at one point what I wanted to be was a billionaire saint."[158]

However, he understood that he could not offer himself to Christ and at the same time remain so attached to the luxurious lifestyle he

[157] Peter J. Boyer, "The Deliverer: A Pizza Mogul Funds a Moral Crusade," *New Yorker*, February 11, 2007.

[158] Pearce, *Monaghan*, 150.

had built. So, the very next day, he began to sell everything: the helicopter, the Gulfstream, and the Bugatti. He sold his Wright collection, and he sold his island resort. In 1992, he sold the Detroit Tigers to the owner of his pizza competitor, Little Caesars. And, in 1998, announcing that he would devote the rest of his life and his resources to the Church, he sold his Domino's Pizza empire for a billion dollars to Bain Capital, telling a reporter for the *New York Times* that "I want to die broke."[159] He believed that he "could get along without the luxuries, that I wasn't addicted to them." In the words of Pearce, he knew that it was time to make a choice "between the good life and the life of luxury, the life of virtue, which is inseparable from the cross of suffering, or the life of comfort, which can easily become the path of least resistance that leads to hell."[160]

Monaghan then set out to expand his Catholic philanthropy. He had already been a generous contributor to Catholic charities in both the United States and Central America in the 1980s, having donated several million dollars to rebuilding the cathedral in Managua, Nicaragua, and supporting a mission in the Honduran mountain town of San Pedro Sula. In 1987, after a fortuitous meeting with Pope St. John Paul, Monaghan founded Legatus, an organization designed to help Catholic executives to spread the Catholic Faith in their business and personal lives. He also provided funding for the founding of the Ave Maria radio station and the Thomas More Law Center, both based in the Ann Arbor, Michigan area. Having served on the boards of trustees of several Catholic colleges, including Catholic University of America and Franciscan University of Steubenville, Monaghan had also been generous to Catholic higher education. It is not an exaggeration to

[159] Alex Prud'Homme, "Taking the Gospel to the Rich," *New York Times*, February 14, 1999.

[160] Pearce, *Monaghan*, 151.

say that Tom Monaghan helped fulfill Father Scanlan's goal of restoring the Faith at Franciscan University of Steubenville.

But Monaghan had bigger plans for Catholic higher education. He had become disillusioned by what he believed was the loss of the Catholic identity at Catholic University of America in the 1980s and 1990s. As a member of the board of trustees, he attempted to motivate the other board members to pay attention to what he knew was the problem of heterodox teachings in CUA's theology department. He was especially disappointed with CUA's common practice of giving honors and accolades to visiting pro-choice politicians and others whose views contradicted Catholic teachings on life and the sanctity of marriage. As Pearce points out, Monaghan became "a nuisance to the lukewarm and indifferent members of the Board, and to the heretics on the faculty, he had become an irritating thorn in their side."[161] Angered by what they considered to be his encroachment on the academic and student life on campus, some of the most heretical and radical CUA faculty members persuaded several of the board members to move against him when his membership on the CUA Board came up for renewal, and he was removed. Although he remained on the board of Franciscan University for a while longer, he began to believe that he was being called to create a new and more faithful Catholic college, one that he could help to shape and could guarantee would remain faithful and would fully honor God.

The Founding and Early Days of Ave Maria

In 1998, Monaghan founded Ave Maria College in Ypsilanti, near Ann Arbor. Then, in 2000, he opened the Ave Maria School of Law in Ann Arbor. He had elaborate plans to combine the schools into Ave Maria University in Ann Arbor Township, but these plans fell through when

[161] Ibid., 172.

Ann Arbor officials denied the necessary zoning change in 2002. Later that year, he announced that the Barron Collier Company, a Florida developer, had donated 750 acres of farmland on the northwest edge of the Everglades to the new university.

And so Monaghan changed his plans away from Michigan and chose instead to build Ave Maria University on that donated land in Florida, while investing another $50 million in a separate partnership with Barron Collier to build the adjoining Ave Maria town. Promising to continue operations in Michigan until 2007, when the current Ave Maria College students would graduate, Monaghan attempted to placate those members of the faculty who had chosen to remain in Michigan, as well as some disgruntled students and alumni. But when he pledged more than $250 million to help build the new campus in Florida, the resentment grew. Angry that their founder's largesse was being transferred south, Michigan faculty and some bitter board members mobilized resistance. In a bid to stall the Michigan campus's closure, Ave Maria College's academic dean sued Monaghan and the school's trustees in 2004, but a state court judge dismissed the suit.

Despite the early turmoil, most Ave Maria College professors relocated to the new Florida campus. Today, the university continues to attract new professors who are committed to providing the kind of serious formation in Catholic and theological tradition that is essential to Catholic higher education, and Monaghan remains committed to helping Ave Maria remain faithful to the Magisterium of the Catholic Church. It really is as simple as that. As a member of the board of trustees at Catholic University of America, Monaghan witnessed the slow decline in faithfulness of the most important Catholic university in the country. He watched CUA lose its way when the administration paid no attention to the growing heterodoxy of its theology professors. He understood better than most what had contributed to the degradation of the student and academic culture at Franciscan before Father Scanlan took control of the wheel, and he simply wanted to prevent that from happening to Ave Maria University.

Not surprisingly, in the world of academia, a world that is saturated with status envy, any success that an orthodox Catholic school might experience is frequently greeted with jeers from envious competitors. The late Georgetown University law professor and prominent dissident Father Robert Drinan, S.J., was especially vitriolic in his response to the news that Tom Monaghan was creating a new and faithful Catholic law school. A promoter of pro-choice public policy supporting expansion of access to abortion during the time he served for ten years in the U.S. House of Representatives as a congressman from Massachusetts, Drinan complained that the founding of Ave Maria Law School was "simply a vehicle to advance a right-wing agenda." Father Drinan accused Ave Maria of "implying that the other 26 Catholic law schools aren't Catholic enough, so they had to take their pizza money and put it elsewhere.... Why not contribute to an existing school?... Why go off and start this free-floating school that has no university or diocese attached to it?"[162]

Likewise, Monika Hellwig, a former religious sister who left the convent to pursue an academic career as a theology professor at Georgetown University, dismissed the need for a new Catholic law school, saying that "Catholic law schools and the Jesuit schools in particular have been offering legal clinics for the poor and addressing Catholic social teachings for years.... They pride themselves on being extremely Catholic."[163] Hellwig ignored the fact that faculty

[162] Katherine Manga, "Ave Maria: A Seriously Catholic Law School," *Chronicle of Higher Education* 46 (February 18, 2000), A18.

[163] Quoted in ibid.

at Georgetown Law School were instrumental in promoting expanded access to abortion. She functioned as a kind of lobbyist/apologist for Catholic higher education during her years as the president and executive director of the Association of Catholic Colleges and Universities (ACCU) before her death in 2005. In her leadership position, she was instrumental in resisting the tenets of *Ex Corde Ecclesiae*, especially the mandatum that required theology faculty to teach in communion with the Church's teaching. In a 2001 article, she compared *Ex Corde Ecclesia* to "the Crusades and burnings at the stake" and predicted that, with time, ecclesial authorities would cease trying to enforce what she saw as opprobrious regulation. She wrote, "Then came 1990 and the apostolic constitution *Ex Corde Ecclesiae,* and increasingly shrill demands from the Roman Curia that universities around the world be reshaped to fit inside the predetermined rules.... Creative expressions of faith in quest of understanding can be reprimanded, punished and exiled, but they cannot be killed by such means. Thrown out at the door of the hierarchic church, and forbidden the designation Catholic, they flow back through the windows to find themselves at home among the people of God."[164] It is no surprise to anyone who knows the sad state of theology on CUA's campus, beginning in the 1960s, to learn that Hellwig received her doctoral degree in theology at Catholic University in 1966.

Tom Monaghan's response to such criticisms from Father Drinan and Dr. Hellwig was to simply state, "There's nothing wrong with most Catholic schools, except they're not Catholic." He defended his academic initiatives by acknowledging that, although there are many Catholic institutions addressing social justice

[164] Monika K. Hellwig, "The Survival of Catholic Higher Education," *America*, July 16, 2001, https://www.americamagazine.org/issue/326/state-question/survival-catholic-higher-education.

issues, "There's no one doing the spiritual, morality, kinds of things. There's more of a need there."[165] He believes that Ave Maria is the only national Catholic law school completely dedicated to providing students with an outstanding legal education enhanced by the teachings of the Catholic Church. For Monaghan, "Law is such an important profession. It is lawyers who effectively run our country. They have so much influence on our society.... It's important that future lawyers are trained in ethics."[166] He knows that this kind of ethical training can only occur on an orthodox campus like Ave Maria, but he also knows that it will be a constant battle to maintain that orthodoxy.

Taking the Lead in Confronting Gender Ideologies

It is clear that Ave Maria University has moved beyond its difficult days of the early 2000s as its focus today remains on meeting all challenges with fidelity. As the transgender movement gained greater visibility and acceptance in mainstream society in 2022 — replete with new mandates from the Biden administration offering federal protections against discrimination for transgender individuals, faithful Catholic campuses have had to respond to threats to their Catholic identity from this quarter. It takes courageous faith for a Catholic college to attempt to counter these types of federal mandates, and the all-too-tempting option is to ignore any confrontation on this front. To its credit, Ave Maria's visionary provost, Professor Roger Nutt, understood and took action to oppose the threat long before any other faithful Catholic colleges and universities did. In 2021, he mobilized the faculty and staff to develop a

[165] Lisa Miller, "Tom Monaghan's Scope, Style, Stir Rancor in His Local Diocese," *Wall Street Journal*, June 21, 2000, https://www.wsj.com/articles/SB961540183229160764.

[166] Pearce, *Monaghan*, 185.

robust policy designed to protect the university from the transgender mandates that he anticipated would be imposed by the federal government. The policy reads:

> As a Catholic institution of higher learning, Ave Maria University adheres to the following essential points of Catholic teaching on the nature of the human person vis-a-vis gender and biological sex:
>
> 1. Human beings are created male and female by God (Gen. 1:27).
> 2. The human person is a body–soul union. The body — created male or female — is a constitutive aspect of the human person.
> 3. Sexual difference is willed by God as part of the divine plan. The complementarity that results from this differentiation is ordered to the human good, particularly to marriage and family life.
> 4. For the sake of their flourishing and fulfillment, all human beings are called to accept their sexual identity, manifested through the body, as a fixed and unchanging element of their psychosomatic identity and personhood.
>
> As a result of these essential points of Catholic teaching, the conduct of all members of the Ave Maria University community, including, but not limited to, students, faculty (full and part-time), staff (administration and coaches, whether full or part-time), will be held accountable to the following expectation:

1. They will conduct themselves in accord with their biological sex at all times, both on campus and when representing the school at off-campus events.

2. They will dress in a manner that corresponds with their biological sex. No administrator, employee, or student of the University may waive this requirement.

3. They will participate in competitive athletics and other University-related events, live in residence, use any bathroom or changing facilities, and address themselves and be addressed with pronouns and proper names that are in accord with their biological sex.[167]

This strong policy, which the university believes will allow it to deal with the transgender issue in a faithful, Catholic way, avails itself of the rich Catholic teaching on the issue of sexuality. It draws upon Scripture (Genesis 1:27), as well as Catholic documents such as *Persona Humana* (Declaration on Certain Questions Concerning Sexual Ethics), Pope St. John Paul II's "Male and Female He Created Them," and various speeches and papal documents from Pope St. John Paul II, Pope Benedict XVI, and Pope Francis. Ave Maria's policy serves as an excellent model for other Catholic universities going forward who seek to keep their mission faithful to Catholic teaching.[168]

[167] *Ave Maria University Student Handbook, 2024–2025*, 84, Ave Maria University, https://www.avemaria.edu/student-handbook.

[168] This policy can be fruitfully contrasted with a policy published by another Catholic school, Villanova University, just outside Philadelphia. In the fall of 2022, its Office for Diversity, Equity, and Inclusion collaborated with the Gender and Women Studies department, among others, to produce a "Gender Inclusive Practices Guide" for faculty and staff insisting on "best practices for being gender inclusive," with attention being given "especially for those who identify within transgender, nonbinary, gender nonconforming,

Faculty Faithfulness Is Key to an Authentically Catholic University

As University of Notre Dame law professor Gerard Bradley reminds us, the faithfulness of the faculty is the principle of a Catholic university: "No college can be much more or will be much less Catholic than its faculty. Without a solidly Catholic faculty, there is nothing a college can do to be Catholic; with a solidly Catholic faculty, there is little more that needs to be done." In sum, "the soul of a university is its faculty."[169] Ignoring such wisdom, most of the Catholic universities that have lost their way have compartmentalized their "Catholicity" by relegating it to the margins of the campus, in the offices of university ministry, social justice, community service, or mission trips. While Professor Bradley supports such social justice activities and acknowledges their importance as one part of the Catholic mission, he reminds us: "You do not set up a university in order to [run] soup kitchens. You do not keep a university going so that young people can go on retreats. Even if every student and staff member works Easter vacation for Habitat for Humanity, that does not make a college Catholic. You need a Catholic *education* for that."[170]

Bradley has suggested that most Catholic-in-name-only universities have adopted the idea that a Catholic university is simply a

---

and/or gender questioning communities." The guide describes "gender inclusivity" as "fundamental to Villanova's mission" and touts the recently available option for all members of the Villanova community to include preferred pronouns in university communications. This methodology being promoted by Villanova, which ignores the rich Catholic heritage on gender present in Ave Maria's policy statement, seems to represent the trend among the majority of mainstream Catholic universities. "Gender Inclusive Practices," Villanova University, https://www1.villanova.edu/content/dam/villanova/vital/pdfs/genderinclusivepracticesvu0822.pdf.

169 Gerard V. Bradley, "Looking Ahead at Catholic Higher Education," *Fellowship of Catholic Scholars Quarterly* 25, no. 2 (Spring, 2002), 21.

170 Ibid., 20.

> generic product in a different wrapping.... Just as a single laundry detergent is chemically and in every other substantive way indistinguishable from other laundry detergents, most Catholic colleges have become indistinguishable from other colleges that you can buy anywhere. The only difference is that Catholic colleges are wrapped distinctively and marketed with a lot of hype about the kind of person you must be because you buy Catholic: concerned, caring, different, spiritual."[171]

Bradley goes on to say that "it is essential that only Catholics who hold the faith teach the theological disciplines. Canon Law required it."[172] But it is not just theology that matters. A truly faithful Catholic university, across all disciplines, can only employ faculty members who support Catholic teachings. That is truly what differentiates the faithful schools from the faithless ones. The truth of the gospel message must be present in all departments of the faithful Catholic university, from the departments of social sciences and humanities to biochemistry, from the schools of education to the schools of nursing. Ave Maria University has always recognized this need for faculty faithfulness, and this criterion is an important part of the hiring process of all faculty members.

Ave Maria's Culture of Life and Dedication to Mary, Our Mother

Like many of the faithful few, Ave Maria University demonstrates its commitment to a culture of life by helping Ave Maria students to attend the annual March for Life in Washington, D.C., each January, and by providing opportunities to pray outside an abortion clinic not far from campus. But that commitment does not end

[171] Ibid., 17.
[172] Ibid., 21.

there. Rather, it is visible in classes like Theology of the Body, Philosophy of Love, and the newest Ave Maria philosophy class offering, Philosophy of Motherhood. Taught by associate professor of philosophy Dr. Janice Chik Breidenbach, the course is designed to address all aspects of motherhood from a philosophical and a Catholic perspective. In an interview published in a 2021 issue of *Ave Maria Magazine*, Dr. Breidenbach, who is herself a mother, said that "the class is intended to obliterate the politicization and compartmentalization of motherhood" by asking the questions: "What is a mother? How is motherhood differentiated from fatherhood? Is motherhood work or leisure?" For Breidenbach, the goal is to urge people to think about what motherhood is: "Motherhood is the quest to assist the child to discover and discern their vocation with God — what their calling is, what their particular path in life is, that God is laying out for them. It's the parent's duty and privilege to assist the child with that." One of the students who is enrolled in the Motherhood course concluded, "It's especially important such a class is taught at Ave Maria University.... We are Ave Maria, we are Hail Mary. We are a school dedicated to *Theotokos* — Mary, the Mother of God."[173] The devil's first attack on mankind was an attack on a woman, and the work of salvation began with the yes of the woman: the Blessed Virgin Mary. It is the goal of the course that Ave Maria students understand motherhood as "anointed, and vocational, and bring this powerful truth into their workplaces and homes, thus changing the world."[174]

This devotion to the Blessed Mother permeates the entire campus. Each evening there is a student-led Rosary Walk on campus. There are also opportunities to participate in several Marian

[173] Ibid., 17.

[174] Annie Schlueter, "Philosophy of Motherhood," *Ave Maria Magazine*, Spring 2021, 14–15.

devotions which are practiced daily by Ave Maria students. As at Franciscan University, during the school year the Adoration chapel on campus is open twenty-four hours a day, seven days a week, for perpetual Adoration before the Blessed Sacrament. There are seven weekend Masses and five daily Masses on campus while school is in session. Confession is available regularly, both in the smaller chapel and in the main church. Campus Ministry works closely with Student Affairs to integrate the practice of the Catholic Faith with a dynamic Catholic student life. For example, there are programs like Theology on Tap that provide informal ways for students to learn about the Catholic Faith.

In addition to campus ministry, there are additional extracurricular opportunities "off-campus" in Ave Maria town, including "Mary's Marines," which is a nationwide movement that unites young women and men in the pursuit of holiness through Marian consecration and Divine Mercy. According to the Mary and Mercy website, the key belief spurring them on the path to their commitment is that "Now is the Time for Mercy."[175] Intended to assist young adults in networking with like-minded others, Mary's Marines was created to build relationships and provide crucial encouragement to one another in their walk with Christ. On campus, they are also involved in getting students to commit to anywhere from fifteen minutes to a full hour of daily Adoration.[176] Mary's Marines are dedicated to working together to share the joy of the gospel: "We understand and practice what it means to be a saint. Living Marian and Loving Mercifully is the true Catholic option in the life of the twenty-first century young adult."[177]

[175] "Mary and Mercy Center," Ave Maria Catholics, www.avemariacatholics.com/mary-and-mercy-center.

[176] "Commit to a Daily Holy Hour," Ave Maria University, https://www.avemaria.edu/marys-marines/.

[177] "About Us," Mercy through Mary, https://mercythroughmary.org/about/.

Coaching as a Calling at Ave Maria University

Of all the faithful Catholic colleges and universities described in these chapters, it is clear that Ave Maria University has been the most committed to intentionally integrating the Catholic Faith into collegiate athletics, promoting the formation of mind, body, and spirit. However, this was not the case in the earliest days of athletics on the Florida campus, as faculty became concerned that many student athletes recruited to participate in athletics at Ave Maria did not understand the Catholic culture of the school. But all of that changed when the leadership changed, and now a renewed sense of intentionality shows in every aspect of every sport. As of 2021, the pregame music for men's soccer games at Ave Maria is a ten-song playlist featuring "Ubi Caritas," "Panis Angelicus," and Bach's "Ave Maria." The university's athletic director, Joe Patterson, who is also the head football coach, told a reporter for *Ave Maria Magazine*, "The first time I heard the pregame playlist, it struck me deeply. What a tremendous reminder of the divine and of our ultimate goal.... Christ gave us a playbook for happiness, we just need to faithfully follow it."[178] For Patterson, "Teamwork is underpinned by the ability to trust. Trust is what opens the door to conversion of heart. Love conquers all and it's this conquering love that exemplifies what is best about sports." This does not mean that Ave Maria is not committed to competing and excelling. After going 0–10 during his first football season, Patterson's football team won the conference championship two years later. The soccer team finished the 2020 season with its best record ever and hosted and won a playoff game. Likewise, the men's and women's cross-country teams finished the 2020 season with second-place finishes in the conference

[178] Joe Patterson, "Coaching as a Calling," *Ave Maria Magazine*, Spring 2021, 20–21.

championships. And the men's basketball team has a win percentage of about seventy. Jamon Copeland, the head men's basketball coach, is a regular at the 12:15 p.m. daily Mass, and he says that he "seeks clarity from our Lord in the Eucharist and from visiting Him in the tabernacle." In the Host, Copeland said that he finds "the wisdom and direction to complete the tasks before me." Sports and faith are intertwined for Copeland because he believes that, when done properly, "sports will reward the same virtues that life rewards. Happiness awaits those who prioritize faith, self-sacrifice, discipline and teamwork."[179]

A New President Answers *Ex Corde Ecclesiae's* Call to Evangelization

In early 2022, Ave Maria University's board of trustees made a conscious decision to strengthen the commitment Tom Monaghan made back in 2003 to fulfilling the tenets of *Ex Corde Ecclesiae* by enlisting Mark Middendorf to be its new president. Previously the executive vice president of Mission Expansion at the Augustine Institute, Middendorf brings a proven commitment to evangelization. His vision is in keeping with Tom Monaghan's primary goal for creating Ave Maria University, which has always been to help as many people as possible to get to Heaven. Evangelization is also the fulfillment of one of the most important components of *Ex Corde Ecclesiae*, as the Holy Father called upon Catholic colleges and universities to respond to the "universal call to evangelization": "Every Catholic University is to maintain communion with the universal Church and the Holy See; it is to be in close communion with the local Church and in particular with the diocesan Bishops of the region or nation in which it is located. In ways consistent with its nature as a University, a

[179] Ibid.

Catholic University will contribute to the Church's work of evangelization."[180] President Middendorf understands this work of evangelization and has devoted most of his life to that goal through creating successful biblically based programs such as FORMED, a digital platform with Catholic film, e-books, and audio talks. He is expanding the university's ability to evangelize and is providing students and faculty with greatly enhanced opportunities.

With the selection of President Middendorf, Ave Maria University is poised to be the premier Catholic university in the country for evangelization and biblical scholarship. President Middendorf is an inspired choice to help Ave Maria meet its founder's ultimate goal, clearly articulated at the conclusion of Monaghan's autobiography, *Pizza Tiger:* "I believe there's something in life bigger and more important than Domino's. I have faith that God will help me find it, and that He'll show me the way to my ultimate goal which is to go to heaven and take as many people as possible with me."[181]

[180] *Ex Corde Ecclesiae,* General Norms, art. 5, sec. 1.

[181] Tom Monaghan, with Robert Anderson, *Pizza Tiger* (New York: Random House, 1986), 346.

Chapter 5

Seeing Things as They Are: Liberal Arts at the Faithful Schools

While most historians — including Philip Gleason — view the period from 1930 to 1960 as the halcyon days of the Catholic Church and her Catholic colleges and institutions because of their numerical growth, organizational vigor, and spiritual vitality, other historians point to signs of trouble during these days.[182] After World War II, Catholics increasingly embraced the American values of pluralism, tolerance, and diversity. And, in the 1960s, what Gleason called a "perfect storm" of academic social and Church currents rocked Catholic colleges: "The priority of individual conscience over the law diffused itself.... Catholics may have been particularly susceptible to the message because of the modernizing trends at the Second Vatican Council. It legitimated change. It reinforced assimilative tendencies."[183]

In 1968, sociologists Christopher Jencks and David Riesman pointed out in their book, *The Academic Revolution*, that "a Catholic elite began to emerge that was American first and Catholic

[182] "Scholar Traces History of Catholic Identity of Universities," *Catholic News Service*, October 28, 2005, https://www.thefreelibrary.com/Scholar+traces+history+of+Catholic+identity+of+universities-a0138535327.

[183] Ibid.

second."[184] Catholic scholars began to seek status by striving for what Jencks and Riesman described as the "Harvard-Berkeley model" of the research university.[185] Academic freedom, increased faculty participation in governance, and the growing abandonment of the neoscholastic approach were elements in that status-striving. And although Jencks and Riesman acknowledged that nearly all colleges and universities aspired to higher status, *The Academic Revolution* held out hope that Catholic higher education would be able to provide educational philosophy and personnel for developing alternatives that managed to "fuse academic professionalism with concerns for questions of ultimate social and moral importance."[186] This hope was never fulfilled by most Catholic colleges and universities.

No one understood this better than Father Robert Gannon of the Society of Jesus, who warned in 1961 that a "new system of thought" had been aggressively and progressively overtaking the institutions of learning. This system, which he named plainly as "naturalism," had at its core the conclusion that "nature is the source of all; all is explained by nature because there is no reason to suppose the existence of the supernatural or the spiritual."[187]

Gannon published these thoughts in an important autobiographical account of the trends he had witnessed take their course over the past half a century in higher education. A product of Jesuit education himself and a scholar who had been at the heart of the Catholic education scene, including a tenure as president of Fordham University,

[184] Christopher Jencks and David Riesman, *The Academic Revolution* (New Brunswick, NJ: Transaction Publishers, 1968), 338.

[185] Ibid., 405.

[186] Ibid.

[187] Robert I. Gannon, S.J., *The Poor Old Liberal Arts*, 2nd ed. (San Francisco: Ignatius Press, 2018), 34.

Gannon invoked the evening of his life as a universal "privilege to relax and think out loud without too much intellectual discipline," reflecting on the many changes he had witnessed over the course of decades.[188]

As an atheistic movement, naturalism stripped away the liberating principles of thought and behavior that Christian humanism had secured as its heritage. Ironically, it was universities that had become beachheads in this war, said Gannon, and they "had been hacking away at the twin foundations of their own house," which were "Christianity and Hellenism."[189] For all this, Gannon ended on a note of optimism, hinting that if Catholic universities—and here he spoke hopefully of his own Jesuit colleges and universities to which he had dedicated his life in serving—understood the spirit of the times, they might still remain viable as institutions of faithful Christian learning.

Of course, Gannon's hopes were not to be realized. In 1969, Fordham decided it would become an "independent institution."[190] The year before Gannon died, in 1978, Fordham made the official request that the Jesuits not speak of the university as their apostolate, but instead of the "Jesuit apostolate at (or in) the university."[191] It would ultimately become clear that Gannon belonged to the last generation of robustly Catholic educators. A scholar who rubbed shoulders with the likes of Father Martin D'Arcy and Christopher Dawson,[192] he was prescient enough to see a shift in the current of Catholic education which many had not yet observed, even if he was overly hopeful about the possibility of turning back the tide. This sea change, by which "the classical Christian tradition of the liberal arts

[188] Ibid., 17.

[189] Ibid., 130.

[190] Thomas J. Shelley, *Fordham: A History of the Jesuit University of New York: 1841–2003* (New York: Fordham University Press, 2016), 403.

[191] Burtchaell, *Dying of the Light*, 609. For a more extended discussion of Fordham's decline, see chapter 10.

[192] Gannon, *Poor Old Liberal Arts*, 141.

merged imperceptibly into the liberal humanistic tradition," only became more perceptible and more complete in the decades following his diagnosis.[193]

Gannon's perspicacity, however, allowed him to identify the nature of the fundamental shift, the undercurrent that was driving the overwhelming torrent of change, even while others fixated on the loss of this or that traditional element of Catholic education. From its beginning, Jesuit education had been ordered toward the holistic formation of the individual. "Learning was not an end in itself but a means whose end was to make men more human and spiritual."[194] Catholic education, at its best, was more than just a course list of scholastic subjects and an education in Greek and Latin. Rather, it enculturated the student into a Catholic mind, a way of viewing the world which casts its light over every discipline.[195]

It was this way of seeing that John Henry Newman described in his lectures, *The Idea of a University*. Perhaps the most influential work in modern times discussing the principles of Catholic education, Newman believed that Catholic education should function as an integrated whole to form students in both the moral and intellectual virtues.[196] A liberal education aimed to offer a formation for the mind, so that "what was an unintelligible wilderness becomes a landscape or a scene."[197] A Catholic educational institution provides that liberal education within the context of divine revelation. In Newman's mind, the Church was

193 Ibid., 34.

194 Ibid., 29.

195 Ibid., 107–108. It was this ideal of education that was to inspire Don Briel when he founded the Catholic Studies program at the University of St. Thomas in 1990.

196 John Crosby, "Newman's Vision of the Intellectual Virtues," (presentation at conference on Liberal Education and John Henry Newman, University of Navarre, Spain, October 2019).

197 Newman, *Idea of a University*, 495.

"in the business," so to speak, of establishing universities so that it could bring the spiritual and the humanist ideals into harmony and bring the moral and the intellectual virtues to perfection. His vision was that universities unite the secular and the sacred, so as "to be at once oracles of philosophy and shrines of devotion," where both the religious and the intellectual searches for truth were reified.[198]

In some important ways, Newman's call was answered by Pope St. John Paul in *Ex Corde Ecclesiae* in which he wrote of the Catholic university's mission to unite the two methodologies: "the search for truth and the certainty of already knowing the fount of truth" (no. 1). Pope John Paul believed, as University of Notre Dame professor Father Wilson Miscamble, C.S.C., correctly observed, that every Catholic university should become "a place where reason and faith supported each other" in the educational endeavor.[199] In this regard, the university models each Christian's search for the truth, as John Paul would state in what arguably became his magisterial magnum opus, the 1998 encyclical *Fides et Ratio*. There he spoke of the universal desire for truth that is implanted in the human heart by God, and how this desire demands the use of both religious and intellectual virtues: "Faith and reason are like two wings on which the human spirit rises to the contemplation of truth; and God has placed in the human heart a desire to know the truth — in a word, to know himself — so that, by knowing and loving God, men and women may also come to the fullness of truth about themselves."[200]

[198] John Henry Cardinal Newman, "Intellect, the Instrument of Religious Training," sermon 1, in *Sermons Preached on Various Occasions* (London: Longmans, Green, 1908), available at The Newman Reader, https://www.newmanreader.org/works/occasions/sermon1.html.

[199] Wilson D. Miscamble, C.S.C., "A Magna Carta Still to Be Adopted," in *Ex Corde Ecclesiae: Reflections After 30 Years*, eds. Anthony Casamento and Michele Riondino (Staten Island, NY: St. Pauls Publications, 2022), 24.

[200] *Fides et Ratio*, introduction.

"The contemplation of the truth" could aptly summarize the purpose of the university, and as such its work must combine spiritual with rational activity. If the notion of a holistic spiritual, moral, and intellectual formation broadly captures the ideal of a Christian liberal arts education, then the curriculum is the ordering structure through which this vision exercises its dynamic force. And here it must be said that a Christian liberal arts education is not simply a variant of its secular counterpart that includes theology as an external addition. It is not necessarily unfolded in a specific core curriculum or in a commitment to reading the "Great Books," though it often takes this shape. It is something more: a manifestation of the educational conviction that "Christ holds the central integrating and organizing place among all the circles of discipline and activities of the university."[201] When I speak of the majority of Catholic universities retreating from the Catholic liberal arts, it is primarily in this sense that I am speaking. A return to the tradition is in the first place a return to a commitment to the centrality of Christ within a university and its manifold activities; it is only secondarily a renewal of any particular educational model that coheres with this.

Once this commitment is in place, however, the choice of educational model is a key one. Following the release of *Ex Corde Ecclesiae*, Father Miscamble recalls that, for several years, he kept returning to two central questions as he thought about how to apply the apostolic constitution's principles at Notre Dame. These questions were simply, "What is taught and who teaches it?"[202] A third question might

[201] Christopher Lushis "Bishop Robert Barron Visits Notre Dame: What Makes a University Catholic?" *Today's Catholic*, March 23, 2023, https://todayscatholic.org/bishop-robert-barron-visits-notre-dame-what-makes-a-university-catholic/.

[202] Wilson D. Miscamble, C.S.C., "What's in a Name? The Meaning of a Catholic University Today" (lecture, Roccasecca Project, University of St. Thomas, Minnesota, April 26, 2022).

be added to Miscamble's list: "How is it taught?" The history of Catholic education has, in a sense, been devoted to answering these questions. Over several centuries, the answers to these questions took form in the medieval institution of the university, which incorporated the Greek tradition of *paideia* into the Christian vision of an incarnational cosmos. This educational tradition of Christianized Hellenism is what the faithful few colleges seem to be revitalizing through their Catholic liberal arts programs.

Why Do the Liberal Arts Matter?

What exactly are the liberal arts, and why are the faithful few Catholic colleges restoring them? The liberal arts derive their meaning from the education worthy of a free people that would give them the wisdom and virtue to live well and to create a just society.[203] In many ways, this form of education traces its root image back to Plato's famous allegory of the cave, in book 6 of his *Republic*. Liberal education in ancient Greece was the education given to citizens of the state and was distinct from the technical education that was suitable for slaves. Whereas technical education was focused on practical skills and information, the Greek *paideia* (from which we derive the Latin word *humanitas*, that is, the *humanities*) formed the whole person and sought "the essence of being human."[204] Throughout all the tumultuous changes that shaped Western civilization, including the transition from a pagan civilization to a Christian civilization, the idea remained that real education consisted in teaching students to live well, and not just to perform in a job. Only recently, in the technologically saturated twentieth and twenty-first centuries, have institutions of higher learning succumbed to the cardinal falsehood

[203] Habiger Institute for Catholic Leadership, *The Heart of Culture: A Brief History of Western Education* (Providence, RI: Cluny Media, 2020), 16, 22.

[204] Ibid., 13.

of education: "the modern failure to distinguish between the process of making a machine and the process of making a man."[205]

These modern institutions have seen a great many successes and legitimate triumphs emerging from their production of highly specialized scholars and engineers. During this time, however, something has been lost that did not need to be: the belief that a transcendent God gives an ultimate unity to all the various intellectual disciplines, and that that same God created an intelligible world for man to organize through his intellect. Gannon says that the very first step toward educating slaves for the modern state is to "cut off the idea that man is made for God." Once the student has been made subject to the ideology of naturalism, "You can hope to have a generation of robots who will be capable of taking a submarine apart and putting it together again but quite incapable of analyzing their own opinions. They will be modernized, paganized, dehumanized, and ready to suffer incredibly for the Absolute State."[206] This, then, is what is at stake in understanding what the liberal arts are, and any effort to reclaim them will have far-reaching implications. "Every educational program is based on a specific anthropology,"[207] and creating a Catholic liberal arts program necessarily means starting from a robust philosophical and theological view of man, nature, and God.

The Greeks passed on to us their confidence in man's ability to form a rational, coherent understanding of the world.[208] This confidence meant that the classical pedagogy was built around the belief that man could bring himself into harmony with reality and that the

[205] Gannon, *Poor Old Liberal Arts*, 162.

[206] Ibid., 150.

[207] Habiger Institute, *Heart of Culture*, 64.

[208] For the anthropology behind the Greek *paideia*, I am indebted to the discussion of this topic in *The Heart of Culture*, 22–26.

purpose of education was to facilitate this harmonization of man with nature. This view also meant that education entailed a degree of moral formation. The Hellenistic tradition believed formation went beyond the intellect, as a physical and moral endeavor, one that brought the whole student into alignment with the natural order of things. The concept of the "natural law" developed from this belief that there were inherent patterns and forms governing how men should behave, just as there were laws dictating the growth of an oak tree or a caterpillar, or regulating the tides of the sea. A rational order governed all things, said the Greeks, each according to its type, and alignment with this order was necessary for each thing to flourish. The Greek word generally used for this rational order was *logos*. In the Hellenistic tradition, the world was governed by the *logos*, or the rational principle.[209] *Paideia*, then, came to mean not simply education in civic duty but also formation according to a universal ideal; that is, how to live virtuously in accordance with the *logos*. When the playwright Terence said, "*Homo sum, humani nihil a me alienum puto*" (I am human so nothing human is foreign to me), he was expressing this universalized belief undergirding the Hellenistic tradition of teaching and philosophy.

The question at the heart of Hellenistic pedagogy, or teaching, was how one ought to bring oneself into alignment with the *logos*. First, it was agreed that any education must be built upon the study of mathematics. Plato wrote above the entry to his academy, "Let no one ignorant of geometry enter here." If there was a rational principle ordering the universe, it made sense that mathematics, with its rational and unchanging laws, was the fingerprint of the

[209] The belief in a *logos*-infused world lay behind the tradition of the Pythagorean, and, to a lesser extent, the broader Grecian emphasis on mathematics as the key to interpreting the universe.

logos.[210] Second, education was held to be a personal matter, as it depended not on the simple transmission of knowledge but on an enculturation of the mind. It was expected that students of the *paideia* would attend the school of a great master. The communities and academies of Pythagoras, Isocrates, Plato, and Aristotle drew crowds of acolytes and became famed across the ancient world as places where students could be conformed to the *logos*.

What Differentiates the *Catholic* Liberal Arts?

The Catholic, or Christian, liberal arts tradition finds its anthropological roots in this Greek tradition of *paideia*. When we speak of the Catholic liberal arts in this book, we mean one that is built upon the same foundation while also being interpreted through a Catholic lens. The Greek liberal arts freed the individual from distraction to ask questions about the good life since, as Socrates famously declared, "The unexamined life is not worth living." The Catholic liberal arts consider the same questions about the meaning of life, but they use Christian first principles. The importance of mentorship under a great master is still present, as is the centrality of the ordering principle, *logos*, but Catholicism brings the two together in the person of Jesus Christ. It could be said that a Catholic liberal arts education is built around two New Testament passages, especially with the understanding that what we are used to hearing translated as *the Word* does in fact appear in the Greek as *Logos*. First, "In the beginning was the Word, and the Word was with God, and the Word was God" (John 1:1); and second, "'For who has known the mind of the Lord so as to instruct him?' But we have the mind of Christ" (1 Cor 2:16). In its conviction that each person is called to an intimate relationship with the *Logos* through Whom the universe was created,

210 Habiger Institute, *Heart of Culture*, 20.

the Catholic liberal arts education fulfills the Hellenistic project beyond the dreams of its original philosophers.[211]

This formative encounter between Christ — present in His Church in the manifold forms of Sacred Scripture, Tradition, and the orders of creation — and the student lies at the center of the Catholic liberal arts tradition. Facilitating this encounter has given shape to the various Catholic educational institutions throughout the Church's history. Although they renew themselves constantly in response to each new culture, these institutions hand on a way of life based on two thousand years of the Church's wisdom. Christopher Dawson summarized the importance of maintaining a robust Catholic education in his incisive *Crisis of Western Education*, where he claimed:

> The essential function of education is "enculturation," or the transmission of the tradition of culture, and therefore it seems clear that the Christian college must be the cornerstone of any attempt to rebuild the order of Western civilization. In order to free the mind from its dependence on the conformist patterns of modern secular society, it is necessary to view the cultural situation as a whole and to see the Christian way of life not as a number of isolated precepts imposed by ecclesiastical authority, but as a cosmos of spiritual relations embracing heaven and earth and uniting the order of social and moral life with the order of divine grace.[212]

211 The beauty of how Christ fulfills the searching of the ancients is captured in very concrete terms in Peter Kreeft, *Socrates Meets Jesus: History's Greatest Questioner Confronts the Claims of Christ* (Lisle, IL: InterVarsity Press, 2002).

212 Christopher Dawson, *The Crisis of Western Education* (Steubenville, OH: Franciscan University Press, 1986), 150.

What is at stake then, is not the perseveration of a particular curriculum or a set reading list (indeed, the Great Books curriculum, a hallmark of "traditional" education, is a largely secular initiative of the 1940s). Rather, it is an education into a culture in which the student learns the Christian vision and way of life and adopts them as his or her own. Once encultured, the student can engage contemporary society with freedom and virtue — and with a certain knowledge of life's purpose.

Liberal Arts at the Faithful Few Catholic Colleges and Universities

The schools profiled on the following pages are set apart, then, by their approach to education. One consequence of the majority of Catholic universities turning away from their Catholic identity was that they lost sight of the importance and purpose of a liberal arts education. This should not be surprising, as it has already been established that one's educational vision flows directly from one's most fundamental convictions about the world and the human person. Once Christ is no longer at the center of a school's mission, He will not long survive as the cornerstone of its curriculum.

Though there are many superficial differences between the pedagogies of the faithful few schools, they share a common vision based on the Catholic educational tradition. Each of these schools centers its education on an encounter with the person of Christ; the differences in their approach are a thousand reflections of the inexhaustible richness of that encounter. The choices of which classes to include in the curriculum, how they are to be organized and structured, and whether to use the Great Books exclusively or selectively, are all significant ones — and some choices are arguably better than others. However, as long as a school's curriculum still focuses on the central question, "What is my purpose as a human?" and seeks an answer from within the Church's tradition, it maintains the fundamental character of a Catholic liberal arts education.

The Humanities and Catholic Culture (HCC) major at Franciscan University is one such example of this fundamental character in Catholic liberal arts education. Created by Professors James Gaston and Stephen Krason in the 1990s, the HCC major is an interdisciplinary liberal arts program that studies the "development of Western civilization and the crucial role religion, especially Catholicism, plays in the creation, unity, and change of human life and culture through the centuries."[213] The program draws heavily upon the work of Catholic historian Christopher Dawson and explores the historical reality of religion as the basis of culture and Catholicism as the basis of Western civilization. At the heart of the program lies the ancient call to "Know thyself," a knowledge that is cultivated through an encounter with, and a conformation to, reality. The schools profiled below share the belief that learning serves the whole person, bringing students into a greater knowledge of themselves through formation in the Catholic intellectual and spiritual tradition.

Thomas Aquinas College

Instead of offering majors supplemented by a core curriculum, Thomas Aquinas College (TAC) offers a fully integrated curriculum, with the aim of presenting each discipline as a means of approaching reality "as a comprehensive whole."[214] This makes it one of only three pure liberal arts schools profiled in this book, the others being Wyoming Catholic College and New Hampshire's Thomas More College of

[213] "Humanities and Catholic Culture Bachelor's Degree Program Overview," Franciscan University, https://shss.franciscan.edu/programs/humanities-and-catholic-culture/.

[214] "A Liberating Education," Thomas Aquinas College, https://www.thomasaquinas.edu/a-liberating-education.

Liberal Arts. As well as offering an interdisciplinary liberal arts model, TAC employs two distinct methodologies that characterize its education: the students only read the Great Books (following the motto "Great Books, not textbooks"), and all classes are conducted in a seminar, discussion style.

Publishing its founding document, *A Proposal for the Fulfillment of Catholic Liberal Arts Education,* in 1969 and welcoming its inaugural class in 1971, TAC emerged right on the heels of the Land O' Lakes statement in 1967 — that document that came to symbolize the divorce of mainstream Catholic education from obedience to Church doctrine and ecclesial hierarchy. TAC's *Proposal* hit back at this spreading secularization and set out a revitalized view of "liberal education in its fullness," which it described as "liberal education undertaken by Christians, and ordered to theology." Defining itself according to "the Christian faith and the tradition of the Catholic Church," the *Proposal* set out a curriculum in which "every student will pursue the same sequence of courses, which will be designed to introduce him to every essential part of the intellectual life."[215]

Since its founding, TAC has seen remarkable success. After capping its capacity for several years, it opened a New England campus in 2019 to accommodate the steadily increasing number of applicants. The school has always prioritized small class sizes, never having more than twenty students in a seminar. It started with only thirty-three students when it was founded;[216] just after its fiftieth anniversary, it welcomed its largest class ever, with over five hundred students between its two campuses.[217] The school has been regularly praised for its

[215] *Proposal for the Fulfillment of Catholic Liberal Arts Education*, 45, 49.

[216] "A Brief History of Thomas Aquinas College," Thomas Aquinas College, https://www.thomasaquinas.edu/about/mission-history/brief-history.

[217] "Thomas Aquinas College," Cardinal Newman Society, https://cardinalnewmansociety.org/college/thomas-aquinas-college/.

excellent education and has been recognized on several lists recognizing academic excellence. Most recently, TAC placed in the 2022 *U.S. News & World Report*'s annual ranking of the top fifty liberal arts colleges in the nation. It was one of only two Catholic colleges on the list.[218]

Even among the schools profiled on these pages, which all offer varying degrees of core curricula, TAC stands out for the depth and breadth of its education. The foundation of its curriculum is the *trivium* and *quadrivium,* the seven disciplines of grammar, logic, and rhetoric (the *trivium*) and then geometry, arithmetic, astronomy, and music (the *quadrivium*) which make up the traditional liberal arts. Freshmen take each of the seven disciplines either as a specific discipline, as in their music and astronomy tutorials, or in a pedagogical approach. For example, the language class teaches the grammatical method, and each seminar's discussion forms its students in rhetoric.

All of TAC's tutorials use the Great Books, as these are the "original works of the greatest minds in our tradition, both ancient and modern."[219] Freshmen read the great literature and philosophy of the Greeks, sophomores the theology of the patristics, juniors the natural science and philosophy of the Renaissance and Enlightenment, and seniors engage the moderns, from Hegel, Tolstoy, and Marx to Faulkner, Schrödinger, and Pope St. John Paul II.[220] However, the books are not considered primarily as objects, and the school stresses that it does not teach these texts as examples of creativity or simply for students "to become more familiar with Western culture and civilization." Rather, the texts are lenses through which the student can more

[218] Anne Hendershott, "Faithful Catholic Institutions Defy Trend of Secularization," *The American Spectator,* June 20, 2023, https://spectator.org/faithful-catholic-institutions-defy-trend-of-secularization/

[219] "The Great Books," Thomas Aquinas College, https://www.thomasaquinas.edu/a-liberating-education/great-books.

[220] "Syllabus," Thomas Aquinas College, https://www.thomasaquinas.edu/a-liberating-education/syllabus.

fully engage the world. These books are prioritized "because, more than any other works, when studied under the light of the teaching Church, they can open up the truth about reality."[221]

This brings the discussion back to a claim at the heart of the Catholic liberal arts education. While many institutions have prioritized technical and professional programs in their schools, the faithful few have preserved the liberal arts not because of a misplaced antiquarianism but because they are seeking to "free the mind from its dependence on the conformist patterns of modern secular society,"[222] and they believe "that men become free by finding, or being found by, the truth and abiding in it. For the Christian believes that Christ Himself is the Truth, and believes Him when He says, 'If you make my words your home you will indeed be my disciples, you will learn the truth and the truth will make you free' (John 8:31–32)."[223]

A consequence of this education, which teaches students true freedom from ignorance and vice, is that it is immensely practical and helps students find success in whatever career or vocation they choose. In contrast to what much of the world would have us believe, John Henry Newman tells us in *The Idea of a University* that a liberal arts education is by no means useless, because "if a liberal education be good, it must necessarily be useful too." This is because it "gives a man a clear conscious view of his own opinions and judgments, a truth in developing them, an eloquence in expressing them, and a force in urging them," and allows him "to master any subject with facility."[224]

[221] "The Great Books," Thomas Aquinas College, https://www.thomasaquinas.edu/a-liberating-education/great-books.

[222] Dawson, *Crisis of Western Education,* 150.

[223] *Proposal for the Fulfillment of Catholic Liberal Arts Education*, 29.

[224] Newman, "Discourse 7: Knowledge Viewed in Relation to Practical Skill," *Idea of a University*, 164, 178, https://www.newmanreader.org/works/idea/discourse7.html.

However, this is a consequence and not the primary intent behind the education. In fact, as program objectives for all its graduates, TAC offers a list of moral and intellectual virtues in which its students will be formed. The moral virtues include "a deeply rooted love for the intellectual life borne from wonder about marvels of the world, both natural and supernatural," and "confidence that progress can be made on the difficult road to wisdom, especially under the light of the Magisterium of the Roman Catholic Church and in the company of friends pursuing wisdom." Its list of intellectual virtues includes the ability to "understand the unity and order of the disciplines," to "grasp something of the order of the universe from prime matter to spiritual being to God," and to "have the skills to converse with others fruitfully and in the spirit of friendship, both in speech and in the written word."[225]

This is the vision, then, that undergirds TAC's intensive, and somewhat radical, education program. It seeks to bring the students into an encounter with reality, and to teach them the virtue that comes from conforming to that reality.

Thomas More College of Liberal Arts

One of the most comprehensive and creative educational programs among the faithful few has historically belonged to Thomas More College (TMC) in New Hampshire. Smaller than TAC, the overall student body at TMC hovers around just a hundred students. TMC was founded to help renew Catholic education in the early 1970s, and it maintains one of the most robust core curricula of any of the faithful few. As noted earlier, it was to TMC that Anthony Esolen fled after

[225] "Program Objectives," Thomas Aquinas College, https://www.thomasaquinas.edu/a-liberating-education/program-objectives.

his tumultuous exit from the formerly faithful Providence College.[226] Upon visiting the college, visitors immediately get a feeling that the place is set apart for a special purpose, as a place where students learn "to see things as they are."

TMC's approach teaches students to ask and answer "the big questions": What is the meaning of life? What is the nature of man? How do we know the things we know? What is right, and what is wrong? These are the perennial questions that give vitality to a liberal arts education, and TMC unabashedly draws on Catholic teaching in its guidance for how to answer them. By integrating the liberal arts education with the Catholic Faith, it can offer the riches of a long tradition of liberal education from the heart of the Church.

The goal of TMC's rigorous program is to train the mind, will, and imagination in the transcendentals and the "way of perfection." This captures the deeply rooted humility, or earthliness, of a liberal arts education, one that does not set out to achieve any particular goal other than cultivating "a desire for wisdom — for an encounter with the real, permanent things." The fulfillment of this desire is a lifelong pilgrimage, and college is only a short though important part of this journey.

To nourish this desire, TMC's curriculum encompasses all the major disciplines: philosophy and literature, history, theology, ancient languages, geometry, astronomy, physics, and biology. A sample of what students read in the humanities includes the works of Aristotle, Plato, the Greek tragedians, Lao Tzu, Augustine and Aquinas, Bacon and Locke, Shakespeare and Dostoevsky, John Paul II and the documents of Vatican II. In the sciences, they study,

[226] See chapter 9 below for more of the story about Anthony Esolen's reasons for departing Providence and the discussion of why Providence was removed from the *Newman Guide*.

among others, Euclid, Ptolemy, Newton, Darwin, Galileo and Copernicus, Einstein and Heisenberg, Mendel and Gould.

The most unique feature of Thomas More College is its commitment to enabling students to gain practical skills and experience in areas beyond what is a rigorous academic curriculum. Much more than "recreational" hobbies or vocational training, the guild system at TMC provides students with the ability to work with talented craftspeople from the community who volunteer their time and expertise to helping students learn skills in areas including woodworking, sacred art, and sacred or folk music. Meeting weekly to provide "hands on" training, students learn from the masters of their trades.[227]

The TMC website describes better than I could the integration of these aspects of education:

> Each guild offers practical experience that is integrated with the College's academic curriculum. Aristotle himself had stated that a purely liberal arts education, without some exposure to the useful arts was harmful to the student. Pope Benedict XVI pointed out that Our Lord, St. Paul, and the Benedictine tradition all reveal the distinctive nature of Catholic education: an education that does not divide what is contemplative from what is practical, what is beautiful from what is useful. The Catholic student must always remember that he is made *imago Dei*, in the image of God, and that God Himself is a Creator of things and so he too must learn to be a maker and steward of creation.

[227] "Guilds," Thomas More College, https://thomasmorecollege.edu/the-core/guilds/.

University of Dallas

When Joseph Sanford was hired as the tenth president of the University of Dallas (UD), he had already spent six years as dean and provost of UD's Constantin College. During that time, he had been committed to furthering UD's reputation as both a deeply faithful and an academically rigorous institution. As president, he shared how he wanted "our students to feel inspired to be outstanding leaders who are dedicated to rebuilding culture because of their intellectual formation and because of their moral and theological formation." As part of that formation, said Sanford, "we're giving real focus to elements of what I was talking about in connection to Christian anthropology — that is to say, the formation of the students as an integrated whole."[228]

While maintaining a rigorous liberal arts core curriculum, UD differs from the previous two schools discussed in its size, the number of degrees offered, and its provision of advanced degrees. Founded in 1956, the school's enrollment by 2022 had reached 1,453 undergraduates and close to 900 graduate students.[229] It maintains a 12:1 student to faculty ratio, with fifty-six majors, over twenty master's programs and certificates, and five Ph.D. programs.[230]

The university prides itself on a well-earned reputation for high academic quality and rigor within each of its programs. It has one of the highest percentages of National Merit Scholars compared with other Catholic colleges and universities,[231] and it is one of only

[228] Virginia Aabram, "New University of Dallas President Jonathon Sanford's Goal: the 'Integrated' Person," *National Catholic Register*, August 26, 2021, https://www.ncregister.com/interview/new-university-of-dallas-president-jonathan-sanford-s-goal-the-integrated-person.

[229] "Facts at a Glance," University of Dallas, https://udallas.edu/about/facts.php.

[230] "Academics," University of Dallas, https://udallas.edu/academics/.

[231] "Academic Rigor," University of Dallas, https://udallas.edu/academics/academic-rigor/index.php.

twenty-three Catholic universities in America to earn a prestigious Phi Beta Kappa chapter.[232] It has also been highly recognized on numerous college rankings, including *U.S. News and World Report, The Princeton Review*, and the *Fiske Guide to Colleges.*[233]

Alongside these accolades, the university offers a nationally recognized core curriculum. This two-year, sixty-credit sequence, while being less comprehensive than either TAC or TMC, provides undergraduate students across all majors with an excellent formation in liberal arts studies. The robust foundations of the classical core were built by Donald and Louise Cowan, whose involvement in UD from the early 1960s ensured a coherent framework of liberal education from the earliest days of the school.[234] For the vast majority of students, the core education culminates in a fruitful study-abroad semester at UD's Rome campus, where much of their coursework is brought to life through firsthand encounters with the architecture and history of classical and Christian culture.[235]

Like TAC and TMC, UD identifies the pursuit of wisdom, truth, and virtue as the threefold object of a liberal arts education.[236] Its mission is the rediscovery of the Christian intellectual tradition, as part of a commitment to the Catholic Church and her authority. To achieve this goal, UD's core provides courses in English, history, philosophy, theology, economics, politics, science, mathematics, language, and fine arts, with an emphasis in

232 "Facts at a Glance," University of Dallas.

233 "Rankings & Points of Pride," University of Dallas, https://udallas.edu/academics/academic-rigor/rankings-and-points-of-pride.php.

234 "Donald and Louise Cowan Center," University of Dallas, https://udallas.edu/centers/cowan/index.php.

235 "Academic Rigor," University of Dallas.

236 "Mission and Vision," University of Dallas, https://udallas.edu/about/mission.php.

each course on the Great Books of Western Civilization.[237] In 2021, the university sought to extend its mission by creating the Saint Ambrose Center for Catholic Liberal Education and Culture. The goal of the center is to bring the university's vibrant educational vision and its core ends of virtue, wisdom, and truth to the world at large.[238]

Conclusion: Enhancing the Catholic Liberal Arts

The ever-prescient Christopher Dawson identified two temptations which he believed could corrupt the Catholic educational project of enculturating students into "the world of Christian thought and the Christian way of life and the norms of the Christian community."[239] The first temptation is to ignore secular culture entirely, creating a "Christian ghetto" which cuts itself off from the wider society.[240] While this could pose as a temptation for faithful Catholic schools, they can avoid it by the strongly evangelical nature of their education — and by their obedience to *Ex Corde Ecclesiae*'s call to be a "place for a *fruitful dialogue between the Gospel and culture*."[241] The other temptation, said Dawson, is "to sacrifice the study of Christian culture to the modern curriculum of studies, so that the Catholic college comes to provide merely an alternative system of secular education under a denominational label. This is an absurd solution, since the only justification for the minority education is that the

[237] "The Core Curriculum," University of Dallas, https://udallas.edu/constantin/core-curriculum/index.php.

[238] "University of Dallas Launches New St. Ambrose Center for Catholic Liberal Education and Culture," University of Dallas, December 7, 2021, https://news.udallas.edu/2021-12-07-University-of-Dallas-Launches-New-St-Ambrose-Center-for-Catholic-Liberal-Education-and-Culture.

[239] Dawson, *Crisis of Western Education,* 146–147.

[240] Ibid., 152.

[241] *Ex Corde Ecclesiae*, no. 43.

minority has something of value to communicate which is not to be found elsewhere."[242]

These prophetic words were published by Dawson in 1961, but his analysis perfectly captures the sorry predicament of mainstream Catholic education today. When formerly faithful Catholic schools stopped trying to answer the question of what it means to be human in light of the gospel of Jesus Christ, they abandoned the distinctive characteristic of a Catholic liberal arts education.

In *Why Liberalism Failed,* Patrick Deneen observed how the abandonment of the liberal arts across mainstream educational institutions poses a very real threat to the continuation of American culture and the American way of life:

> The liberal arts were long understood to be the essential form of education for a free people, especially citizens who aspired to self-government. The emphasis on the great texts—which were great not only or even because they were old but because they contained hard-won lessons on how humans learn to be free, especially free from the tyranny of their insatiable desires—has been jettisoned in favor of what was once considered "servile education," an education concerned exclusively with money making and a life of work, and hence reserved for those who did not enjoy the title of "citizen."[243]

In most schools today, including ostensibly Catholic ones, any commitment to a rigorous investigation of "the big questions" has been jettisoned as a relic of a bygone age. The consequence of this, as Deneen observes, is that our culture offers an education fit for slaves, and not citizens,

[242] Dawson, *Crisis of Western Education,* 152–153.
[243] Deneen, *Why Liberalism Failed,* 13.

which creates atomized individuals who are experts in their field but who have never been taught even to be amateurs at being human.

Looking at how the formerly faithful schools lost the Catholic liberal arts, it is possible to anticipate the pressure points that will threaten the liberal arts at the faithful few schools or hamper the liberal arts from developing easily at other colleges and universities. One particular danger lies simply in not having clarity about the structure and purpose of the school's liberal arts commitment. This can lead to carelessness in guarding the integrity of its liberal arts education. A college cannot risk being halfhearted in its approach to a Catholic education; for any such college, with an unclear vision of the why and the what of its program, a liberal arts education is likely fast to be seen as a distraction holding it back from investment in more popular areas of college life, such as the development of sports facilities and the expansion of professional programs, as well as a barrier to the development of contemporary policies on diversity, equity, and inclusion (DEI). It was just such a slide of a liberal arts education into a politically influenced, "woke" education that led Anthony Esolen to abandon his tenured position at Providence College in favor of work at a faithful school.[244]

While the liberal arts have been abandoned in many institutions, the hope is that not only will the current faithful few schools maintain their commitment to the liberal arts, but that other institutions will rise and join a full-flowering renaissance in Catholic higher education. Until then, however, it will have to be enough that these schools transform the hearts and minds of one student at a time, enculturating them into their Catholic heritage.

This, in the final account, is what the faithful few schools seek to accomplish through their liberal arts programs. Rejecting the

[244] Smith, "Anthony Esolen in His Own Words."

tyranny of modern, secular culture, this kind of Catholic education seeks to bring students to strive for a moral and intellectual perfection through formation in the True, the Good, and the Beautiful. This work cannot be done without a dependence on divine grace. In fact, the inculcation of a profound humility necessarily undergirds this model of education, whose primary duty is faithfully to pass on the rich and diverse heritage of Catholic culture, to immerse "students in the whole sweep of the Catholic intellectual tradition — what *Ex Corde Ecclesiae* refers to as 'the Church's own culture.' "[245] When a school transmits this culture, as the faithful schools so passionately seek to do, it gives its students tools to build a new culture for Christ, a culture that can rise splendid and glorious from the ashes of the old.

[245] Archbishop Michael Miller, C.S.B., "Criteria for Assessing Catholic Identity," address at Franciscan University of Steubenville, Ohio, April 20, 2017.

Chapter 6

"In the Light of the Spirit": The Struggle for Academic Freedom

In 2017, the Veritas Center for Ethics in Public Life at Franciscan University hosted a conference on higher education that featured a panel discussion on "The Politicization of the American University and the Crisis of Free Speech and Reasoned Academic Discourse." Another panel explored the limits on academic freedom within the context of the faithful religious colleges and universities like those profiled in this book. No one realized just how prescient that conference was, considering what was about to occur on the Franciscan campus in 2019, when a tenured professor of literature at Franciscan University assigned to his undergraduate students what was judged by many faithful Catholics to be a blasphemous book that denigrated the purity of the Blessed Virgin Mary.

The controversy over the profane book emerged when it was revealed in the Catholic media that a Franciscan University professor had required his Franciscan undergraduate students to read Emmanuel Carrère's *The Kingdom*. The Carrère novel not only included an explicit discussion of Carrère's personal online pornography addiction, but also rejected — in graphic detail — the purity and innocence of the Holy Virgin Mary. Carrère's *The Kingdom* portrayed

Mary, the mother of Jesus Christ, as someone who engaged in deviant sexual behavior. In the novel, Carrère graphically describes how his pornography addiction is "intimately linked" to his speculation on the vulgar sexuality of the Virgin Mary. The book contains a lengthy passage in which the author compares the Blessed Mother with his favorite porn actresses performing autoerotic acts. Students — and a number of parents — were gravely concerned when they learned that the blasphemous book had been used in an undergraduate classroom. These same students and parents were bewildered when Franciscan's academic administration issued an official statement that appeared to defend the professor's academic freedom to assign such a novel to undergraduate students. A tremendous backlash emerged on social media and in letters and phone calls to the university from Catholics who were scandalized by the fact that a novel like this could have been used, and defended, on the faithful campus. In response to the deluge of complaints from parents, students, and donors, Franciscan's president, Fr. Sean Sheridan, T.O.R., issued a strong statement finally condemning the assignment. It stated that the professor "did not intend to scandalize, but *The Kingdom* is so directly pornographic and blasphemous that it has no place on a Catholic university.... I regret that the University's earlier statement did not make this clear.... Above all, I would like to apologize to Our Blessed Mother and Her Son and to anyone who has been scandalized by this incident."[246]

This case illustrates the challenges of defining academic freedom on a faithful Catholic campus. Responding to the Franciscan

[246] Christine Niles "Concerns Remain After Franciscan Univ Apologizes for Blasphemous Book," Church Militant, January 9, 2019, now available at Catholic Citizens of Illinois, https://catholiccitizens.org/uncategorized/83009/concerns-remain-after-franciscan-univ-apologizes-for-blasphemous-book/.

University controversy in an interview with *Inside Higher Ed,* Paula Moore, the spokesperson for the Association of Catholic Colleges and Universities, pointed to the value of *Ex Corde Ecclesiae* in granting each Catholic university "the institutional autonomy necessary to perform its functions effectively and guarantees its members academic freedom, so long as the rights of the individual person and of the community are preserved within the confines of the truth and the common good." Moore added that the "basic mission of Catholic higher education is the search for truth, understanding that God is the ultimate truth." With this granted, she continued,

> professors at Catholic colleges and universities are free to raise questions or even disagreements in intellectual areas where there is a formal Catholic position — so long as they also present official Catholic teaching accurately and respectfully.... Catholic colleges rely on their faith — its ideals, attitudes and principles — to inform their decisions about teaching, research, and other activities. For students, the result is not only intellectual growth and academic excellent, but also faithfulness to the Church.[247]

We will also see how these debates around academic excellence and faithfulness have played out on campuses of the faithful colleges, and what policies these schools have adopted to support the university's commitment to the twin guiding lights of faith and reason, so they might "shine forth in the light of the Spirit."[248]

[247] Colleen Flaherty, "Banning a Book, in the Name of 'True Academic Freedom,'" *Inside HigherEd,* January 15, 2019, https://www.insidehighered.com/news/2019/01/15/franciscan-u-bans-book-portrays-virgin-mary-sexual-and-ousts-department-chair-who.

[248] *Ex Corde Ecclesiae,* no. 5.

Ex Corde Ecclesiae, Canon Law, and Academic Freedom

Ex Corde Ecclesiae addresses the question of academic freedom in article 2, section 5:

> A Catholic University possesses the autonomy necessary to develop its distinctive identity and pursue its proper mission. Freedom in research and teaching is recognized and respected according to the principles and methods of each individual discipline, so long as the rights of the individual and of the community are preserved within the confines of the truth and the common good.

The Holy Father then sketches out these "confines of truth and the common good" by articulating the four "*essential characteristics*" of a Catholic university as *Catholic*: a Christian inspiration of individuals and institution; ongoing reflection on the whole body of knowledge in light of the Faith; fidelity to the Christian message; and an institutional commitment to helping the Church achieve its "transcendent goal which gives meaning to life." Academic freedom, then, receives its fullest meaning in the telos of the Catholic university. Academic freedom's proper use is to operate within the context of an institutional fidelity to both the teaching of the Church and her mission of the salvation of souls. In fact, *Ex Corde Ecclesiae* shifts the question of academic freedom from the rights of the teacher primarily to that of the student, maintaining that students enrolled in a Catholic university have the right to be educated in the truth of the Church's moral and religious principles and social teachings. Students also have the right to participate in the life of faith in all aspects of their campus experience. It is key for a university that it understand its purpose as part of the evangelical efforts of the Church as a whole, "born from the heart of the Church," and not as some isolated entity.

In his essay "Canonical Issues and US Catholic Universities," Jesuit canon law scholar James Conn gives an excellent account of both the particular canons and their historical development that guide the relationship between the university and the ecclesial hierarchy, norms which ensure that the academic freedom of the institution and the members within it are respected, while detailing the responsibility of viewing that freedom as a furthering of its Catholic mission.[249] The relevant text, canon 810.1, requires that those made competent by university statutes (i.e., normally the university administrators, not ecclesial authorities) must ensure that hired teachers are distinguished by "integrity of doctrine and probity of life," on top of their "scientific and pedagogical qualifications." This guarantees that the university professors at a Catholic institution are committed to upholding the truth and the way of life of the Church, even if they themselves are not Catholic. Conn goes on to explain the canon's requirement as a means of safeguarding the "critical mass of persons who are so committed" to the Faith. Here Conn is referencing a norm from *Ex Corde Ecclesiae* article 4, section 4, that insists that non-Catholics teachers can never form a majority within a Catholic university.[250]

Conn next deals with the second paragraph of canon 810, which articulates the obligation of the Catholic hierarchy to be attentive to whether the "the principles of Catholic doctrine are observed faithfully in these same universities." What this should foster, Conn explains, is a good-faith collaboration between the clergy and university leaders that protects the university's mission and identity.

249 James J. Conn, S.J., "Canonical Issues and US Catholic Universities," in *Fidelity & Freedom:* Ex Corde Ecclesiae *at Twenty-Five*, eds. Stephen M. Hildebrand and Sean Sheridan, T.O.R. (Steubenville, OH: Franciscan University Press, 2008).

250 Ibid., 172–173.

However, as Pope John Paul made clear in *Veritatis Splendor*, paragraph 116, such episcopal authority extends — in radical circumstances — to removing the title "Catholic" from a teaching institution if it has demonstrated itself uncooperative.[251]

Part of what makes Conn's account of the relevant canon compelling is the caustic history that lies behind these seemingly uncontentious governances. He reveals how, during the drafting of the 1983 revisions to canon law, significant lobbying attempts were made by a coterie of presidents of U.S. Catholic universities, who pushed for greater autonomy on behalf of their institutions.[252] This effort was part of a major initiative by universities in the second half of the twentieth century, especially by American colleges and universities, to distance themselves from any magisterial or ecclesial obligations. This lobbying, though it largely failed to alter the drafting of the canons, was waged with more success during the drafting of the national *ordinationes*, or norms for implementation, by the United States Conference of Catholic Bishops (USCCB). Conn describes how this "significantly flawed" document was supposed to merely render more specific the objective principles already established for the universal Church by canon 810. Instead, the USCCB provided "no concrete means or procedures" to guide the U.S. national situation.[253] It chose rather to soften the Vatican's language, and its guidelines gave significant interpretive discretion to the educational institution. Conn notes, for example, how the eight "essential elements of Catholic identity" that were given as normative content in an early USSCB draft were, in the final version, shifted "to its introductory, non-juridical section."[254] This shift allowed a new relationship to be cemented in American educational institutions. Now,

[251] Ibid., 176–177.
[252] Ibid., 171.
[253] Ibid., 173–174.
[254] Ibid., 176.

regardless of the official religious affiliation of the university, the Church was relegated to the role of an exterior force that could be negotiated with or ignored, rather than an interior presence that lent vitality to the school's mission.

The Role of Tenure on a Faithful Catholic Campus

One particular institutional quality that most faculty members — even those on faithful Catholic campuses — maintain as necessary to guarantee academic freedom is that of tenure. As Naomi Schaefer Riley's book *The Faculty Lounges: And Other Reasons Why You Won't Get the College Education You Paid For,* points out:

> If you ask any professor why he needs tenure, the first words out of his mouth will undoubtedly be some variation of the phrase: "to guarantee academic freedom." Believe me, I've tried this dozens, if not hundreds, of times. I have asked professors on both ends of the political spectrum and those whose work falls squarely in the middle. They have all given me the same response, at least to start. If professors don't have a guaranteed job for life (or what usually amounts to it), the argument goes, they will not be able to speak or write freely. Those with unpopular views — or views that upset the administration or the trustees or other members of the faculty — will be run off campus.[255]

But many faithful Catholic scholars question whether *absolute* academic freedom is a principle worth defending on a faithful Catholic campus.

[255] Naomi Schaeffer Riley, *The Faculty Lounges: And Other Reasons Why You Won't Get the College Education You Paid For,* (Lanham, MD: Ivan R. Dee, 2011), 19–20.

This question was picked up in a series of symposia at Franciscan University in 2014 and 2015 that commemorated the twenty-fifth anniversary of *Ex Corde Ecclesiae*. The conferences discussed how the document offered a road map for Catholic universities in how they practice their Catholicism; the role of academic freedom within the university was a focal point of vibrant conversation.[256]

Riley herself pointedly asks in her book, Shouldn't those faculty who are not fully onboard with the mission and the beliefs of a faithful Catholic campus be encouraged to leave? Certainly, it seems as if this attitude was at least partly adopted by Father Michael Scanlan, and he was very successful in bringing faculty in line with the school's Catholic mission when he assumed leadership over the then-struggling Franciscan University. Besides, as Riley recalls, tenure in even the earliest secular universities had little to do with academic freedom and was simply intended mostly to protect the economic security of a group of people who devoted long years to training for a job that didn't provide much remuneration. For that matter, tenure wasn't a particularly unusual arrangement in the workplace. In 1950, most people worked for the same company for their entire lifetime. It didn't seem unreasonable for professors to have a similar kind of security. Besides, in the early days of the Catholic university, professors didn't need tenure to protect their academic freedom because academic freedom was not much of an issue. The earliest Catholic colleges were specifically designed to train priests, and the mission was clearly stated: to prepare men for the priesthood. There was no question about whether the truth of Catholic teachings should be taught on a Catholic campus. It was just taken for granted.

[256] Papers from these symposia can be found in Hildebrand and Sheridan, eds., *Fidelity and Freedom*.

Today, we can no longer assume that what is taught on most Catholic campuses is the truth. This commitment to the search for the truth is what truly differentiates the faithful few Catholic colleges and universities from the rest, as John Paul highlights: "*By its Catholic character,* a University is made more capable of conducting an impartial search for truth, a search that is neither subordinated to nor conditioned by particular interests of any kind."[257] And although we have reassurances that what is taught on a faithful Catholic campus is in communion with the Church, tenure — which was originally intended to be a barrier to protect academic freedom in the classroom — has all too often become a protective shield that defends radical professors who are intent on bringing heretical teachings into their classrooms.

It is very difficult — almost impossible — to fire a tenured professor, even when that professor publicly denigrates the mission of the university. On a faithful Catholic campus, administrators should have the ability to censure professors who violate their implied assent to support the mission of the Catholic college or university. This is because the courts have traditionally considered that, in private religious institutions, professors and administrators have a contract. And, like any other employer, the university is required to live up to the terms of that contract. If the contract says that the institution is a Catholic university and that faculty members are to support the Catholic mission of the university, then those who are unwilling or unable to support that mission can be fired. But in practice, firing a tenured professor who runs afoul of the mission is much more difficult than the court decisions suggest. The American Association of University Professors (AAUP) has a long list of censured religious institutions who are deemed to have restricted the academic freedom of their faculty members. No university — even a faithful Catholic

[257] *Ex Corde Ecclesiae,* no. 7, emphasis added.

university — wants to be included on that list. Catholic University of America has been on the list of censured universities over an academic freedom issue related to a dissident theology faculty member for more than three decades, despite its repeated attempts to be removed from that list since its initial inclusion in 1990.[258]

Trying to directly address the issue of the limits of academic freedom, a faculty committee at Franciscan University drafted a strong academic freedom policy in 2019 that protects the mission of the faithful university while still protecting the academic freedom of the individual faculty members:

> Since the exercise of freedom does not imply the right to say or do anything, an instructor is not free to jeopardize the moral formation of his/her students by placing them in situations in which moral danger is certain or highly probable (while recognizing an appropriate degree of student maturity as adult learners) or to engage in activity that is illegal, unethical, contrary to Catholic morals, contrary to University policy, detrimental to student overall well-being, or harmful to the common good of the University.[259]

In a response to queries about tenure at Franciscan University, Stephen Hildebrand, vice president of Academic Affairs, said "All faculty are bound to our academic freedom policy which is not the typical AAUP policy but our own, drawn from the Gospel and the teachings of the Church.... The Scriptures affirm 'for freedom Christ has set us free' (Galatians 5:1).... We are called to freedom ... yet freedom should

258 "Censure List," American Association of University Professors, https://www.aaup.org/our-programs/academic-freedom/censure-list.

259 "Academic Freedom Policy for Franciscan University," drafted by the faculty and approved by the board of trustees, spring 2019.

be used for loving service and not as a pretext for evil (1 Peter 2:16)." Franciscan's policy reminds faculty that,

> As a faithful Catholic institution, Franciscan University of Steubenville insists that instructors, in the exercise of their professional tasks as teachers and researchers, respect the institution's religious commitment and abide by the norms and guidelines of our mission statement, and our values as a Catholic University. As such we confess the Catholic faith as a source of truth and moral enlightenment. Our ultimate exercise of freedom is guided by the teaching of Scripture and the Church, which remind us that true freedom respects the truth and tends toward love of God and neighbor.[260]

Like Franciscan University, Belmont Abbey College has a tenure system, and, like Franciscan, faculty support for the Catholic mission and identity of the institution is the most important component of that tenure system. According to David Williams, vice provost for Academic Affairs and dean of the faculty at Belmont Abbey,

> It would be fair to say that no faculty member takes up a position at Belmont Abbey without being well aware of our fidelity to mission. Moreover, Catholics teaching in the Theology department must also hold a mandatum given by competent authority according to the *Application of Ex Corde Ecclesiae* to the United States. Should this mandatum be revoked, whether before tenure or after it, the faculty member would have to leave the college.[261]

[260] "Franciscan University's Academic Freedom Policy," November 15, 2019, in faculty handbook.

[261] David Williams, interviewed by David Willey, 2022.

Williams added:

> With respect to the tenure evaluation process, consonance with mission is an essential aspect of the initial third year review.... A key factor in any evaluation is evidence of attained integration between faith, life and teaching. In ways appropriate to their disciplines, all Catholic faculty should be faithful to, and all other faculty should respect Catholic doctrine and morals in their research and teaching. And when the tenure review takes place typically in the sixth year, the same standard is applied in the recommendations given to the President by our rank and tenure committee and by the Provost's Office. Following tenure, each faculty member is reviewed on a three-year cycle. Should the review find the faculty member severely deficient, there would be a year to correct the problem. If it were not corrected or well on the way to correction, the faculty member's contract would not be renewed.[262]

Although some of the larger faithful Catholic colleges and universities profiled in this book, including Belmont Abbey College, Catholic University of America, University of Dallas, and Franciscan all award tenure to faculty, most of the faithful few we studied do not have a tenure system in place on their campuses.

In contrast, while Ave Maria University does not offer tenure to faculty members, job security is provided once faculty members are promoted to the rank of associate professor, when they are provided with a three-year rolling contract. According to Dan Davy, dean of the faculty, in an attempt to provide some guidance to new faculty,

[262] Ibid.

"Assistant Professors are hired on annual renewable contracts no later than February 1 in their first year and November 1 in the subsequent academic years."[263]

Like Ave Maria, Wyoming Catholic College attempts to provide a sense of security to faculty. According to academic dean Kyle Washut, there is a

> streamlined renewal process which is similar to tenure but distinct in key ways. Faculty go through two contract renewals after they are hired. During the middle of the second year of a four-year contract, an intensive review is conducted and the faculty member is told the likelihood of them being renewed. The next year, the review is repeated, and a renewal decision is made. In the event that there is a renewal, faculty are given repeating four-year contracts.... If however, at any point upon a determination by the Academic Council and the President, that the faculty member has engaged in conduct of moral turpitude, an improper relationship with a student that is damaging to the mental or physical welfare of that student, publicly rejecting or defying the authentic teaching authority of the Catholic Church or the Pope's authority as head of the Catholic Church, or continuing to teach, after a written warning from either the Academic Dean or President, matters which are contrary to the doctrine of the faith held by the Catholic Church, then the contract can be terminated.[264]

Perhaps the most unique "non-tenure" system we studied was the one that was recently implemented at Thomas More College of the Liberal

[263] Dan Davy of Ave Maria, interview by David Willey.
[264] Kyle Washut, interview by David Willey.

Arts. As described by Jay Thompson, fellow and dean at TMC, the new system

> provides stability to those faculty members who have faithfully served the College for a long period and who have excelled in their duties.... Thomas More has two ranks of full-time faculty: Fellows and Instructors. Newly appointed Fellows and Instructors are reviewed by the Dean and the Dean's Council for three years. Reappointment is not assumed during this period but must be made and confirmed by the President in writing on an annual basis for each of the three years. After three years and upon the judgment of the Dean's Council an individual can be recommended to the President for continuance beyond a single year appointment.[265]

The status of "Fellow" may only occur after two years of full-time teaching or five years of combined part-time teaching and administrative work. Renewal of appointments for fellows after a successful third year review becomes automatic on the first of June of each successive year. Still, Thomas More faculty can be terminated for "failure or inability to perform assigned duties in a satisfactory manner, the commission of any act seriously offensive to justice or to the reputation of the College, persistent lack of collegiality, recurring or irreconcilable disagreement with the objectives and policies of the College as manifested by one or more acts of insubordination, or public dissent from the magisterium of the Roman Catholic Church."[266]

[265] Jay Thompson, interview by David Willey, 2022.

[266] Ibid.

In June 2023, the board of trustees at Thomas More College considered a proposal for a form of tenure which would award tenure to

> Fellows and stably appointed faculty who have served the College for 15 years or more and who are above the age of 55.... This tenure lasts until the individual is 70 years old (or whatever the SSA determines as retirement age). Senior faculty hired with experience at an institution of higher education other than Thomas More College will have previous full-time service counted by half up to an equivalence of ten years. Even a senior hire must serve a minimum of five years prior to consideration.[267]

Even with this proposed tenured system, a tenured individual at Thomas More "does not have guaranteed life-time employment, but prior to retirement age, he can only lose full-employment 'for cause.' In the event of an economic crisis, tenured individuals should be retained so long as the College can adequately staff all courses."[268]

Academic Freedom and *Ex Corde Ecclesiae*

Deeply intertwined with the debate around tenure is the question of the exact nature of an authentically Catholic academic freedom. For most — but not all — of those teaching on the faithful few campuses, *Ex Corde Ecclesiae* provides the boundaries of academic freedom. Franciscan's symposia on the twenty-fifth anniversary of the document dedicated several sessions to outlining the Catholic position on academic freedom. Within this discussion there was certainly disagreement about how to interpret the role of academic

[267] Ibid.
[268] Ibid.

freedom in light of revelation. One presenter, Terrence Tilley of Fordham University, invoked Heft's "open circle" as a potential model, where the Catholic intellectual tradition serves to provide "principles [that] center the circle as a whole." Tilley acknowledged that there are certain parameters that theologians, at the very least, must follow; namely, the need to always present the Catholic position as an option for students, even if it is alongside a personally held, dissenting belief. He insisted on the "necessity" of "the procedural version of academic freedom" as held by secular universities, even while admitting its insufficiency. And he claimed that "Catholic colleges and universities cannot be institutions of higher learning without procedural safeguards such as those of the AUUP ."[269]

Against this reading of academic freedom, Dr. Reinhard Hütter from Catholic University of America reframed the notion of academic freedom around the fact of revelation, aligning himself with John Paul's articulation of the tension within each Catholic university between "the search for truth, and the certainty of already knowing the fount of truth."[270] Hütter cut to the heart of the matter when he identified legitimate academic freedom as constitutive of the mission of a Catholic university: "*Ex Corde Ecclesiae* constitutes nothing less than a most prescient magisterial gift that enables Catholic universities in America to recuperate their constitutive identity—the idea of a Catholic university—and their mission, propelled by the complementary double center of the gift of revealed truth and the realization of authentic academic freedom."[271]

[269] Terrence Tilley, "Academic Freedom, Divine Revelation, Catholic Universities," in *Fidelity and Freedom*, 97, 109–111.

[270] *Ex Corde Ecclesiae*, no. 1.

[271] Reinhard Hütter, "Academic Freedom and Revealed Truth: Applying the Spirit and Letter of *Ex Corde Ecclesiae* to Catholic Universities in Contemporary America," in *Fidelity & Freedom*, 78.

For Hütter, the majority of modern "Catholic" universities keep their identity only through a "vague but discernible Catholic image" on their website, while, in their efforts to be competitive with secular schools, they eradicate Catholicism from the institution and leave the Faith no room in the administration, student life, or curricular commitments of the school. These schools, said Hütter, are "not unlike certain postmodern architecture, where the aesthetic of the facade conceals a completely different interior structure of mere functionality."[272] They provide only a negative view of academic freedom, seeing it as purely freedom *from* interference and indifferent to the truth or falsehood of any claim.

On the other hand, Catholic universities that understand their mission, as articulated by *Ex Corde Ecclesiae,* to dedicate themselves to the "cause of truth"[273] see academic freedom as a perfection of this mission and as consecrated to Truth, whose meaning is Christ. Understood in this light, Hütter contended, the "free search for the whole truth about nature, man, and God is nothing but the very realization of authentic academic freedom."[274]

In this context, it is possible to understand the radical move made by the faithful few, a move which is in fact a return to a position which eighty years ago was held by all. It is not that they simply have different conclusions from secular schools, but that the standard by which they measure the pursuit of those conclusions is different. For a secular school, "academic freedom" is the sole tool of secular reason and the guarantor of truth. In contrast, Catholic universities draw a circle at whose center is revelation. Academic freedom finds its authentic place within this circle, where it is measured by and in support of the deposit of faith.

[272] Ibid., 73.

[273] *Ex Corde Ecclesiae,* no. 4.

[274] Hütter, "Academic Freedom and Revealed Truth," 84.

The Debate Continues

While this book argues that this is the faithful Catholic interpretation of academic freedom, there is still a reluctance by many in the Catholic education world to accept the role that revelation plays in setting constraints on academic freedom. This reluctance played out recently in a professorial debate in the pages of *The Irish Rover*, one of the independent student newspapers at the University of Notre Dame. On one side was professor of political science Patrick Deneen, who published an article entitled "Against Academic Freedom." On the other side, Professor Daniel Philpott, whose views on academic freedom are a bit more complex — and rather convoluted. Philpott suggests that although academic freedom is a "given" for faculty within the classroom and within their published work or speeches, he believes that there should be a distinction between the sphere of administration and the sphere of inquiry on the Catholic campus. Philpott, who also teaches political science, has no problem with Church teachings reflecting the norms and practices of the "sphere of administration." He writes: "The sphere of administration addresses residential life, student clubs, pastoral ministry, human resources and employment, curricular requirements and behavior standards where norms and practices ought to reflect the Church's teachings." But Philpott rejects such adherence to the Church's teachings when it comes to the "sphere of inquiry" on campus. In a kind of "academic freedom for me, but not for thee" argument, Philpott maintains his need for complete academic freedom as a faculty member, claiming that "academic freedom governs directly" in the classroom, student publications, faculty publications, artistic performances, and public speech. In contrast, for Philpott,

> a faithful Catholic university would structure its employee health care and benefits policies consistently with

> Catholic norms of marriage and sexuality, while in the classroom and the student newspapers, students would be free to question these norms and yes, to defend them.... Behind a Catholic university's fidelity to Catholic morality in its policies is its belief that the truth will make you free; behind its fearless commitment to open inquiry in its classrooms is its confidence that freedom leads you to truth.[275]

But does it lead to truth? From Philpott's perspective, the Catholic university should be a "two-tier" organization, with faculty and students engaging in "open inquiry" and enjoying the academic freedom to reject Catholic teachings, and the administrative offices on campus adhering to Catholic teachings. For these "open inquiry" faculty and students, there is the freedom to reject Catholic teachings on life issues, marriage, family, gender identity, and sexual orientation. But Philpott would require that those in human resources and student affairs create policies that are consistent with Catholic teachings.

Unfortunately, such a system is completely unworkable. In fact, the two-tier system Philpott suggests has already been violated at Notre Dame, as there is abundant evidence that neither the sphere of administration nor the sphere of inquiry feel any need to conform to Catholic teachings at Notre Dame. Notre Dame student W. Joseph DeReuil pointed this fact out recently in an article on academic freedom published in *The Irish Rover* in 2022 when he suggested that academic freedom is protecting pro-abortion faculty at Notre Dame as they "disseminate information about how students might subvert the law, both human and divine, to kill their unborn children through abortifacients.... These loud

[275] Daniel Philpott, "Let's Argue," *The Irish Rover*, January 20, 2022, https://irishrover.net/2022/01/lets-argue/.

pro-abortion messages are sustained 'because Notre Dame supports my academic freedom' explained one pro-abortion professor, Tamara Kay." DeReuil lamented the fact that the academic freedom of the university has provided cover for a myriad of abuses of the Catholic identity of the once-faithful Catholic university. DeReuil recalled that, only a few years ago, Notre Dame students petitioned the administration for a campus-wide pornography filter on university WiFi — a common sense measure to support already existing university policy and one that has been implemented at many of the faithful few. But Notre Dame students were told that the policy proposal was rejected because such a filter "would violate academic freedom." DeReuil also suggested that "academic freedom is the reason given that Notre Dame sells tarot cards and sexualized children's books in the campus bookstore."[276]

Responding to Philpott's suggestion of a "two-tier" system of academic freedom on the Catholic campus, Patrick Deneen acknowledged that academic freedom may seem like the best protection for the ideas and beliefs of those professors whose conservative Catholic views may violate the liberal zeitgeist of the campus. However, by tracing the philosophical and historical origins of the idea, he revealed that

> the origins of academic freedom that predominates at universities today was in the first instance, explicitly and intentionally advanced in opposition to the distinct identity of Christian institutions and society.... Its aim was not ultimately to promote all views, but to advance a set of substantive commitments that were implicit in a liberal

[276] W. Joseph DeReuil, "The Limitations of Academic Freedom," *The Irish Rover*, October 12, 2022, https://irishrover.net/2022/10/the-limitations-of-academic-freedom/.

> conception of freedom that was directly opposed to the classical and Catholic understanding of liberty.[277]

Deneen reminds readers that many of today's Catholic defenders of academic freedom invoke the arguments of John Stuart Mill's *On Liberty* as the foundational text in defense of intellectual freedom, including academic freedom, but Mill was clear that

> what this ideal of liberty aimed to do was to displace traditional forms of culture and long-standing belief in favor of progress. Liberty was not merely good in itself but was to serve the advance of social and human transformation.... Once liberated from the stultifying confines of traditional society, Mill argued the human capacity for self-creation would be unleashed.... He believed that once liberty unleashed opportunities for self-creation, not just a few individuals would benefit, but ultimately a new social order — indeed, moral and even quasi-religious order — would emerge.[278]

Deneen points out that an earlier generation of Catholic educators "discerned the substantive commitment contained within the doctrine of academic freedom and denounced it as a practice that would ultimately undermine not just the religious underpinnings of Catholic institutions but would also displace the existing belief system of the United States with another creed altogether." Most Catholic universities understood this threat — until Father Hesburgh's declaration of independence at Land O' Lakes when he demanded "institutional

[277] Patrick Deneen, "Against Academic Freedom," *The Irish Rover*, March 17, 2022, https://irishrover.net/2022/03/against-academic-freedom/.

[278] Ibid.

autonomy" from the authority of the Church. In fact, Deneen points out that, in 1959, the Jesuit-founded Fairfield University "proudly boasted that as a Catholic institution it has taught and will always teach the principles on which rest all law, order, and right government." In those days, Fairfield University specifically rejected academic freedom as a "pretext to teach systems which destroy all freedom."[279]

It is ironic that this same Jesuit Fairfield University until recently boasted one of the most heterodox theology professors in the country in the person of Professor Paul Lakeland — the former director of Catholic Studies at Fairfield, who retired in 2023. In his book *Liberation of the Laity*, Lakeland, a former Jesuit priest who is married, argues for an accountable church with a liberated laity. By this, he means liberated from the authority of the teachings of the Church. Referring to what he often calls the "Alternative Magisterium," Lakeland has lobbied for optional celibacy, women priests, and gay priests. A frequent presenter at conferences such as Voice of the Faithful and CORPUS, both of which dissent from magisterial teaching, Lakeland has been a long-time critic of the institutional Church.

Criticism of the privileged status of priests and bishops is the constant theme of Lakeland's complaints in all of his writings and speeches. Moving beyond the university in his advocacy, Lakeland was the leader and spokesperson in an attempted state takeover of the Catholic Church's governance in the state of Connecticut in 2007, in which two state senators introduced Bill 1098: "An Act Modifying Corporate Laws Relating to Certain Religious Corporations." The bill would have allowed the state of Connecticut to control individual parishes' governance and financial affairs, relegating priests and bishops to an advisory role in their own parishes. Had the law passed, it would have required the state to provide

[279] Ibid.

governance over the Catholic Church in the entire state of Connecticut. On the surface, the proposed bill looked like an unconstitutional takeover by the state, but the real force behind the bill was a small but well-organized group of Catholics — including, most notably, Fairfield University's Paul Lakeland, and the membership of Voice of the Faithful, CORPUS, and other disgruntled Catholics. These Catholics, unhappy with Church teachings on moral and governance issues, attempted to enlist the state as a partner in radically transforming the Church from within. Paul Lakeland was on the front lines in leading the charge for the legislation that was designed to re-make the Church from the inside by toppling the hierarchy. Yet Fairfield University's Jesuit leadership thought so highly of Professor Lakeland's advocacy work that it provided him with an endowed chair and a faculty position for life with the academic freedom to teach his theology students that the Catholic Church is a draconian site of oppression and inequality for women, the LGBTQ community, and former priests who have left the priesthood to marry.

Deneen understands how unfettered academic freedom gives rise to a Paul Lakeland. He understands that places like Fairfield University and many of the more than two hundred Catholic colleges and universities are defined by what Deneen calls the

> substantive commitments arising from Mill's aspirations of academic freedom: progress, social transformation, moral perfection. While seemingly neutral, the modern research university consists of definite boundaries and substantive commitments. Faculty who aspire to join such an institution must conform to the research ideal whose fundamental orientation is toward progress and transformation of society. These Millian ideals are now contained in the

> foundational commitments of the institution and over time will—and do—transform every institution in keeping with its deepest substantive beliefs.[280]

Deneen also understands that the consequence is obvious:

> The distinct missions and identities at places such as Notre Dame will cease to exist as it continues to model itself on the alternate religion of the modern university—those contained in the very commitments contained in the philosophy of John Stuart Mill. Like a frog being slowly boiled, the same process that has replaced an older faith tradition with a new faith at nearly every college and university in America is advancing daily at Notre Dame, now accelerated by its enthusiastic embrace of the new theology of wokeness that is rapidly replacing whatever remained of its Catholic identity.[281]

Academic Freedom Policies for the Faithful Few

For Deneen—and for the leaders and most of the faculty of the faithful few—the important question is to determine exactly what it is that makes a Catholic university a "faithful" university: Does the Catholic college community itself share an understanding of the *boundaries* of that Catholic community? Faculty lectures on the values of abortion or same-sex "marriage" would be outside of these boundaries on a faithful Catholic campus. They would be unthinkable on such a faithful campus. Moving beyond theoretical conversations

[280] Deneen, "Against Academic Freedom."
[281] Ibid.

on academic freedom, the important question when evaluating a Catholic college's faithfulness is whether its campus ethos is one of commitment to living out the teachings of the Church. This does not mean that we reject conversations over academic freedom, but it does mean that the faithful few have made a commitment to Catholic teachings — authentic Catholic teachings — in every area of the university, not just isolating this commitment to the offices of student life or campus ministry. Conveying to students ideas that are clearly contrary to the teachings of the Church should be unthinkable.

This is how it is at Christendom College, according to long-standing faculty member Dr. Robert Rice. Joining the faculty just four years after the college was established, Rice played a distinguished part at Christendom for almost forty years, during which he served as department chair for English, academic dean, and vice president for Academic Affairs. When we interviewed Rice, he explained to us that it is a given at Christendom that academic freedom is only to be understood within the context of faithfulness to the Magisterium. All Christendom faculty take an oath of fidelity to the Magisterium when they are hired, and this oath is renewed each year. "When *Ex Corde* came out, we received it with glee," said Rice. "We were already living its principles, but when it was released we adopted the document as part of our mission."[282]

This attitude, which emphasizes Catholic identity in every department, is also held by Dr. Sanford, the president of the University of Dallas. In a 2022 interview, he spoke of UD's firm commitment to a Catholic identity that informs every discipline, a commitment which confirms legitimate academic freedom and ensures UD's high academic standards: "We take practical measures to ensure our Catholic identity and mission is at the fore,

[282] Dr. Robert Rice, interview by David Willey, 2022.

from recruiting committed and mission driven faculty members and ensuring that each of our theology teachers, in particular, receive a mandatum from the Bishop of the Diocese," said Sanford. "Unreservedly, the University of Dallas is faithful to the Magisterium, and as our mission statement says, is wholly 'dedicated to the pursuit of wisdom, of truth, and of virtue as the proper and primary ends of education.'" Sanford emphasized UD's "mission driven faculty" because of the university's holistic vision of a Catholicism that informs every educational discipline, as well as all of its administrative decisions: "We do not see the Catholic portion of a Catholic liberal arts education as a 'value-added' component. It is not the salt in the stew. It is not the icing on the cake. A truly Catholic education is a liberal arts education through and through; that is, an education that frees us to live virtuously, that enables us to think for ourselves so that we can direct all our efforts to the greater glory of God."[283] Such an education does not promote free inquiry for its own sake, but rather sees free inquiry as directed to its proper end; namely, truth and virtue.

While all the faithful Catholic universities directly address the ways in which *Ex Corde Ecclesiae* shapes academic freedom on their campuses, Wyoming Catholic College provides some of the most specific guidelines for faculty on academic freedom. Promising the "spirit of freedom and charity," it "encourages its faculty to recognize that they enjoy genuine academic freedom, in accordance with the rich Catholic tradition of human rights set in the context of the search for truth and the need to preserve and further the common good." At the same time, professors at Wyoming Catholic "are firmly

[283] Jesse Russell, "The Pressing Task for Catholic Universities: An Interview with Dr. Jonathan J. Sanford, *Catholic World Report*, August 18, 2022, https://www.catholicworldreport.com/2022/08/18/the-pressing-task-for-catholic-universities-today-an-interview-with-dr-jonathan-sanford/.

resolved never to teach anything contrary to faith and morals as taught by the Church's Magisterium."[284]

Understanding its unique relationship with the Church, Wyoming Catholic recognizes that this relationship is essential it its institutional identity. As such, it recognizes that the College

> participates most directly in the life of the local Church in which it is situated; at the same time, because it is an academic institution and therefore part of the international community of scholarship and inquiry, each institution participates in and contributes to the life and the mission of the universal Church, assuming consequently a special bond with the Holy See by reason of the service to unity which it is called to render to the whole Church. One consequence of its essential relationship to the Church is that the institutional fidelity of the University to the Christian message includes a recognition of and adherence to the teaching authority of the Church in matters of faith and morals.[285]

Ultimately, the schools which are defending an application of academic freedom that is in obedience to the Magisterium understand that freedom is always directed to an end, and that academic freedom is no different.

Now, it is important not to confuse academic freedom and freedom of speech, which are different freedoms aimed at different (if connected) goods. Specifically, free speech guards the good of the conscience. The individual's conscience should not be violated by

[284] "About: Catholicity," Wyoming Catholic College, https://wyomingcatholic.edu/about/catholicity/ex-corde-ecclesiae/.

[285] Ibid.

being forced to say what they do not believe, nor should they be prevented from saying what they do believe.

Academic freedom, on the other hand, guards the search for truth. It is not simply free speech in the classroom or academy; instead, it exists to protect the good of truth in the university. The reason why it is so important to protect academic freedom is simply because there is much that we do not know. Even what we do know, we know imperfectly and with uncertainty. Academic freedom is important because it allows each person to contribute the light of his own intellect to the pursuit of truth.

Still, there is an exception to this uncertainty: namely, the truth of revealed religion. We hold to this exception because the certainty of this truth depends not on us, but on the trustworthiness of the revealer: God. If academic freedom finds its raison d'être in the pursuit and defense of truth, it would violate its own end to attack divinely revealed truth. In taking this position, these universities set themselves against the vast liberal consensus, which believes that academic freedom, by definition, is without constraints. In taking this stand, the *Newman Guide* schools are returning to the traditional Catholic stance on academic freedom and so are aligning themselves with the educational vision set out by Pope John Paul II.

Chapter 7

The Sanctuary Lamp: The Culture of Worship at the Faithful Few

Christendom College

On February 7, 2023, Christendom College mourned the tragic passing of alumna Mandy Hain, class of 2007, who died after a long battle with cancer. According to those whose lives were touched by Mandy, her love of beauty, her deep faith, her extraordinary artistic talent, and her loving presence inspired and enriched the lives of many. Until her death, Mandy had devoted countless hours to painting the crossing-tower ceiling in the college's spectacular new Christ the King Chapel. She wrote and painted the beautiful letters of the inscription, "Sanctus, Sanctus, Sanctus," and provided the gold leaf detail of the Latin inscription, "This is the House of God and the Gate of Heaven," that sits above the entrance to the chapel. Mandy also painstakingly restored each of the Stations of the Cross to prepare them to be hung in the new chapel. These stations had been hung in the "older" campus Chapel of Christ the King that had been dedicated in 1995. Mandy cleaned, repaired, and repainted — including regilding each in gold leaf — each of the Stations of the Cross before they were mounted on the walls of the new chapel. All of this work was done while Mandy was enduring the ravages of the terminal illness that eventually took her life. According to *Instaurare,* the magazine of Christendom College, "Painting the crossing tower's ceiling was an enormous undertaking, and one that also brought considerable pain at times. Mandy often spoke about offering up her sufferings gladly and the redemptive element of being an artist, pointing to the importance of raising one's eyes to God."[286]

In reflecting on her work on Christendom's magnificent new chapel, Mandy said: "Beauty brings us to its Source and makes us better without effort on our part. It is truly part of God's order of mercy and redemption in this way. This is a dream I have for the students — that they encounter real beauty within the heart of Christendom, the Chapel of Christ the King."[287] It is the beauty of the chapel, and the beauty of the liturgy that emerges from within the walls of that chapel at Christendom that inspires the faith of Christendom's students. Those who helped to build the chapel understand — as Mandy Hain did — that "Beauty bring us to its Source."

On April 15, 2023, Christendom's new chapel was dedicated — reflecting the tireless work of fundraising and the sometimes arduous physical labor of dozens of carpenters, stone cutters, artisans, and generous volunteers who donated their time and treasure. Creating the chapel was a community commitment that involved hundreds of contributors. In fact, in a blustery cold week in late January 2023, the faculty, students, and staff volunteered to help unload the nearly three thousand pieces of the

[286] "Christendom Mourns the Passing of Alumna Artisan Mandy Hain," Christendom College, February 8, 2023. For a visual presentation on Mandy Hain and her work on the chapel, see "The Artist," video, 3:43, *Artisan Highlights,* Christ the King Chapel, https://chapel.christendom.edu/.

[287] Ibid.

magnificent new organ for the choir loft. After a three-week installation period, Charles Kegg and the Kegg Pipe Organ Builders began voicing each of the over 2,800 pipes. This voicing involves minute adjustments to each pipe, acoustically marrying the pipe to the chapel, a process that has been described as more artistry than mere tuning.[288] Spanish sculptor Edwin Gonzalez carved the commissioned Pietà sculpture for the chapel. This extraordinary piece of art occupies a niche in the north transept. Gonzalez is also creating the bronze Christ the King statue that will occupy the top of the granite column at the center of the piazza, directly in front of the new chapel.

All this artistry truly brings all of us to the beauty of the Source that Mandy Hain so beautifully spoke of. The leaders of Christendom College — beginning with Christendom's founder, Dr. Warren Carroll — have always known of the importance of beauty inspiring the faith of its students. And although the soaring spires of Christendom's new chapel have not been able to be replicated on all the campuses of the faithful few Catholic colleges and universities profiled on these pages, each of these schools try to find ways to inspire students through beautiful liturgies.

According to a published essay on the history of Christendom College by Tom McFadden, vice president of Enrollment and Marketing at Christendom — and as we discussed in chapter 2 — the college took its name from the word which embodies the Christian social and political ideal: a society, a culture, a government in which Christ the King reigns. Dr. Carroll envisioned Christendom College as a new institution that would "take on the task of rebuilding Catholic higher education. It would be dedicated to full Catholic truth and

[288] "Christ the King Chapel Update," *Instaurare: The Magazine of Christendom College*, Spring 2023, 3.

would be genuinely innovative in developing a Catholic curriculum, taught in an authentically Catholic cultural environment." Christendom was designed to "'restore all things in Christ' by forming men and women to contribute to the Christian renovation of the temporal order. This mission gives Christendom College its name."[289]

Christendom College aimed to be a "mini-Christendom … a society, however small, in which Christ does truly reign." Carroll envisioned the college as an example and a model, as well as a center of study on what Christendom is and how it might be built anew even in our secularized age. He recognized the damage that had been done to Catholic higher education with the Land O'Lakes statement in 1967. He realized — similar to how Franciscan University's Father Michael Scanlan realized and Ave Maria University's Tom Monaghan realized — that there was no longer a place in these now secularized universities for what had always been the primary purpose of Catholic education: "to lead young minds out of narrow perspectives into the world of known truth and under the guiding light of the Catholic faith."[290] For Dr. Carroll, the "watchwords" of Christendom College are: "Truth Exists. The Incarnational Happened." In one of his last public lectures at the college, on April 26, 2010, the founder reminded students and faculty of those watchwords, saying, "You must go to your death fearlessly proclaiming that truth exists. That is why you must avoid, as you would avoid a plague victim, any man or institution that permits the teaching that truth does not exist. This is our modern message of death and destruction and it is why averring the Incarnation happened makes you a Christian. It's why I was not a Christian until I could say it."[291]

[289] McFadden, *Restoring All Things*, 5.

[290] Ibid., 9.

[291] Ibid., 20.

Dr. Timothy O'Donnell was appointed as the president of Christendom College in 1992. The crowning achievement of his work there is the spectacular Chapel of Christ the King. Announcing his plans to begin to build it even at his inauguration, O'Donnell launched an ambitious fundraising program in which the college committed 15 percent of every dollar of unrestricted donation to the Chapel Fund. According to Tom McFadden, prior to the announcement of the Chapel Fund, O'Donnell had met with Christendom College's executive vice president, Mark McShurley, who insisted that a major gift would have to be received in order to launch this project. The two men prayed to the Blessed Mother for her intercession and, within thirty minutes of the conclusion of their meeting and prayer, McShurley received a phone call from an anonymous donor who wanted to pledge $250,000 to the Chapel Fund.[292]

The following month, on the feast of Christ the King, a special ground blessing ceremony was held on the site of Christendom's planned new chapel. A month later, the ground was broken for the Chapel of Christ the King. According to McFadden,

> Petrine Construction began work on the Christ the King project on December 18, 1992. The Chapel was patterned after the oldest Catholic Church in the Shenandoah Valley, the Sacred Heart Church built in 1870, located in Winchester, Virginia, and built by Irish immigrants. Much of the interior furnishings came from Sacred Heart Church, including the beautiful stained glass windows.[293]

Generous benefactors stepped forward to help with the construction of the chapel. The pews were bought from a Philadelphia church that

[292] Ibid., 22.
[293] Ibid.

was closing. "The old high altar, made of pure Carrara marble, donated in 1991 by then-Bishop of Arlington John R. Keating, was from the old Sacred Heart Church in Winchester."[294]

On April 8, 1995 — less than three years after the ground-breaking — the Chapel of Christ the King was dedicated and blessed by most Cardinal Jan Schotte, Pope John Paul II's secretary general to the World Synod of Bishops. At the solemn dedication, Cardinal Schotte read a personal message from the Holy Father and presented the college with a chalice and paten from the pope. The message read: "I know what they are doing there and I want them to have this chalice and paten from me so I may be always present to them in this way. Take it to them."[295]

Today, the spirit and the mission of Warren Carroll and the early founders and donors continues. A graduate of 2020 shared with us how Carroll's oft-quoted motto about Truth and the objectivity of the Incarnation permeates campus life to this day, and how it continues to unite academics and the spiritual life in the classroom. It served as a reminder that "faith and reason went hand in hand," she said. "Everything I learned in the classroom I could bring to prayer and vice versa. Each faculty member is dedicated to teaching and spreading the Truth, which means being practicing Catholics outside the classroom as well as teaching the truth within."

And there are plenty of opportunities for prayer. "There's no way to capture how integral access to the sacraments was for my spiritual life," she confessed. With the old chapel located in the center of campus, and with up to three Masses a day, the opportunities for a sacramental life were always available. The "11:30 daily Mass would be packed, and even the early 7:30 daily Mass would have a good

[294] Ibid., 23.
[295] Ibid.

number of students," she reminisced. "I was also struck by how long the confession line would be regularly, as well as frequent holy hours and first Fridays that would be full to the rafters." [296]

Christendom College offers students an opportunity to attend Mass twice each day, every day, and also offers students the opportunity to attend Mass in the Extraordinary Form twice weekly on campus in the magnificent Chapel of Christ the King (although this is currently under review due to the motu proprio *Traditionis Custodes*). There is also a holy hour every weekday, and the students have access to the chapel, where the Eucharist is in repose in the tabernacle twenty-four hours a day. There are Confessions twice daily and before all Masses. There is a daily Rosary in the Christ the King Chapel.

Franciscan University

As we saw in chapter 2, Franciscan University's Father Mike Scanlan understood better than most the importance of liturgy on a faithful campus, especially demonstrated in his intentional efforts to renew the liturgical life on campus, despite the administrators who thought such efforts were a waste of time. He knew then, as those who are blessed to be on the Franciscan campus today know, that it is the spiritual life at Franciscan — and at all of the faithful few — that makes all the difference. It is the inspiring liturgies several times each day and the rousing praise and worship services throughout each semester that make that difference. And, most importantly, it is the ability to be present with the Blessed Sacrament in the Portiuncula at any time on any day. Franciscan students sign up for a weekly holy hour commitment at the start of each semester, and "The Port," as students call it, is open for continuous Eucharistic Adoration except during school breaks.

[296] Interview by David Willey of a 2020 Christendom College graduate.

Built on the Franciscan campus in 1987, the Portiuncula is a re-creation of the thirteenth century Portiuncula chapel that was built by St. Francis where he heard the words "Rebuild my Church" from the mouth of the Lord, speaking through the San Damiano crucifix in a tiny, dilapidated church outside Assisi. The Port is a "grace-filled haven for quiet meditation and eucharistic adoration.... Nestled in a grove of trees opposite Christ the King Chapel on campus, the Portiuncula beckons students and visitors alike to come and spend an hour with the Lord in prayer."[297] By decree of the Vatican, the Franciscan University Portiuncula is designated as a site of holy pilgrimage. Anyone who goes there is eligible to receive a plenary indulgence on five occasions throughout the year, if they devoutly visit the Port, pray for the intentions of the Holy Father, including the Our Father and the Creed, as well as have an interior disposition of complete detachment from sin; have made a sacramental confession; and have received the Holy Eucharist within seven to ten days of visiting.[298]

Today, the message of "Rebuild My Church" continues to echo in everything that Franciscan does. Like St. Francis, Franciscan University leaders know that this commission is much bigger than constructing dormitories and academic buildings. It means caring for the poor, reigniting people's faith, and spreading the gospel in a world that has fallen into disrepair. In 2021, the "Rebuild My Church" strategic plan provided a new blueprint for outlining the university's commitment to rebuilding this culture, a commitment renewed in the 2024 "Be Light" plan.

Tending to the spiritual needs of its students is key to Franciscan's success as a leader of the faithful few. The spiritual life on campus is

[297] "The Portiuncula," Franciscan University, https://chapel.franciscan.edu/pray/the-portiuncula/#1558116888884-332f9d8e-aec6.

[298] Ibid.

vibrant, with four daily Masses each weekday. The most popular daily Mass is at noontime; it is usually filled to capacity, and it is spirit-filled, as students join faculty and staff to pray the Rosary before Mass, and many remain in the pews after Mass for private prayer before they return to their afternoon classes. Saturday morning is reserved for the Pro-Life Masses, in keeping with Father Scanlan's commitment to the unborn. And each Sunday throughout the semester there are five Masses, which, until recently, included a weekly Extraordinary Form Mass. All are usually filled to capacity. Confession is available throughout each week and there is a community Rosary each weekday evening in the center of campus in Rosary Circle. In addition to these opportunities for communal prayer and structured worship, students find a peaceful place for private prayer at the Tomb of the Unborn Child. Set across from the Portiuncula, the tomb was designed to be a peaceful place to pray for infants in the womb, expectant mothers, those healing from abortion, and all the vulnerable of the world. Guarded by a perpetual flame and encircled by a stone patio and wooden benches with two granite kneelers, students are constantly reminded by the presence of this tomb of the need to protect the most vulnerable. Throughout the school year, the Students for Life Club gathers each Wednesday evening to pray the Rosary at the tomb.[299]

What distinguishes Franciscan University from the other faithful few is its commitment to charismatic prayer on campus. At the "Festival of Praise" offered on one Saturday evening each month throughout the semester, students are invited to an evening of Adoration, uplifting praise and worship music, and an inspiring talk—"allowing the Holy Spirit to work in and among" those gathered.[300] It is the joyful and

299 "Tomb of the Unborn Child," Franciscan University, https://chapel.franciscan.edu/pray/tomb-of-the-unborn-child/.

300 "Festivals of Praise," Franciscan University, https://chapel.franciscan.edu/campus-evangelization/.

spirit-filled praise and worship services that have given Franciscan the reputation as a "charismatic" Catholic university. According to Father Scanlan's autobiography, "The charismatic renewal embodied the kind of dynamic faith that I thought should shape college life, a faith marked by free praise of the Lord, spiritual gifts, commitment to one another's welfare, and a life of prayer."[301]

The monthly praise and worship services attract more than one-third of the student body; several of the Franciscan students we spoke with have found them to be the most engaging and transformative spiritual occasions on campus. One student, a 2019 graduate, spoke of Father Scanlan's charismatic legacy being a major attraction to him when he attended Franciscan. "It was the way they worshiped that attracted me to Franciscan," he shared, "that and the strong Catholic community I knew I'd find. The Holy Spirit, and His charisms, are absolutely present on the Franciscan campus." He believed that the combination of deep charismatic spirituality and constant availability of the sacraments was what made his and many others' time at Franciscan truly great. "Sacraments are offered so frequently at Franciscan, they make it *hard* for you to miss Mass and Confession," he laughed. "Having that emphasis on prayer at a college, at a time when everyone is trying to figure out what will make them happy in life — it's making the statement that there's something more important here. It's a reminder that Jesus is the only one who will fill us."

He also shared that through the charismatic spirituality at Franciscan, students are constantly reminded that worship of God is a conscious decision. Whether you're in the Portiuncula, one of the frequent praise and worship sessions around campus, or just in a dorm chapel, you learn to pray with your whole heart and all your attention. "It's everything," he said decisively. "If Franciscan taught

[301] Scanlan, *Let the Fire Fall*, 146.

nothing else but was just a place where young men and women came to learn to pray and live a life immersed in the sacraments — it would still be an incredible institution."

Recalling fond memories of his time at Franciscan, he said they involved him texting some of his guy friends so that they could get together to praise, and to pray for an outpouring of the Holy Spirit on campus. "We prayed our guts out, asking the Holy Spirit to come down and continue to transform Franciscan. It's a beautiful thing to have five contacts in your phone who you can text anytime and worship with," he said with a smile. "And we weren't even that unusual!"[302]

Clement Harrold, a recent Franciscan University graduate, published an article in *First Things* about the spiritual and liturgical life at Franciscan: "From the pulpit and in campus ministry, a radical openness to the Holy Spirit is emphasized, as are the healing power of grace, the power of testimony, the necessity of praise and the importance of joy in the Christian life." Entitled "Tradismatic Trentecostalism," the article captures the richness of the liturgical life on campus. As this young graduate attests, "My years at Franciscan changed my life, precisely thanks to the university's commitment to joyful liturgy, confident prayer, and authentic Christian community."[303]

And although the charismatic character remains, Harrold points out that Franciscan has also embraced the spiritual-liturgical recovery that has occurred for many young Catholics throughout the West. Often referred to as "traditionalist," the movement describes the desire to return *ad fontes* — to the sources — and reclaim the full sacramental and ecclesial patrimony that has too often been denied us. Responding

302 Interview by David Willey of a 2019 Franciscan University graduate (2022).

303 Clement Harrold, "Tradismatic Trentecostalism," *First Things*, March 2022, https://www.firstthings.com/article/2022/03/tradismatic-trentecostalism.

to student needs and desires, Franciscan has embraced many of the traditions and rituals of the earlier Catholics — those who worshiped prior to the Second Vatican Council — without rejecting the good to be found in the charismatic movement and the devout yet lively *Novus Ordo* Masses that Franciscan is best known for. Harrold recalls: "During my time serving on student government, for example, we conducted polling that showed that more than 90 percent of students at Franciscan supported the putatively 'trad' measure of introducing patens in the distribution of Holy Communion — an indication that old labels might need revision."[304] Additionally, a few years ago, the T.O.R. friars undertook a major work of beautification in the campus chapel, which included returning the tabernacle to the center of the sanctuary, also something that is sometimes seen as a hallmark of the "trad" agenda. As the director of chapel ministries, Father Shawn Roberson, T.O.R., explained to Harrold, "Franciscan is, at its heart, a Christ-centered university and as such it strives to have good and vibrant liturgical celebrations whether that is in the *Novus Ordo*, Traditional Latin Mass, or the Byzantine Rite. Our fundamental witness is our active participation in the liturgical life of the Church."[305]

One of the students Harrold interviewed summarized it well by saying that "Franciscan exemplifies the reality that tradition and charism are not opposed to each other but are fundamental pillars which build up the Church." Harrold, who is a student of the Latin language and sees great beauty in the ancient rite, typically attends the *Novus Ordo* and routinely listens to praise and worship music, much of it written by evangelical Protestants. For Harrold, there is a false dichotomy of charismatic and traditional divisions in the Church — a dichotomy that is not present on the

[304] Ibid.
[305] Ibid.

Franciscan campus. In fact, Harrold points out that "the 'tradismatic' spirituality found within the student body of Franciscan is a vibrant synthesis, one that modern Catholicism ought to prize." And he reminds us that John Henry Newman himself promoted the kind of Catholic synthesis that is so visible at Franciscan when he wrote in his *Development of Christian Doctrine* that "one aspect of Revelation must not be allowed to exclude or to obscure another; Christianity is dogmatical, devotional, practical all at once; it is esoteric and exoteric; it is indulgent and strict; it is light and dark; it is love and it is fear."[306]

Newman's words are taken to heart at each of the faithful few Catholic campuses profiled in this book. Although *Traditionis Custodes*—the motu proprio issued by Pope Francis in 2022 which restricted the Extraordinary Form—has had a dampening effect on offering the Traditional Latin Mass on some of our most faithful campuses, most of the faithful few have been able to continue offering it on their campuses. Sadly, Franciscan University was required by its presiding bishop to suspend offering the Traditional Latin Mass on campus in 2023 because of the motu proprio. Still, in response to student requests, the university offers a bus once each month from campus to St. Peter's Church, a nearby parish church in Steubenville that is already home to many of the more traditional Franciscan students, faculty, and staff, for Mass in the Extraordinary Form.

Thomas Aquinas College

In her 2005 book *God on the Quad: How Religious Colleges and the Missionary Generation are Changing America,* Naomi Schaefer Riley described visiting Thomas Aquinas College in Southern California—founded in

[306] Ibid.

1971 — and attending one of the college's Sunday Masses. "The whole thing is in Latin," she recounted.

> Every student at Thomas Aquinas is required to learn Latin Grammar and study the Mass. There are a few readings in English, but there is no separate English Mass for students to attend. The reason offered by Rev. Wilfred Borden, an Irish-looking man of about seventy with reddish eyebrows, is not simply to preserve a tradition. "Latin is concise," he asserts. "So many English words have different shades of meaning."

"Even Catholics who have attended Latin Mass," Riley concludes, "might find TAC's a bit more formal."[307]

A non-Catholic, Riley noted that the "most joyous" part of the Mass she attended was when three congregants who were in the process of converting to Catholicism were introduced. Ninety percent of students who enter Thomas Aquinas College are Catholic, and half of the remaining ones convert during their time there. A section of the Mass is devoted to asking the community to support them in this venture and appealing for God's blessing on them. Riley observes that the issue of how to treat non-Catholics at TAC is "a topic for discussion even in this monastic and homogeneous community.... Some TAC students don't see the zeal to convert non-Catholics as an unqualified good. And even the [then] President of the school acknowledges that some students may have a tendency to go overboard but he does expect that proselytizing should be a part of the lives of TAC students and graduates." One of the priests Riley interviewed concluded, "If you

[307] Naomi Schaeffer Riley, *God on the Quad: How Religious Colleges and the Missionary Generation are Changing America*, (Chicago: Ivan R. Dee, 2005), 81–82.

think the faith is true and if you think that it's appropriate to live your life for Christ, it's also appropriate to want to draw others into it."[308]

In an attempt to discern whether there were controversies on campus, Riley spoke with several of the students who responded that the "big controversy" at TAC is "the Plato versus Aristotle controversy." One of the students Riley spoke with said that he chose Thomas Aquinas because he "wanted to have a better foundation of belief in Christianity before I tackled the skepticism." Riley told them that at some of the religious schools she was studying — including Wheaton College—there was an atmosphere that forces students to question their beliefs, even if ultimately it is in the service of strengthening them. She added that this results in a certain population of "doubters" at these other schools:

> Puzzled, these TAC upperclassmen can't seem to understand why a religious school would want to engender doubt among its students. I try to explain that that is not Wheaton's final goal, but sometimes, the professors there tell me, it is a necessary step on the way to bringing serious intellectual strength to their students' faith.
>
> "There are no doubters here," one of the students tells me resolutely. And the other quickly concurs. After a moment, the first adds that even if there were, we wouldn't be able to "see into another student's soul."[309]

Riley finally asked the TAC students whether "they ever witnessed someone experiencing, perhaps, a crisis of faith? They give me a unanimous no."[310]

[308] Ibid., 83.
[309] Ibid., 89.
[310] Ibid.

The General Attitude of Worship at the Faithful Few

While this book has focused in detail on the few schools discussed above, I could say just as much about the authentic atmosphere of Catholic worship at each school in the *Newman Guide*. The portraits of Christendom, Franciscan, and Thomas Aquinas are representative of the Catholic environment at each of the faithful few. And so, in the rest of this section, I provide a quick glance at some of the most enriching details of the liturgical life found at a number of these colleges and universities.

As expected, spiritual life at Ave Maria University includes daily Masses and Confession. There is a chapel in every residence hall, twenty-four-hour Eucharistic Adoration, faith-centered student households, and the availability of the Extraordinary Form of the Mass. Thomas More College of Liberal Arts in New Hampshire, in addition to the daily Masses that are scheduled around classes to offer students ample opportunities to attend, the Extraordinary Form of the Mass is offered weekly. There is also a nightly recitation of the Rosary, and students are invited to participate in chanted Morning and Evening Prayer each day. At Wyoming Catholic College, both the Ordinary and the Extraordinary Forms of the Mass as well as the Byzantine Rite are offered on campus. There are no classes during the times of daily Mass, and Eucharistic Adoration and Confession are offered daily.

At Belmont Abbey in North Carolina, daily Masses are held at the historic Abbey Basilica. The Liturgy of the Hours with the monks is also open to the students. Eucharistic Adoration is available each weekday. The presence of the monks lends a stable, grounding quality to the all-too-often-distracted lives of the students on campus. A student from the class of 2023 spoke to us about her experience of the monks bringing "a beautiful sense of order and peace" to life on campus. For her, "Having the monastic community on campus provided the perfect opportunity to delve deeper into the more contemplative aspects of my faith, gifted me with a better understanding of prayer and how to structure my prayer life, and encouraged me to learn more about the liturgy and about the Benedictine tradition." She also spoke of how the witness of the monks would bring many of the non-Catholic students into full communion with the Church. In their faithful celebration of the sacraments and their commitment to the Catholic intellectual life, the monks "enrich the campus and have had a profound effect on my own spiritual life," she concluded. She shared with us that, because of the formation she received at Belmont, she has continued to be serious about her spiritual life since graduation.[311] In our experience, this is a common phenomenon among students who attend the faithful colleges.

Likewise, Benedictine College in Atchison, Kansas, offers daily Mass and Confession with Eucharistic Adoration on weekdays. It also offers prayer at the Marian grotto and Liturgy of the Hours with the monks. Students at the Catholic University of American have access to several daily Masses at a number of chapels on campus. They also are able to attend Mass at the Basilica of the National Shrine of the Immaculate Conception, which is next door to the campus, and offers several daily Masses, six Masses each Sunday, and a Saturday afternoon vigil Mass. Walsh University offers students daily Mass as well as two Masses on Sundays. According to Walsh University's Ben Walther, director of Campus Ministry, it offers Eucharistic Adoration on campus daily for thirty minutes before Mass as well as scheduled times throughout the week. At their weekly nights of worship and Adoration (Wednesday nights from 8:00 to 10:00 p.m.), students either pray Night Prayer or the Rosary together. Walther added that there are also student groups on the

[311] Interview with Belmont Abbey student by David Willey.

Walsh campus who pray the Rosary together outside of the scheduled time at Adoration.

When we inquired about the liturgical life at the University of Dallas, Karen Bless, assistant to the chaplain and rector at the University of Dallas, wrote to us that the university's Church of the Incarnation holds twenty hours of Eucharistic Adoration each week throughout the school year. Confessions are available to students for eight scheduled hours each week, although students may also request Confession as needed from any of the Cistercian priests who live in an abbey across the highway and come to campus both as professors and students. There is a scheduled Rosary every Monday through Friday, led by different departments on campus. During the academic year, there are two daily Masses on the Dallas campus. There is one daily Mass on Saturdays, four Sunday Masses, and one anticipatory Mass on Saturday evening.[312] We spoke to a graduate of 2022, who simply described the liturgy as "just part of the framework of how we do things at UD." Daily Mass is always crowded, and she laughed that "on holy days of obligation, everyone knows that you're late to class because of Mass going over or because of the long Communion lines." She also spoke warmly of other aspects of the sacramental life, remembering one priest in particular who would frequently hear confessions until 1:00 a.m., because so many students were waiting in line. Campus ministry also organizes several retreats every year for the students. In the fall, the "Genesis" retreat is held for new students, to help orient them spiritually as they start life on campus. Then, every spring, there is the national retreat program called "Awakening," which focuses on growing spiritual community and fellowship on campus, built around Eucharistic Adoration and Confession. There are no opportunities for students

[312] E-mail interview with Karen Bless, August 16, 2022.

to participate in the Extraordinary Form of the Mass on UD's campus, but a number of students travel to a nearby Extraordinary Form parish that is shepherded by the Fraternity of St. Peter.[313]

Conclusion

On April 15, 2023, at a Mass packed with a cardinal and a bishop, dozens of priests, and hundreds of alumni and benefactors, Christendom's Christ the King chapel was finally dedicated.[314] "It's by going back to our roots and our foundation that we can find the way forward now for our country, for our society. Everything from the spires that you see rising up above, pointing to Heaven, to the gothic crossing tower, all of those windows and arches inside the building point us to where we're all destined: toward Heaven," said Timothy O'Donnell, Christendom's president at the ribbon-cutting ceremony the afternoon before the dedication. At the event was also Alice Carroll, wife of Christendom's founder, the late Warren Carroll. Carroll cut the ribbon, and then a letter was read from the late Pope Benedict XVI, who had blessed the chapel's cornerstone in 2008 and who had recently written a letter to share his joy at the chapel's completion. "I hope that all who enter this college chapel will feel the richness of our common patrimony that we have as human beings and as Christians and recognize the incredible heritage that is ours," shared O'Donnell, quoting the Holy Father.[315] O'Donnell later announced that his retirement would follow the 2023–2024 school year, and his decades of faithful service to the school find a suitable

[313] Ibid.

[314] "Christendom College's New Christ the King Chapel Dedicated," Christendom College, April 17, 2023, https://www.christendom.edu/2023/04/17/christendom-colleges-new-christ-the-king-chapel-dedicated/.

[315] Ibid.

legacy in the completion of this magnificent church, the spires of which are visible for miles across the Shenandoah Valley.[316]

The dedication of the chapel to Christ the King is also a fitting homage to Warren Carroll. His founding vision for Christendom was for it to be a place that formed students as active builders of the Christian social order. As noted earlier, Carroll named the college *Christendom* as a sign of this commitment to a Catholic society, and the new chapel's dedication to Christ the King is an inspiring invocation of its founder's mission. This holistic vision, which sees colleges as a place of religious as well as intellectual formation, is representative of the mission of all the *Newman Guide* schools, and it explains the great emphasis that each of them places on its campus's sacramental life. These schools have realized on their campuses what Cardinal Newman spoke of when he said: "I wish the same spots and the same individuals to be at once oracles of philosophy and shrines of devotion. It will not satisfy me, what satisfies so many, to have two independent systems, intellectual and religious, going at once side by side, by a sort of division of labor, and only accidentally brought together."[317]

The small, red tabernacle flame that burns in each school's chapel is a reminder that Christ's presence makes these campuses into shrines of devotion as well as oracles of philosophy. The lamps issue a continuous invitation to holiness for each person at the school and, like the spires of Christ the King Chapel, they are a reminder of each Christian's heavenly destination.

[316] "Christendom College President Dr. Timothy O'Donnell Announces Plan to Retire after 2023–24 Academic Year," Christendom College, May 1, 2023, https://www.christendom.edu/2023/05/01/christendom-college-president-dr-timothy-odonnell-announces-plan-to-retire-after-2023-24-academic-year/.

[317] Newman, "Intellect, the Instrument of Religious Training."

CHAPTER 8

Responding to the Secularizing Threats to the Faithful Few

CONCERNED ABOUT FALLING ENROLLMENTS and a nearly $3.5 million operational deficit in 2018, Washington, D.C.'s Catholic University — long considered the national university of the Catholic Church in the United States — hired a group of consultants who reportedly told CUA's leaders that the university's religious identity was actually a liability in recruiting students. According to the *Chronicle of Higher Education*, Eric Collum, a senior associate at the secular higher education consulting firm, Art & Science, LLC, told a gathering of the Catholic University faculty that their commitment to a Catholic identity "hurts" their brand. Faculty were advised that "students are open to having their experience enriched by Catholicism but not necessarily defined by Catholicism. They want to go to college; they don't want to go to church."[318]

In an article entitled "Is Catholic University's Chaste Brand Scaring Off Students?" the *Chronicle of Higher Education* reported that the consultants suggested that Catholic University should focus

[318] Jack Stripling, "Is Catholic University's Chaste Brand Scaring Off Students?" *Chronicle of Higher Education* 64 (April 16, 2018), https://www.chronicle.com/article/Is-Catholic-U-s-Chaste/243137.

on "research opportunities for undergraduates, and guaranteed on-campus housing," and should expand opportunities for "athletics and fun." To turn things around, the faculty were advised to position the university as a "global Catholic research university" rather than a "narrowly defined" religious institution.[319]

For a time, it appeared to some that Catholic University may have taken the consultants' advice to heart. While Christopher P. Lydon, the university's vice president for enrollment management and marketing, told *Chronicle of Higher Education* reporters that "to lay it all at the feet of Catholic identity seems a narrow interpretation," he acknowledged that "the consultants found that we had no more market share to gain through Catholic identity alone." And although Andrew V. Abela, then provost at Catholic University, denied that there is any evidence that the Catholic identity might be hurting the university, the *Chronicle* suggested that Catholic University may already be making changes to rebrand itself.

For example, a 2016 marketing video titled "Cultivating Catholic Minds" was moved in February 2018 from its prominent spot on the university's home page to a separate tab labeled "Faithfully Catholic." It was a video depicting papal visits, pious students at Mass, and priests and nuns. While this may have been a coincidental move since the video had been on the homepage for the prior two years, the *Chronicle* reporter concluded by noting that faculty members said that removing the "Cultivating Catholic Minds" video was "an acknowledgment that the university had gone too far in portraying itself as churchly." And indeed, since then, the Faithfully Catholic tab on that website has completely disappeared now.

This pressure to rebrand away from a "churchly" identity is an example of the many ways that schools that take their Catholicism

[319] Ibid.

seriously are harried by the temptation to secularize. These secularizing trends present themselves from all sides and require a constant and prayerful vigilance for all the *Newman Guide* schools. However, as will become clear from the stories in this chapter, the most aggressive attempts to secularize the faithful few have emerged from a small number of disgruntled alumni. Although the majority of graduates from these schools blossom in their faith during their years on campus, with many going on to serve the Church and their communities in a myriad of ways after graduation, there are some graduates who appear to have struggled with their faith while at college or after graduation. And, in an effort to lash out at what they may believe is a source of their unhappiness, some of these graduates have used a variety of means to attack their alma maters. Their methods have ranged from social media crusades to petition campaigns — all with the goal to criticize the faithful Catholic colleges and universities for their continued commitment to the fullness of the gospel and the teachings of Church on faith and morals. Of these attacks, issues involving gay, lesbian, and transgender rights feature most prominently. In a number of cases, young graduates have pressured their former schools to compromise on Church teaching on gender and sexual orientation.

This chapter should serve as a reminder of a point often made but too frequently ignored: the path toward secularization is not an inevitable drive of progress but rather a deliberate, conscious campaign. This campaign is aimed at deconstructing public religious practice and seeks to privatize religious belief.[320] Notre Dame sociologist Christian Smith argues in *The Secular Revolution: Power, Interests, and Conflict in the Secularization of American*

[320] This argument was addressed and demonstrated in great detail in Hendershott, *Status Envy*.

Public Life that the very theory of secularization popular among academics is itself an agent of secularity. It is "an ideology actively sympathetic to 'progress,' which legitimates and therefore at least indirectly facilitates the decline of religion."[321] Smith proposes, as a corrective, that secularization studies draw more heavily on "the sociology of revolutions and social movements." Examining the various influences identified by revolutionary sociology, such as activists, material resources, issue framing, organizational mobility, and strategy, Smith boldly argues that "the historical secularization of the institutions of American public life was not a natural, inevitable, and abstract by-product of modernization; rather, it was the outcome of a struggle between contending groups with conflicting interests seeking to control social knowledge and institutions."[322]

I agree with Smith's thesis and believe that the pressures toward secularity that is present on faithful Catholic universities today fit the model of the struggle identified by Smith. Whether posing as the face of "progress," or using the more in-vogue terms of "tolerance," "diversity," and "inclusion," the stories in this chapter represent an ideological assault on faithful Catholic institutions.

Threats at Catholic University of America

Catholic University of America seems to have experienced various struggles over the past few years, with conflicts over sexual orientation and gender identity arising among its students and a small number of faculty. In 2018, several students protested a panel

[321] Christian Smith, introduction to *The Secular Revolution: Power, Interests, and Conflict in the Secularization of American Public Life*, ed. Christian Smith (Los Angeles: University of California Press, 2003). In the passage quoted here, Smith is approvingly characterizing the argument of Peter Glasner.

[322] Ibid., vii.

discussion on transgender issues sponsored by the Institute for Human Ecology because the students believed the panel was biased in favor of Catholic teachings. Panelists included Ryan Anderson, author of *When Harry Became Sally: Responding to the Transgender Moment,* as well as theology professor John Grabowski and university chaplain Father Jude DeAngelo. Although reports on the event indicated that Ryan Anderson expressed his views opposing the anti-Catholic transgender trends, Father DeAngelo disregarded Catholic teachings on gender identity and gender ideology. He said that he does not advocate nor express opposition to individuals contemplating transitioning, adding that regardless of a person's gender identity, society must always recognize each person as a "child of God." Meanwhile, student protesters waved a Human Rights Campaign flag, and a transgender student from CUA criticized Anderson for "research that was very inconclusive." In an article about the event for the university's independent student publication, *Tower,* Adriana Penafil, president of the university's club for LGBT students and their allies, CUAllies, assured students that "for those looking for a safe space, know that CUAllies' doors are always open.... Take care of yourselves, and know that this campus, this community is a better place because you are in it."[323]

While the CUAllies group was formed in 2009, it has not received official standing as a student club, something that would have enabled it to receive student funds. The group has made several attempts to obtain this recognition; without it, they ostensibly are not allowed to rent rooms on campus for meetings or receive funding for events, and they are prohibited from advertising club meetings or events on fliers on campus. But the reality is that the group has indeed been meeting

[323] John Connolly, "Navigating the Transgender Debate at Catholic," *The Tower,* September 2018, http://cuatower.com/2018/09/navigating-the-transgender-debate-at-catholic/.

on campus and has been advertising their meetings and speaker events. They have also been allowed to raise funds for their activities using the CUAllies identity. Ash Samuels, the current president of the group told a reporter for the *Washington Blade* that the club uses campus space at the Center for Cultural Engagement, where director Javier Bustamante has allowed them to meet and advertise LGBT events.[324] In March of 2021, when the CUAllies made yet another attempt to gain recognition, the Catholic University's Student Government Association passed a resolution encouraging the club to request official status. But the request was again denied by then-president John Garvey. Samuels told the *Washington Blade* that the Dean's Office advised the club to wait until the following year to reapply, as a new president would at that point have replaced President Garvey.[325] As of this writing, there has still been no official decision made whether or not to recognize the club.

President Garvey encouraged faithful Catholics in his first year on campus by announcing a return to single-sex dorms, part of an effort to address the growing hookup and binge drinking cultures emerging from co-ed dormitories. He later approved a Catholic University student government resolution to block the top two hundred pornography sites from university Wi-Fi.[326] In an inspiring inaugural address on January 25, 2011, President Garvey promised to promote a "serious Catholic intellectual culture" at the university, claiming

[324] Meghan Brink, "Catholic University LGBTQ Student Group Remains Unrecognized," *Washington Blade*, February 3, 2022, https://www.washingtonblade.com/2022/02/03/catholic-university-lgbtq-student-group-remains-unrecognized/.

[325] Ibid.

[326] Daniel Payne, "Catholic University Will Ban Hundreds of Porn Sites from School Network," *The College Fix*, April 26, 2019, https://www.thecollegefix.com/catholic-university-will-ban-hundreds-of-porn-sites-from-school-network/.

that the deans, faculty, and staff were all committed to the vision of Catholic higher education articulated in *Ex Corde Ecclesiae*. They would continue, Garvey said, working as a community of scholars "united in a common effort to find goodness, truth and beauty," and he went on to echo *Ex Corde* paragraph 14 when he said, "The intellectual life, like the acquisition of virtue, is a communal, not a solitary, undertaking. We learn from each other. The intellectual culture we create is the product of our collective effort. A Catholic intellectual culture will be something both distinctive and wonderful if we bring the right people into the conversation and if we work really hard at it."[327]

However, bringing the "right people" into the conversation is much harder than President Garvey may have realized. The issue of who the right people are to bring into campus conversations has been a problem that Garvey appears to have been unable to resolve throughout his entire career, long before his arrival on the Catholic University campus. Quite simply, John Garvey has not been very discerning at all when it comes to hosting and honoring those who persist in defying Catholic teachings on life, sexuality, marriage, and now, gender identity. The open circle method which dominated Heft's policies at Dayton and promotes an inclusive approach to the detriment of authentic Catholic identity (through adherence to dogma and obedience to the Magisterium) has eaten away at Catholic University throughout Garvey's presidency.

In 2007, before his tenure at CUA, John Garvey rejected the U.S. Catholic bishops' policy that decreed that Catholic institutions

[327] President Garvey's Inaugural Address, delivered at the conclusion of the Inauguration Mass: "Mass 01-25-2011 – Inauguration of John G. Garvey, JD as 15th President of CUA," January 25, 2011, video, EWTN, January 26, 2011, starting at 2:25:55, https://www.youtube.com/watch?v=ws67EBea3p4.

must not honor those who act in defiance of our fundamental moral principles. While he was serving as dean of Boston College's law school, he gave an honorary degree to Representative Edward J. Markey, a pro-abortion politician from Massachusetts. Just a few years prior to that, *Catholic News Agency* reported that Garvey tried to dispel concerns that Boston College's Catholic identity would require "a certain orthodoxy" by claiming that "no school that regulates ideas can justly call itself a university."[328] Garvey also lauded the leadership of the late Father Robert Drinan, S.J., the pro-choice representative from Massachusetts who promoted anti-life policies that expanded abortion during his political career. In fact, during his tenure as dean of Boston College Law School, Garvey published an article in the *Boston College Law School Magazine,* along with the former Speaker of the House, Nancy Pelosi, and former Senator John Kerry, praising Father Drinan's "moral leadership." That entire Spring/Summer 2007 issue was devoted to honoring the pro-abortion priest-politician Father Drinan.[329]

In all these matters, by ignoring the USCCB's advice and extolling those whose actions are gravely sinful, Garvey was making himself a source of scandal. The *Catechism of the Catholic Church* (CCC) identifies scandal as "an attitude or behavior which leads another to do evil" (no. 2284). The Church holds each individual to a high level of responsibility for his actions, and public actions hold a special kind of responsibility because it is through these that other people either "may see your good works and give glory to your Father who is in heaven" (Matt. 5:16), or be

[328] "New CUA President Believes that the Pledge of Allegiance May Violate Vatican II's Teaching on Religious Freedom," *Catholic News Agency*, June 16, 2010, https://www.catholicnewsagency.com/news/19994/new-cua-president-believes-pledge-of-allegiance-may-violate-vatican-iis-teaching-on-religious-freedom.

[329] *Boston College Law Magazine* (Spring/Summer, 2007), https://core.ac.uk/download/pdf/71452573.pdf

led into sin. Of this, Jesus warns, "Whoever causes one of these little ones who believe in me to sin, it would be better for him to have a great millstone fastened round his neck and to be drowned in the depth of the sea" (Matt. 18:6). Commenting on this passage from Matthew, the *CCC* notes: "Scandal is grave when given by those who by nature or office are obliged to teach and educate others" (no. 2285). This is true of politicians who, while claiming the label "Catholic," legislate policies contrary to the moral code of the Church; it is *especially* true of those in positions of authority to "teach and educate others" at Catholic institutions, such as the positions Garvey held, first as dean of Boston College Law School and next as president of CUA.

Unfortunately, the open-circle philosophy is what ultimately guided President Garvey's tenure at Catholic University. In 2016, the controversial Father James Martin, S.J., was welcomed to campus to speak to undergraduate students about his advocacy work with the LGBT Catholic community. Father Martin was invited again in 2017 to speak at the Theological College's Alumni Days on campus, but a backlash from faithful Catholics ensued and the invitation was rescinded. In response, President Garvey appeared to side with those who supported Father Martin's return to campus and issued a statement against the faithful Catholics who protested Father Martin.[330] Claiming that the Theological College had made the decision to rescind the invitation to Father Martin "independently" of the university, President Garvey issued this statement:

> The campaigns by various groups to paint Father Martin's talk as controversial reflect the same pressure being applied by the left for universities to withdraw speaker invitations....

[330] "University Statement on Father James Martin, S.J.," Catholic University of America, September 16, 2017, https://communications.catholic.edu/news/2017/09/statement-martin.html.

> Universities and their entities should be places for the free, civil exchange of ideas. Our culture is increasingly hostile to this idea. It is problematic that individuals and groups within our Church demonstrate this same inability to make distinctions and to exercise charity.... We regret the implication that Catholic University supported yesterday's decision [by the Theological College]."

It appears to some faithful Catholics on that campus that, on most matters, President Garvey typically sided with the campus progressives against those promoting the traditional Catholic stance. For instance, LifeSiteNews reported that the current dean for its School of Social Services, a Garvey appointee, appears to support homosexuality and gender ideology.[331] A scathing article published in LifeSiteNews by Theresa Nixon, a former staff member at Catholic University, suggests that President Garvey appears "more intent on pleasing the left than addressing the concerns of staff and faithful Catholics who have long supported CUA."[332] It is difficult to know whether or not that is true; however, what cannot be denied is that Catholic University is committed to embracing some of the most progressive movements in secular culture.

Under President Garvey's direction, Catholic University has actually been ahead of the curve in embracing Critical Race Theory on campus. In 2017, Catholic University held a "Teach-In" on how to combat racism. This is a laudable goal, and it is consistent with the

[331] Martin Bürger, "New Social Work Dean Appears to Tweet Support for Gender Ideology," LifeSiteNews, July 27, 2020, https://www.lifesitenews.com/news/catholic-univ-of-america-hires-professor-who-appears-to-tweet-support-of-gender-ideology/.

[332] Theresa Nixon, "Catholic University Has Become Catholic in Name Only," LifeSiteNews, August 4, 2020, https://www.lifesitenews.com/opinion/catholic-university-of-america-has-become-catholic-in-name-only-former-employee/.

Church's social teaching, which condemns any "sinful inequalities" affecting men and women on the basis of race and states that "every form of social or cultural discrimination in fundamental personal rights on the grounds of sex, race, color, social conditions, language, or religion must be curbed and eradicated as incompatible with God's design" (*CCC*, no. 1935). However, the speaker chosen to provide the teach-in was Eleanor Hancock, the director of White Awake, a group which describes itself as being committed to "combat[ing] white supremacy by focusing on educational resources and spiritual practices designed to facilitate white people's engagement in the creation of a just and sustainable society."[333] Instead of combating racism, Hancock presented divisive, radical left-wing rhetoric on the evils of white people. White Awake emerged from a "small group of Insight Buddhist practitioners in Washington, DC who, as white allies to practitioners of color within their local sagha, wanted to educate themselves about race. The group called themselves 'White Awake' and held two six-month sessions exploring white privilege."[334]

The leaders of White Awake are involved in Buddhist meditation, although one of the members of the advisory council of White Awake, Katrina Messenger, is a Wiccan who is also the pro-choice president of the Maryland Chapter of NOW (the National Organization for Women, a progressive feminist organization).[335] It is unclear why a group such as White Awake, which teaches spiritual and social values entirely at odds with Catholicism, would have been chosen by Catholic University to teach against the real evil of racism.

333 "Catholic University Social Service School to Hold Teach-In on How to Combat Racism," Catholic University of America, September 7, 2017, https://communications.catholic.edu/news/2017/09/teach-in-on-how-to-combat-racism.html.

334 Ibid.

335 "White Awake: Waking Ourselves for the Benefit of All," https://white-awake.org/about/.

In 2021, there was yet another racial controversy on Catholic University's campus, and again, the situation was exacerbated by President Garvey. This one centered on a new painting which depicted George Floyd as Jesus Christ. Floyd, a black man who died in May of 2020 in the custody of white police officers in Minnesota, has become a symbol of racial injustice and police brutality. By 2021, his violent death had triggered months of protests, primarily led by the Black Lives Matter movement. In a public statement in 2000, Garvey had already expressed an affinity for the protestors' perspective, while discouraging the violence into which the protests sometimes descended: "I want to join my voice to those who have expressed sorrow and anger at the death of George Floyd. The manner of his death was inexcusable.... If you are participating in the protests, please be witnesses of peace."[336]

The artist of the painting in which Floyd appears as Christ, Kelly Latimore, told reporters that he wanted to paint a portrait of a black Virgin Mary cradling a black Jesus, both of them with golden halos encircling their heads, and Jesus resembling George Floyd. The painting, which appears to emulate Michelangelo's *Pietà,* is entitled "Mama." Like the original *Pietà,* it depicts the Virgin Mary cradling her dead son in her arms. Though this painting was clearly blasphemous, for "failing in respect ... due God and his holy name," (CCC, no. 2148) as well as being scandalous (CCC, no. 2284) for portraying a flawed human being as Christ, copies of the picture were installed in two places on the Catholic University campus: one in the offices of Campus Ministry, and the other prominently placed in the hallway adjacent to the Mary, Mirror of Justice Chapel in the CUA Law School. Students and some faculty

[336] John Garvey, "Our Faith Condemns Racism and Discrimination," June 1, 2020, Catholic University of America, https://garvey.catholic.edu/communications/letters/on-death-of-george-floyd-and-dc-protests.html.

members protested and called for its removal.[337] One CUA student told a reporter for the *Daily Signal*:

> The icon has no place at The Catholic University; it is blasphemous and an offense to the Catholic faith, but it is not surprising at all that it was put there.... It is just another symptom of the liberalization and secularization of our campus.... There are many students, faculty and staff who are concerned about this, but there is nothing we can do.... And if we sound the alarm, we will be labeled racists.[338]

Catholic University's chapter of Young Americans for Freedom started a petition to remove the painting from the two locations on campus. But then, a short time later, the portrait was stolen from its location at the law school.[339]

President Garvey's response to the blasphemous icon made the issue immeasurably worse; he first began by denying that George Floyd was even the Jesus-like individual in the picture. Angrily dismissing the concerns in an open letter to the CUA community, Garvey stated that "many [including the artist herself] see the male figure as George Floyd, but our Law School has always seen the figure as Jesus." And although he acknowledged that some "critics called

337 Sarah Bahr, "A Painting of George Floyd Roils Catholic University," *New York Times*, December 24, 2021, https://www.nytimes.com/2021/12/24/arts/design/george-floyd-painting-catholic-university.html.

338 Margaret Mary Olohan, "Catholic University Celebrates Painting of George Floyd as Jesus," *Daily Signal*, November 22, 2021, https://www.dailysignal.com/2021/11/22/george-floyd-jesus-painting-catholic-university-of-america-washington-dc/amp/.

339 Joe Burkas, "Painting at Center of George Floyd Controversy Stolen from Catholic University," *Catholic News Agency*, November 24, 2021, https://www.catholicnewsagency.com/news/249701/painting-at-center-of-george-floyd-controversy-stolen-from-catholic-university.

the image blasphemous because they saw it as deifying or canonizing George Floyd," Garvey dismissed the criticism as coming from "people unconnected to the university" and immediately replaced the law school's missing picture with yet another copy of the blasphemous George Floyd depiction of Christ, stating, "We hope to continue to build on campus a culture that is engaged in thoughtful dialogue and debate, not the sort of bully tactics epitomized by this theft." The second picture was stolen a few days later.[340]

A month later, President Garvey, responding to overwhelming criticism both of the university and of his remarks, apologized for the "needless controversy and confusion" over the school's display of an icon that "many saw" as depicting George Floyd as Jesus Christ. Refusing to take responsibility for the decision to display the picture, Garvey wrote that while defenders of the work said "it was meant to provoke thought about seeing Christ in the most distressed among us," he acknowledged that the interpretation of the work as George Floyd "led to accusations that the work was blasphemous, something that is contrary to the respect due God and his holy name."[341]

On this basis, conservative critics contend that Garvey has guided the school according to the dictates of some of the most progressive ideologies. There have been consequences for this type of political advocacy. The *Washington Post* reported that between the fall of 2013, Garvey's second year as president, and 2021, the university's total enrollment had fallen from 6,725 students to 5,059, a 25

[340] John Garvey, "Law School Icon: A Letter to the Campus Community," Catholic University of America, November 24, 2021, https://garvey.catholic.edu/communications/letters/law-school-icon.html.

[341] Joe Burkas, "President Apologizes for Needless Controversy Over Stolen Icon," *Catholic News Agency*, December 20, 2021, https://www.catholicnewsagency.com/news/249936/john-garvey-cua-george-floyd-icon.

percent drop.[342] There was a $3.5 million operating budget deficit in 2018 and, in the midst of the COVID pandemic in 2020, Garvey announced a $26 million shortfall to the university community.[343] By 2021, he had issued a number of austerity measures, including a 4 percent pay cut for all faculty members and a 4 percent pay cut for all staff and administrators earning more than $50,000 per year. There was also a 5 percent budget cut across all departments, which resulted in the elimination of some positions.[344]

While the budget deficits for 2020 and 2021 were partially results of the COVID pandemic, the fact is that there were serious deficits in 2018, long before the COVID deficits. It is clear that Catholic University of America has been struggling for a while. Admittedly, it must be difficult to avoid concessions to progressive movements on a campus in the heart of Washington, D.C., a place where progressive politics dominate. The fact of the matter is, however, that Catholic University's previous president, Father David O'Connell, managed to keep the university from succumbing to toxic Washington politics. Indeed, during his tenure from 1998 to 2010, O'Connell was able to bring the university back from a loss of Catholic identity, revitalizing the campus and renewing the university's commitment to faithful, Catholic education. It has happened before, and it can happen again. Catholic University is, however, clearly at a crossroads. President Garvey certainly accomplished many wonderful things at Catholic University, as it has a strong cohort of faithful Catholic faculty there, along with orthodox Catholic

342 Lauren Lumpkin, "Catholic University Names Peter Kilpatrick President," *Washington Post*, March 29, 2022, https://www.washingtonpost.com/education/2022/03/29/catholic-university-peter-kilpatrick-president/.

343 John Garvey, "Budget Adjustments: Letter to the Faculty and Staff," Catholic University of America, October 8, 2020.

344 Ibid.

academic administrators at the highest levels committed to reclaiming and retaining a strong Catholic identity. But the presidency is the most important position on campus for ensuring that the Catholic identity remains strong. Garvey's compromises inevitably weakened the robustness of Catholic University's faithful identity, and it will be the responsibility of the next president to restore a justified sense of confidence that the school is being faithful to its mission as a Catholic institution.

There was initial concern aroused when the presidential search committee replacing Garvey included names of those supporting progressive views, including Cardinal Joseph Tobin of Newark, a supporter of Gay Pride Masses in his diocese. However, the candidate eventually chosen, Peter Kilpatrick, encouraged all with his commitment to revitalizing the Catholic identity on campus. He has previously shown himself to be committed to a culture of life and an advocate for the unborn; in 2013, he received the *Magister Vitae* Award, a pro-life award that is given to "an outstanding faculty member at the University of Notre Dame whose teaching, scholarship and life exemplify what it means to build a culture of life at Notre Dame and in the world."[345] In an encouraging interview with the *National Catholic Reporter*, Kilpatrick has said that he "considers himself 'apolitical,' adding that many would consider his pro-immigration views to be liberal and his stance on life issues to be conservative." He said, "I think all of my positions are very Catholic." The article goes on: "Regarding the university's Catholic identity and mission, Kilpatrick told the reporter that the university's guiding principles call for the Catholic University — which was founded in 1887 as the nation's pontifical university — to be a place 'where both faith and reason are

[345] "Meet President Kilpatrick," Catholic University of America, https://president.catholic.edu/meet-president-kilpatrick/index.html.

held up and integrated as we pursue truth,' " and "That integration of faith and reason, I think, calls us as stewards of the truth to pursue research and to help build that up."[346]

Kilpatrick was inaugurated in July of 2022, and it is difficult to predict how, as time goes on, he will handle the growing campus demands for "full inclusion" of LGBT students and faculty, especially transgender students and faculty. He did initially decline to rule out recognizing the CUAllies club, saying he would meet with its representatives before deciding.[347] While CUA has not made a public statement about the status of their LGBTQ allies club, there appears to be growing acceptance on campus. For example, longtime CUA politics professor John Kenneth White published a pro-LGBTQ article in which he criticized Catholic teachings on same-sex behavior, writing that, "Reports from the field find that many Catholic parishioners have

[346] Brian Fraga, "New President of DC's Catholic University Sees Return to School's Roots" *National Catholic Reporter*, March 29, 2022, https://www.ncronline.org/news/people/new-president-dcs-catholic-university-sees-return-schools-roots.

[347] In an interview with the *The Pillar*, he commented, "On the one hand, we can't deny or walk away from Catholic teaching. We can't do that. On the other hand, we owe persons of same-sex attraction our love, our affection, we have to honor their dignity and we have to engage them in dialogue so that we understand what their hopes and fears are and how we can help, as I said earlier, bring them to completion as persons. So I look forward to meeting our gay and lesbian students, engaging them in dialogue, trying to understand exactly where they're coming from and then judging for myself, how I can help this university move forward on an issue which is troubling to many." See " 'Integration of Faith and Reason' Key for New CUA President Peter Kilpatrick," *The Pillar*, March 29, 2022, https://www.pillarcatholic.com/integration-of-faith-and-reason-key/.

A later article from LifeSiteNews perhaps sheds more light on the issue, revealing that Kilpatrick promoted LGBT pride in his previous position as provost of the Illinois Institute of Technology: "New Catholic University of America President's Background Includes Support for 'LGBTQ+ pride,' " LifeSiteNews, March 30, 2022, https://www.lifesitenews.com/news/new-catholic-university-of-america-president-supported-lgbtq-pride/.

identified the church's position on homosexuality and the exclusion of homosexuals from their pews to be deeply troubling." Professor White must know that no one is "excluded" from the pews of the Catholic Church. But he appears to want acceptance for the behavior and has supported greater inclusion for the LGBTQ community at CUA. Lauding Pope Francis's call for synodality, White sees synodality as "an invitation to welcome those on the margins of society," claiming that "Many homosexual Catholics grieve the lack of acceptance from a church they love but often find unwelcoming."[348]

It is important at this time that every effort is made to help Catholic University recover its Catholic identity. A historic university, founded in 1887 by the Catholic bishops to be *the* pontifical university of the Catholic Church in the United States, it would truly be a tragedy if this flagship university continued down the path to secularization.

Threats at Franciscan University

While Franciscan University is not the only one of the faithful few to have received criticisms from a small number of graduates about what they call the university's "rigidity" in supporting Catholic teachings on gender, same-sex behavior, and abortion, it has also experienced several large-scale social media attacks from radical feminist grads as well as a handful of disgruntled gay and lesbian alumni. In 2012, an organized attack on the university arose from a private Facebook group called Franciscan University Gay Alumni and Allies. The alumni were angered by a social work course on the Franciscan campus entitled "Deviant Behavior." In the class's course description, homosexual

[348] John Kenneth White, "Catholic University of America Professor: Embrace Synodality to Engage with LGBTQ People," *Outreach*, July 13, 2023, https://outreach.faith/2023/07/catholic-university-of-america-professor-embrace-synodality-to-engage-with-lgbtq-people/.

behavior is included in a long list of forms of "deviant behavior," and the protestors demanded that it be removed from the list.

Initially, the university fought back by criticizing the group for using the Franciscan University name in the title of their LGBT Facebook group. The group deleted the word "University" but retained the name "Franciscan Gay Alumni and Allies" on their social media pages. Through a savvy use of social media, the attackers were successful in garnering national attention for their campaign. They adopted the ideology of mainstream LGBT activists; that is, they rejected the notion that homosexual behavior is in any way deviant, and they knew their success would depend on winning this point. This is why they demanded that homosexuality be removed from the list of "deviant behaviors." Toward that goal, two alumni in the Facebook group issued a press release attacking the course and demanding that the university remove or significantly revise it "to stop contributing to the culture of hate and ignorance" through its claim that homosexual activity is in any way "deviant."[349]

In an effort to maximize the damage to the university, the alumni also encouraged other Facebook members to contact the university's accreditors to demand that it lose its accreditation as long as it continued to view homosexuality as a form of deviant behavior. They were alarmingly successful in jeopardizing that accreditation. Because of the organized protests from concerned alumni, Stephen Holloway, the director of the office of accreditation at the Council on Social Work Education, told a reporter at *National Public Radio* that the course was a "matter of concern.... The fact that homosexuality was identified in the course description as deviant behavior raises a

[349] Quoted in Anne Hendershott, "Redefining Deviance: The Gay Assault on Franciscan University," *Crisis*, November 13, 2012, https://crisismagazine.com/opinion/redefining-deviance-the-gay-assault-on-franciscan-university.

flag. Understanding diversity and difference and their dynamics in society are critical for social workers to be effective in working with diverse populations." Holloway warned that the Council requires that social work education "advance human rights and economic justice," and he added that social workers must work toward the "full participation of individuals who are gay, lesbian, bisexual, transgender or two-spirit in social work education."[350]

The incident demonstrates how difficult it is for faithful Catholic institutions to instruct students in perennial Church moral teaching in areas where sinful behaviors have been normalized by the secular world. A social work program on a faithful campus like Franciscan has a challenge in being "allowed" to define social justice for individuals who are part of the LGBT community. For those outside the Church, social justice may demand access to marriage for same-sex couples, or assistance in transitioning for those who believe they are transgender. But for a faithful Catholic college, true social justice demands that those who experience same-sex attraction or gender dysphoria must be supported in charity and love — and this means not encouraging them in the lies that society wants to teach them about how such life choices will bring them happiness and fulfillment. On the contrary, the teachings of the Church must always be followed, not out of some sense of dictatorial authority, but because they are true, and in fact are the only path to authentic peace. The Church has remained consistent in her teachings on these matters. While it requires that homosexual persons be treated with "respect, compassion and sensitivity" (CCC, no. 2358), it also clearly states in the same paragraph that homosexual acts are "intrinsically disordered."[351]

[350] Ibid.

[351] The *Catechism* argues this point from the perspective that such acts "are contrary to the natural law.... Under no circumstances can they be

Not surprisingly, these teachings were not in the least bit persuasive to the leaders of the Franciscan Gay Alumni and Allies Facebook group. One of the group leaders who issued the press release protesting the social work course, a 1991 Franciscan psychology graduate, told a *National Public Radio* interviewer that "as a lesbian and as a psychological professional, I found a couple of things offensive about the course." She was joined in her protest by a 1990 graduate who, despite the harsh rhetoric in the press release, recalled Franciscan as a "powerful, creative, intense place of immense blessings." He went on, "I continue to believe I received a solid, quality education. I have since changed my thinking on certain theological and philosophical issues, but this has not resulted in my viewing the University any differently." Although this former student has left the Catholic Church, he said that he remains grateful for the "sincere and kind and talented professors" at Franciscan. When asked if he had been open about his same-sex attraction during his years at Franciscan, he responded: "Yes, with many students and friends and a few clergy members. The issue of my orientation did not play a role in my classroom experiences and was not mentioned." Still, he added, he was "concerned for the gay and lesbian students who may currently be on campus and may encounter this course and description and have it added to the possible and unnecessary shame or alienation they may experience."[352]

In an early response to the controversy, Daniel R. Kempton, then Franciscan's vice president for Academic Affairs, released a statement

approved" (*CCC*, no. 2357). Explaining this further, the *Catechism* states that such acts "close the sexual act to the gift of life" and "do not proceed from a genuine affective and sexual complementarity." Such a view, though deeply unpopular in the modern secular culture, remains the consistent teaching of the Church, and as such requires faithful adhesion by those claiming to be part of the Church.

[352] Excerpt from an interview with Gregory Gronbacher, in Hendershott, "Redefining Deviance."

to reporters at *Inside Higher Education* indicating that "principles of academic freedom apply to the course.... While critics of the university are entitled to their opinion that their understanding of homosexual behavior is scientifically confirmed and thus should be imposed on all universities, we respectfully disagree." Citing the same paragraphs from the *Catechism of the Catholic Church* that I have also cited, Kempton continued that "while gay people should be treated with respect and dignity, homosexual acts are intrinsically disordered. They are contrary to the natural law. They close the sexual act to the gift of life. They do not proceed from a genuine affective and sexual complementarity." At Franciscan, Kempton said, "offering that perspective is essential and academic freedom should protect that idea. Our faculty members have the right to present a variety of views in the classroom, but Franciscan University opposes the promotion of propositions and values contrary to Catholic teachings." Kempton made it clear that, "In sum, our faculty can present a variety of views on a topic but cannot promote values contrary to Catholic teachings."[353]

Although the initial response was strongly supportive of the university's right to continue its defense of Catholic teachings on sexual behavior, there was still pressure on campus to respond more positively to the graduates' concerns about inclusivity on campus. And indeed, later that year, Franciscan's social work program administrators did end up giving the LGBT alumni exactly what they wanted: they changed the course description by deleting homosexuality as a form of deviance. Whether homosexuality was included as a topic within the content of the Deviant Behavior course was left up to the individual professor teaching the course. This conciliatory gesture appeared temporarily to have pacified the LGBT alumni.

[353] Scott Jaschik, "Anti-Gay Bias or Academic Freedom?" *Inside Higher Education*, September 4, 2012, https://www.insidehighered.com/news/2012/09/04/dispute-franciscan-u-over-course-calling-homosexuality-deviant.

But they were not silent for long. In 2018, a new social media-generated scandal emerged, driven by many of the same individuals who had been involved in the Deviant Behavior course controversy. In this new scandal, three feminist alumnae, led by a disgruntled former employee, claimed to be concerned over what they perceived as a "growing conservative political ideology" on campus. This incident again garnered national attention in the Catholic media when they promoted an open letter and petition to remove the Veritas Center for Ethics in Public Life from campus. The Veritas Center was founded in 2013 as a place to bring faithful Catholic scholarly reflection to bear on the most pressing ethical questions in contemporary culture — questions of marriage and sexuality, war and peace, life and death, as well as economic and social justice. These topics can be controversial at times and, since the Veritas Center always takes a strong stand supporting magisterial teachings in all of these areas, it has drawn the ire of those who view the center as inappropriately taking political stands on hot-button topics. The hostility directed toward the faculty leaders of the Veritas Center by a handful of feminist alumni was a consequence of its support for Catholic teachings on the sanctity of life, the sacredness of marriage, and the primacy of the family. The mission of the Veritas Center is "to promote natural moral law, illuminated by the light of faith, in order to defend both human freedom and dignity."[354]

In their open letter, and in the petition they widely promoted on Twitter, the alumnae leaders accused the Veritas Center and the two Franciscan professors leading it of being "strongly ideologically aligned with the far right of American politics." As "proof," the petition pointed to some articles published by the professors that were

[354] "The Mission of the Veritas Center for Ethics in Public Life," Franciscan University of Steubenville, https://institutes.franciscan.edu/veritas-center/.

critical of Catholic politicians voting in favor of abortion and other articles that expressed concerns about the Affordable Care Act and its contraception mandate. The protestors were also angry about articles that supported traditional marriage (i.e., between one man and one woman), articles that were critical of the faulty implementation of Title IX, and articles on Catholic teachings on the transgender movement and radical feminism.[355]

The Franciscan administration consistently maintained that the Veritas Center professors were publishing positions consistent with and supportive of Catholic moral teaching, and no steps were ever taken to curtail their academic freedom. Regardless, in an effort to placate the critics, there was no public support ever given to the Veritas faculty, and the unfortunate consequence was that the professors affiliated with the center were marginalized on campus. The publications and work of the Veritas Center also slowed because faculty were reluctant to affiliate with the center by publishing articles and doing presentations under its banner. Worse, the feminist alumnae were also given permission to bring their petition against the faculty affiliated with the Veritas Center to campus, setting up a table outside the bustling J. C. Williams student center, in an effort to convince current students to sign a petition pressuring the administration to silence the "offending" professors and remove the Veritas Center from campus.

We see, then, that even at a campus like Franciscan's, topics such as the sanctity of life and marriage, and work advancing the Catholic position on such topics, have become contested terrain.[356] The

[355] "Steubenville Alumni Attack Conservative Profs," *Church Militant*, April 19, 2018.

[356] In 2021, the center saw something of a revival as Sohrab Amari joined as a visiting fellow. In October of 2022, the center hosted a major conference on political theology, which brought together leading theologians

university administration refrained even from publicly criticizing the petitioners, and, though the professors were still allowed the academic freedom to publish articles faithful to Catholic teachings on moral and social issues, the vacuum of support sucked much of the oxygen from its work for a few years. Fortunately, it has recovered in the intervening years, and today it is as strong as ever.

Franciscan's academic administration attempted to support both sides in the controversy by inviting the protestors to campus to work cooperatively with the Veritas Center faculty leaders they had targeted for criticism. Father Sean Sheridan, T.O.R., the university's president at the time, issued a letter which thanked the alumnae for their concern and invited the three main leaders of the protest of the Veritas Center to work collaboratively with Veritas Center leaders to plan "a forum to discuss how a diversity of opinions can be expressed in a manner that brings faithful intellectual clarity and concomitantly builds and sustains unity within the body of Christ." The conciliatory letter continued, "I invite you to assist Franciscan by providing suggestions for planning such a symposium.... Please know that you and all those who signed the open letter remain in my prayers."[357] While such a strategy angered some of Franciscan's more conservative constituents, the intentions appeared to be noble, and the collaboration might have worked if both sides were actually truly interested in collaborating.

Although several meetings occurred between Veritas Center staff, university faculty, and the alumnae protestors, the collaboration

---

from around the country. In all, it appears that the future is bright for the Veritas Center, as it reclaims much of its previous support as a promoter of Catholic orthodoxy in the public square.

357 Father Sean Sheridan to Claire Gilligan, Anne Snoddy, and Theresa Williams [response to "Expression of Concern" from "alumni and friends of FUS"], May 4, 2018, https://docs.google.com/forms/d/e/1FAIpQLScouIg8NH4d4M8RMoE3_DsuMEZBRte3q3tWRp7R8Sj09SHYMg/viewform.

was not a success. The three protest leaders and the former adjunct professor continued a relentless social media attack on Veritas Center personnel and then proceeded to bully Veritas Center board members by publicly denigrating their involvement with the center. The collaboration was ended, and the critics abandoned their protests once they realized that Franciscan University administrators and the university's board of trustees would not acquiesce to their demands to remove the center.

Today, the Veritas Center retains a strong presence on campus, bringing Catholic teachings to bear on contested social issues. The most recent conference in the fall of 2022 was the largest academic conference ever held on the Franciscan campus. Entitled "Restoring a Nation," the conference brought together scholars to discuss "The Common Good in the American Tradition."[358] Previous conferences have explored some of the most contested terrain in contemporary society. In 2019, the Veritas Center hosted a major conference with more than three hundred attendees on "Faithful Catholic Perspectives on The Transgender Movement"; and in 2021, the center devoted its annual conference to discussing the threats to parental rights and religious freedom — some of which were parental rights related to the gender identity of their own children.

As part of a proactive, administration-wide response to pressures to accommodate the transgender ideology, a working faculty group was created and charged with developing a policy consistent with Catholic teachings on gender. A force driving this action was the impending threat in 2022 of governmental mandates requiring transgender affirmative policies; Franciscan, along with other Catholic universities, sought to implement its own policies ahead of the

[358] "Restoring a Nation: The Common Good in the American Tradition," October 7–8, 2022, Veritas Center for Ethics in Public Life, Franciscan University, https://institutes.franciscan.edu/restoring-a-nation/.

upcoming changes. The U.S. Education Department has expanded its interpretation of federal sex protections to include gay and transgender students, reversing the Trump-era policy and opposing proposals from many states seeking to bar transgender "girls" from school sports.[359] This new policy promised federal sanctions against schools and colleges that fail to protect gay and transgender students from discrimination of any kind. Consequently, colleges and universities are not allowed to forbid biological males who believe they are female from participating on female sports teams, with the policy promising to "take action" against the colleges and universities if students are denied equal access to academic or extracurricular opportunities because of their sex. Schools found to have violated the new policy can face a range of severe penalties, including a total loss of federal education funding.

Franciscan University's president Father Pivonka was so concerned by the threats to Catholic identity posed by this mandate that he published an opinion column in *USA Today* lamenting the threats such a policy presents to Franciscan students. With Catholic teachings as the foundation, Father Pivonka described the "inestimable value and dignity" of the male body and the female body stating that: "The body matters.... That's why, as a university president, I am concerned for my female athletes. They will work hard, be diligent in their training, and on race day, lose to transgender athletes. Tragically, it becomes another example of how the system is rigged against women because they were born women. Our female athletes deserve better."[360]

[359] The Associated Press, "Biden Administration Extends Protections to Transgender Students," NPR, June 16, 2021, https://www.npr.org/2021/06/16/1007344321/biden-admin-extends-protections-to-transgender-students.

[360] Dave Pivonka, "The Body Matters," *USA Today*, April 28, 2022, https://www.usatoday.com/story/opinion/voices/2022/04/28/transgender-athletes-conversations-university-president/7217994001/?gnt-cfr=1.

In an effort to make Catholic teachings clear to all, Father Pivonka assembled all faculty and staff members for a mandatory opening meeting of the 2022 fall semester. The most important issue discussed at that meeting was the importance of remaining faithful to the Church's teachings on faith and morals. In an important statement, Father Pivonka addressed attacks from the outside that threaten the university's faithfulness, attacks which often come in the guise of "cancel culture":

> It seems to me, you can't cancel somebody who hasn't subscribed to something. Here at Franciscan University, we don't subscribe to the world that says you can't know truth, that you can't know goodness, that you can't know beauty. We don't subscribe to the world that says young people don't matter. We believe that you matter, profoundly you matter. Our desire for you here is that you discover who you are ... who God wants you to be.[361]

So far, Franciscan has managed to ride out the secular threats which have arisen in the past decade as it remains a strong beacon of orthodox Catholic higher education — and, under Father Pivonka's leadership, there is promise of a continued faithfulness.

Threats at University of St. Thomas in Houston

There has been something of a power struggle around the Catholic identity and the place of the founding religious order at the University of St. Thomas in Houston. Founded by the Basilian Fathers in 1947 and currently included in the *Newman Guide*, St. Thomas drew

[361] Mariely Madero de Gessler, "Wow! THIS!" post with picture quoting Father Dave's address, August 26, 2022, https://www.facebook.com/photo?fbid=10226135653291034&set=a.1194336351771.

national attention when it attempted to remove the last remaining full-time Basilian faculty member from campus. Claiming that it was making necessary faculty cuts for financial sustainability, the school did not renew contracts for thirty faculty members, including three tenured professors, for the 2020–2021 academic year. As the *Catholic News Agency* reported, "One dismissed tenured faculty member is philosophy professor Father Joseph Pilsner, CSB, the former Dean of the School of Arts and Sciences, and a member of the Basilian Fathers, the religious community that founded the university in 1947 and has served the school to this day." Father Pilsner, a popular professor on the campus, was the last full-time Basilian faculty member on the Houston campus.[362]

In response to the removal of Father Pilsner, University of St. Thomas alumni organized protests, and Texas First Lady Cecilia Abbott resigned from the university's board of trustees after nearly a decade of service.[363] Christopher Evans, the vice president for Academic Affairs, claimed that the decision was a "fiscal reality" and that "the absence of Basilians on the faculty is more a reflection of the Basilians themselves." Others, both on and off campus, are not so sure.

There are indications — even beyond the Father Pilsner controversy — that the University of St. Thomas has begun moving toward secularization. According to an article in the *Celt Independent,* the online student newspaper of the University of St. Thomas, there has been an LGBT student club called Pursue Excellence and Cherish

[362] Matt Hedro, "Changes at Houston's St. Thomas University Leave Some Doubtful," *Catholic News Agency,* December 20, 2019, https://www.catholicnewsagency.com/news/changes-at-houstons-university-of-st-thomas-leave-some-doubtful-97546.

[363] Brittany Britto, "First Lady of Texas Cecilia Abbott has Resigned from Houston College Board," *Houston Chronicle,* December 18, 2019, https://www.houstonchronicle.com/local/education/campus-chronicles/article/First-lady-of-Texas-Cecilia-Abbott-has-resigned-14916556.php.

Everyone (P.E.A.C.E.) present on campus since 2015. Founded by University of St. Thomas alumnus Travis Jackson, the website for the group states that the club's mission is to "enhance the mandate of the Catholic Church, to respect all human dignity, and support the diverse UST community." The website also states that the club "holds on-campus events to create awareness and provide information on human rights issues and aims to advance the University's mission and acknowledge the human dignity of every UST student."[364]

According to the *Celt*'s article, "Does PEACE Have a Chance?" the LGBT club at UST struggled for years to gain acceptance as a university-approved club. Patrick Stoner, a former president of the club, told reporters for the *Celt* that it

> aims to operate under the doctrine of the Catholic Church … and focuses on sexual identity issues.… We talk about LGBT history, we talk about what to do if you're coming out or if your friend is coming out. We're not in there telling people how to get a boyfriend.… All we're trying to do is educate people that just because someone is gay, bi-trans, or lesbian, it does not mean there is anything lesser, or broken or wrong with them.

Travis Jackson, the founding president of the P.E.A.C.E. club, recalled the "slow and difficult" process of gaining approval for the LGBT club: "We didn't give up because we believed, why doesn't the University have this club?" Apparently, the Student Council of Clubs supported the club's formation but could not continue the approval without authorization from the university's administration under then-president

[364] *Celt Independent* Staff, "Does PEACE Have a Chance?" *Celt Independent,* June 21, 2019, https://celtindependent.com/2019/06/21/does-p-e-a-c-e-have-a-chance/.

Robert Ivany. Eventually, "after months of meetings," Ivany approved the club but emphasized that it had to be under the jurisdiction of Campus Ministry. At that time, Jackson told the reporter for the *Celt*, "Campus ministry did not support" the LGBT club, but he was "glad that the current leadership does."[365]

Indeed, it does. University of St. Thomas's current director of Campus Ministry, Nicole Labadie, a graduate of the University of Notre Dame's Master's in Divinity Program, said in an interview in the same *Celt* article that she considers herself an ally of the LGBT community and the campus P.E.A.C.E. club: "I love the idea of P.E.A.C.E. and I think they're doing a really great thing because at the core of what the Church teaches is that human beings are called to relationship.... We are made in the image and likeness of God who is relationship, and we have this desire for communion with other people." She added that discrimination against homosexuals is unjust and noted that the *Catechism* affirms that those with same-sex attraction are also called to fulfill God's will in their lives: "If we look at the example of Christ, He welcomed people as they were but He challenged them to grow.... Identifying as gay, lesbian or bi isn't what's at issue, you're created with a certain kind of attraction, but what is sinful is acting on it."

Members of the LGBT club say that it has been welcoming. One LGBT student member said that, after coming from a Catholic family where she felt she had to hide her bisexuality, she now "feels safe to reveal her bisexual feelings" at UST. Another student said that although most people on campus are accepting of him, he wishes the school would show "greater outreach" toward the LGBT community: "I'm just really surprised that we're on Montrose, two streets from gay bars and clubs and there is not a larger amount of openly LGBT students on campus."[366]

365 Ibid.

366 Ibid.

This shift was recognized by New Ways Ministry, the heterodox Catholic LGBT advocacy group, which celebrated the University of St. Thomas's "embrace" of LGBT-themed events on campus in a 2019 article posted on their website entitled "Catholic University in Houston Cautiously Embraces LGBTQ Events."[367] According to the *Celt Independent*, the new student organization, Diversity and Inclusion, was allocated $1,500 by the UST Student Government Association to host two LGBT-related events, with the stipulation that the chair of the Student Government Association's Catholic Identity Committee be included in the event planning process, along with Campus Ministry. Diversity and Inclusion committees often devolve into LGBT advocacy organizations on campuses because they see their role as one that offers support and inclusion to those who may feel marginalized.[368] It is a laudable goal to offer authentic support to the marginalized, but, as I have pointed out throughout this book, it is difficult to resist the pull of advocacy. Although St. Thomas has instituted policies and procedures designed to ensure that the LGBT events would be held "in a manner consistent with UST's Catholic identity," most Catholic colleges and universities — even the formerly faithful ones — have found that this is much more difficult than it would first appear.

Overall, it would seem that UST is on a trajectory toward ever greater compromise on the LGBT issue. There remain a significant number of faithful Catholics among its staff and faculty; however, the

[367] Jonathan Nisley, "Catholic University in Houston Cautiously Embraces LGBTQ Events," *NewWays Ministry*, June 29, 2019, https://www.newwaysministry.org/2019/06/29/catholic-university-in-houston-cautiously-embraces-lgbtq-events/.

[368] Brittany Christiano, "SGA Approves Funding for LGBT Events on Campus with Stipulations," *Celt Independent*, May 16, 2019, https://celtindependent.com/2019/05/16/sga-approves-funding-for-lgbt-events-on-campus-with-stipulations/.

administration will need to choose a more united and coherent effort if it is to remain a faithful school. Unfortunately, as the recent history of Catholic higher education demonstrates, the path of least resistance to secularization is broad, easy, and well-traveled.

Threats at Walsh University

Another Newman Society-recommended university, Walsh University, located in North Canton, Ohio, has an LGBT community that has long been lobbying for recognition of their own support group.[369] Efforts to form a recognized LGBT club at Walsh have spanned more than a decade, and, as at Franciscan University, a contingent of activist LGBT alumni have continued to lobby for a LGBT club on campus that offers support as well as opportunities to hold campus-wide events. One 2013 graduate, Dave Eaton, claimed that Walsh leaders "forced him and his friends to submit extra paperwork that wasn't required for other new student organizations when they sought to create a gay-straight alliance around 2012."[370] According to the local newspaper, the *Canton Repository*, Walsh leaders required that they

> prove students wanted the club on campus and required the signatures of at least 10% of the student body. Eaton said they gathered the signatures, as well as a faculty advisor in a few days. They also drafted their mission statement in the framework of upholding Catholic values and chose to name the group after the paired Christian martyrs, Saints Sergius and Bacchus.... "We weren't looking to pass out condoms and have a Pride

[369] Kelli Weir, "Walsh University LGBTQIA+ Students Pushing for Change, Recognized Club," *Canton Repository*, April 5, 2021, https://www.cantonrep.com/story/news/2021/04/05/walsh-university-lgbtqia-students-seek-recognized-club-acceptance/4819353001/.

[370] Ibid.

> parade, but to have a space on campus," said Eaton. . . . But the approval never came.[371]

Efforts revived in 2015 when LGBT students said that, although they were meeting on campus, they were "tired of meeting at night in classrooms just so they could talk freely." Caitlin Kohler, who identifies as nonbinary and goes by the name Wren, led the effort, saying, "We just really wanted to be seen and recognized at Walsh. . . . We just wanted to be validated in the eyes of our institution." Though the group was given permission to meet in the counseling office with a counselor present, the students balked at this, complaining the proposal would create more of a support group than a "real club." This, despite them initially stating that they wanted a "support group" and a place to share experiences and "talk freely." They rejected the offer, also stating a concern that they would be prohibited from hosting events or advertising. Kohler graduated in 2016, and the efforts among the students faded yet again.[372]

But, according to the *Canton Repository,* faculty support for a gay-straight alliance on campus emerged as two Walsh faculty members, working through the Walsh University Diversity Council, arranged for a student trip to the University of Notre Dame to meet with leaders of that university's LGBTQ+ club, PRISMND. Even Notre Dame's ally club, however, did not offer the breadth of opportunities that former Walsh faculty member Amanda Gradisek, a professor of English, envisioned for Walsh University, with Gradisek telling *Canton Repository* reporters that "Notre Dame's group was far from perfect, given the compromises they had to make."[373]

[371] Ibid.

[372] Kelli Weir, "Walsh University Outlines New Inclusion Efforts, No LGBTQIA+ Club Mentioned," *Canton Repository,* July 17, 2021, https://www.cantonrep.com/story/news/2021/07/16/walsh-outlines-eight-inclusivity-actions-steps-no-lgbtqia-club-yet/7989845002/.

[373] Weir, "Walsh University LGBTQIA+ Students Pushing for Change."

The most recent lobbying efforts, involving the "Oasis Club," have been underway since early 2021. Described as a "safe space for LGBTQIA+ students and their allies to meet, discuss issues and talk about service initiatives," the proposal for the club was submitted in May of 2021 by "Kaylyn Liossis, a senior at Walsh who identifies as pansexual or queer, and Hannah McFeeters, a senior who identifies as an ally."[374] The university has not responded to the proposal. In an attempt to encourage the administration to act to approve the proposal, Walsh students created a petition to "call on Walsh University to allow and accept an LGBTQ+ safe space club on their campus and to give that club the emotional and financial support.... We are simply asking for the same support given to all other clubs on campus. Without a safe community for LGBTQ students at Walsh, students find themselves isolated, alone, excluded and rejected from the overall campus community."[375]

Walsh's student activists have promised that they will not "back down" this time. One told a *Canton Repository* reporter: "My friends are a feisty group.... We don't back down."[376]

It is indeed likely that these students won't back down. Refusing all offers of a "support group" for the LGBT students on campus, campus advocates pledged to "hold out" for a real LGBT club with real LGBT events supported by the university and advertised to all

[374] Taylor Bruck, "LGBTQ Students, Allies, Seek Recognized School Club at Walsh University," *Spectrum News 1*, September 26, 2021, https://spectrumnews1.com/oh/columbus/news/2021/09/22/lgbtq-students-and-allies-seek-recognized-school-club-at-walsh-university-.

[375] This petition is sponsored by the left-wing "Religious Exemption Accountability Project." It is titled, "Call on Walsh University to Allow a Safe Space Club for LGBTQ+ and Allied Students!" on Action Network, https://actionnetwork.org/petitions/call-on-walsh-university-to-allow-a-safe-space-club-for-lgbtq-and-allied-students.

[376] Weir, "Walsh University LGBTQIA+ Students Pushing for Change."

students on campus. In interviews, they pointed to the LGBT club (P.E.A.C.E.) at the University of St. Thomas in Houston as an example of a *Newman Guide* school hosting a club on campus that holds events and receives funding from the university's student affairs budget.[377] As the *Canton Repository* reported, Walsh's

> President Collins and his cabinet released a message that said hate will not be tolerated nor accepted in any form at Walsh and that each person will be treated with dignity, respect, kindness, sensitivity, and compassion.
>
> Without naming specifics, they committed to engaging in dialogue and taking action that will further the university's efforts with diversity, inclusion and equality.
>
> "In Christ we make up one body, where all matter and all belong," the statement reads.[378]

As of the writing of this book, Walsh had still not officially declared recognition of the Oasis Club, and it remains to be seen whether it will resist the growing clamor of voices calling for pro-LGBT policies or not.

Conclusion

The secularizing trends are evident, even at some of the faithful few profiled on these pages. Even at the *Newman Guide* schools, college leaders can be tempted to believe that the road to upward mobility for their schools bypasses the Church and her teaching authority. The stories told in this chapter reveal the agency behind the secularizing trends. However, these stories on the campuses of Catholic colleges should not be isolated from the general cultural trajectory

[377] Ibid.
[378] Ibid.

toward liberalization, particularly regarding issues of sexuality. The tactics of persuasion that aim at liberalizing attitudes and policies around LGBT behavior have been articulated by the advocates Marshall Kirk and Hunter Madsen in their influential work, *After the Ball: How America Will Conquer Its Fear and Hatred of Gays in the '90s*. In this work, Kirk and Madsen call for the LGBT community to overcome the stigma of sexual deviance using a three-pronged tactical approach: desensitization, jamming, and conversion. This approach prescribes that they "inundate the heterosexual world with a 'continuous flood of gay-related advertising'"; that they use shaming and "conditioning procedures" to embarrass anyone questioning of the morality of same-sex behavior; and that they convert attitudes using techniques that target "the mechanism of prejudice."[379]

This emphasis on the role of advocacy groups in secularizing Catholic universities helps avoid what Christian Smith critiques as the "conceptual over-abstraction" model of secularization that strips these movements of their human agency.[380] However, I would like to take Smith's thesis a step beyond the purely sociological circle of human agency. As Catholics, we know that, just as Christ and the Spirit guide and protect the Church, so too the devil organizes evil in a constant assault against the good and true. And while the final victory is guaranteed, we do well to recognize that, here on earth, "We are not contending against flesh and blood, but against the principalities, against the powers, against the world rulers of this present darkness" (Eph. 6:12). The threat is real, and it can be diabolical, and schools must resist it at every turn if they are to remain faithful to their identity and mission. The faithful few are remaining faithful by rejecting these very trends.

[379] For a more detailed discussion of Kirk and Madsen, see Hendershott, "Redefining Deviance."

[380] Smith, *Secular Revolution*, 14.

Chapter 9

How Darkness Entered the Once-Faithful Colleges

THIS CHAPTER RECALLS AGAIN the observation cited in chapter 4 by Father Richard Neuhaus, the late editor of *First Things,* that when a Catholic college or university is "haggling over its mission statement, it is a sure sign that it has already lost its way." Father Neuhaus understood the very real temptation that many Catholic colleges face to ensure their sustainability in a competitive environment by broadening their appeal to reach those who may not want a faithful Catholic college experience. For some of the once-faithful schools that I introduce here, a strong Catholic identity appears to have become an embarrassment and a burden that they no longer want to bear. Schools like Providence College, DeSales University, and Mount St. Mary's in Maryland were once proud to be listed in the *Newman Guide.* But, for a number of reasons that we will discuss, these schools are no longer on that list.

Even as many of the formerly faithful Catholic colleges and universities have been defining down their Catholic identity in their marketing materials, Franciscan University of Steubenville, still proudly branding itself as "Passionately Catholic," is enrolling its largest incoming freshman classes. According to Joel Recznik, vice president of Enrollment, Franciscan received 20 percent more applications in 2019 (just before the pandemic hit) than it had in the previous year. Recznik attributes the higher numbers of freshman applications to "Franciscan's Catholic intellectual and faith mission."[381] Likewise, Ave Maria University welcomed the largest class in the history of the school in fall 2022, and then broke all records for incoming students in the fall of 2023. Both schools, along with all the other *Newman Guide* institutions, have embraced the tenets of *Ex Corde Ecclesiae* — and they are growing.

In 2020, the thirtieth anniversary of what was supposed to be the implementation of *Ex Corde Ecclesiae,* there were very few Catholic college administrators willing to even discuss the document and even fewer bishops willing to enforce it. College administrations have refused to comply with the document's requirement that all Catholic teachers be faithful to the Church's teaching and that all administrators respect and promote their college's Catholic identity and be accountable to their bishop. When they are not actively rejecting *Ex Corde Ecclesiae,* most Catholic college and university administrators have, for the past few decades, elected to ignore it.

But the faithful administrators at Ave Maria University have refused to allow that to happen on their campus. Instead, Ave Maria's provost spearheaded a project to publish the papal document in a beautifully bound book and distribute it widely across campus. In fact, the reason that Ave Maria University's leaders decided to appeal to the Holy See through the Apostolic Nuncio in Washington, D.C., for permission to reprint the papal document was because printed copies of it are almost impossible to obtain. It was republished by Ave Maria University Press in 2022; Provost Roger Nutt wrote in the foreword:

381 "Franciscan University Anticipates Largest Ever Freshman Class," Franciscan University, March 27, 2018, https://franciscan.edu/franciscan-university-anticipates-largest-ever-freshman-class/.

> *Ex Corde Ecclesiae* has been an inspiration and guide to the university since its founding. The document is used for orientation of new faculty and other formation opportunities on campus.... It is our hope that this Ave Maria University reprint of *Ex Corde Ecclesiae* will facilitate interest in John Paul II's vision for Catholic higher education and provide greater clarity to all the faithful about what the Church expects from her universities."[382]

With a statement like this from Ave Maria's provost, it is clear that the university's academic leaders understand the important mission of a faithful Catholic university.

Unfortunately, as we have seen and discussed, other formerly faithful schools have lost sight of that mission. Some seem either to have deliberately chosen the path of secularization or to have failed to pay attention to the slow slide to secularization. For still others, it was a conscious decision to trade a strong Catholic identity for what they imagined would be higher status and increased enrollments.

A few of the formerly faithful schools even hired consulting firms to help them rebrand themselves to appeal to a broader pool of applicants. As pointed out in the previous chapter, secular consulting firms like Arts & Science, LLC, have suggested that "Christian colleges must adapt to new strategies and messaging: 'Do you want students who are trying to find a Church? Or are you looking for students who are interested in finding a college that will also address their faith?' "[383] For

[382] Rogert W. Nutt, foreword to *From the Heart of the Church: Ex Corde Ecclesiae* [Apostolic Constitution of John Paul II] (Ave Maria, FL: Ave Maria University Press, 2022).

[383] Liam Adams, "At a Time of Change These Baptist Colleges Are Staying the Course." *Chronicle of Higher Education* 63 (December 21, 2017), https://www.chronicle.com/article/at-a-time-of-change-these-baptist-colleges-are-staying-the-course/.

some Catholic colleges, this meant removing any clerical influence in the academic arena, as we saw at St. Thomas. But such attempts are sometimes met with fierce resistance from the founding orders.

Providence College Has Lost Its Way

We began chapter 1 with the poignant story of Renaissance literature scholar Anthony Esolen's decision to renounce his tenure and leave Providence College in the Spring of 2017: Providence's most prominent and prolific professor during his three-decade career, translator of Dante's *Divine Comedy* and author of dozens of scholarly books and hundreds of scholarly articles, left Providence for one of the faithful few. Esolen left Providence because it had lost its commitment to a faithful Catholic identity and its dedication to a liberal arts education. In his interview that I cited earlier, Esolen said he had become weary of "shoring up a crumbling wall":

> I have countless memories of fine students at Providence College, some of whom are now my close friends; and to my colleagues in Western Civilization — of whom many have retired and some have passed away — I owe a debt I can never repay, for their friendship and support and instruction. But I am too old to want to spend the evening of my career trying to shore up a crumbling wall, when those who are in authority at the college are unwilling to listen to our pleas or even to meet with us so that we can make the pleas in person, but instead pass out lemonade to the professors with the sledge hammers.[384]

Esolen's essay concluded that he "prefers to be in on building something exciting for the Church and for sheer ordinary humanity." He understands

[384] Smith, "Anthony Esolen in His Own Words."

that faithful Catholics are indeed like St. Augustine's pilgrims, strangers in a strange land seeking the City of God. For Esolen, as for Augustine, pilgrims to the City of God are strangers in the world, even though the world's founder is God Himself. Sadly, for Esolen, Providence College had become an Earthly City that was motivated by the earthly love of self. In an earlier essay, before his departure, he had lamented the "narcissism" that was guiding the curriculum at Providence College. In "The Narcissism of Campus Diversity Activists," Esolen concluded that in the curriculum and the culture at Providence College, "Everything is about ourselves. We don't want to study other cultures. We want to make other people study about us, and from our preferred point of view. I say to students, 'Here let me teach you about Milton,' the author of the greatest poem in the English language. The students reply, 'No, let us teach you about us.' Dear Narcissus, there is a great and beautiful world beyond that pool."[385]

Esolen concluded by stating that he did not have a problem with professors who teach about various human matters, including present-day politics and the struggles for justice for every human being. What he does have a problem with is when present-day politics usurp the bulk of the curriculum in the humanities, as he saw happening at Providence College. In an interview published in *National Catholic Register*, Esolen responded to the interviewer's query on his "long-running battle within Providence College regarding its direction as a Catholic institution" by saying:

> I could live with a somewhat Catholic school that was really committed to the humanities, such as we were for many years. I could live with an unreservedly Catholic

[385] Anthony Esolen, "The Narcissism of Campus Diversity Activists," *Crisis*, February 24, 2016, https://www.crisismagazine.com/opinion/the-narcissism-of-campus-diversity-activists.

> school where the humanities needed shoring up. But to live at a used-to-be-Catholic school no longer committed to the humanities where all the big decisions are basically secular in their inspiration and their aim, on a campus that is highly politicized and therefore treacherous — no, that's not for someone of my years. I wrote, 10 years ago, that we had never really lost our identity and that what we had lost we were well on the way to recover. I could not write those words now.[386]

It is especially disheartening for faithful Catholics that Providence appears to have made a conscious decision to attempt to take the secular route to higher status as it was only a decade ago that the Cardinal Newman Society and others were praising the school's courage in resisting the appeals to make Providence more "inclusive" by welcoming those who might be hostile to the Faith. In an especially courageous act in 2000, Providence College suspended three male students from the college for an entire semester because they posted blue "abortion rights" fliers across the campus that pictured a statue of the Virgin Mary. According to the *Chronicle of Higher Education*, the fliers read: "How's this for an immaculate concept: Keep Abortion Safe and Legal," and showed a marble statue of the Virgin Mary.[387] *The Chronicle* reported that the Father Philip A. Smith, then the college's president, upheld a decision by a college judicial officer and the vice president for Student Services to suspend the three students. In response, the *Associated Press* reported that "about 50 angry students congregated for a silent

[386] Smith, "Athony Esolen in His Own Words."

[387] Sara Hebel, "Providence College Suspends 3 for Abortion-Rights Flier Depicting the Virgin Mary," *Chronicle of Higher Education* 46 (March 6, 2000), https://www.chronicle.com/article/providence-college-suspends-3-for-abortion-rights-flier-depicting-the-virgin-mary/.

protest outside the school's administration building, carrying signs with messages like, 'The first amendment does not stop at the gates of PC. Protect your rights.' "[388] According to the *Associated Press* article, Providence psychology professor John Colby complained, "We're supposed to be here to share ideas and debate.... We're providing for the opportunity for people to express different points of view. It's not as though they committed some crime." But the same article also provided the opposing voices from the Providence campus, including a student who said, "The right to free speech is not all encompassing. The fliers were a defamation of the image of the Virgin Mary. It's a Catholic institution's duty to uphold the teachings of the faith." President Smith called the flier a "deliberate misuse of a venerated person." And in fact the school released a statement to that effect: "The deliberate misuse of the image of the Blessed Virgin cannot be defended under the guise of free speech. We don't dispute their opinion, but rather how it was expressed." In response, the suspended students wrote a letter to the college newspaper claiming that their intention was meant to "shock not insult.... We hoped that the explicit nature of the imagery would add a more personal dimension to the issue."[389]

In 2013, Providence College again demonstrated a bold defense of its Catholic identity when Hugh F. Lena, serving as the provost at that time, canceled a scheduled lecture that was to support same-sex "marriage." The lecture was to be given by John Corvino, the chair of the philosophy department at Wayne State University in Detroit and author of the book *What is Wrong with Homosexuality*? (Oxford University Press, 2013). He had already

[388] Michael Mello, "Rhode Island Students Protest Suspension," *Associated Press*, March 16, 2000, https://apnews.com/article/71e7371331b1ae9c1ea2f2582487cc30.

[389] Ibid.

delivered the talk at several Catholic college campuses around the country.[390] When the provost offered to reschedule the lecture to be sure that an opposing viewpoint on authentic Catholic teachings on marriage could also be presented, he cited the document published by the American bishops in 2004, *Catholics in Political Life,* which states clearly that "Catholic institutions should not honor those who act in defiance of our fundamental moral principles. They should not be given awards, honors or platforms which would suggest support for their actions."[391] The cancellation led to a firestorm of protests from students and faculty at Providence. In an email to the faculty that was later leaked to the students, Lena wrote, "While academic freedom is at the heart of teaching in a Catholic university, the United States bishops maintain that in accord with *Ex Corde Ecclesiae,* the Catholic community and Catholic institutions should not honor those who act in defiance of our fundamental moral principles."[392]

Provost Lena received tremendous pushback from the more progressive faculty and students on campus — much worse than the response to the pro-abortion fliers that had been posted just a decade earlier.[393] According to an article published in the *New*

[390] Anne Hendershott, "Dr. Lena and Providence College Made the Right Decision," *Catholic World Report*, September 25, 2013, https://www.catholicworldreport.com/2013/09/25/dr-lena-and-providence-college-made-the-right-decision/.

[391] United States Conference of Catholic Bishops, "Catholics in Political Life," https://www.usccb.org/issues-and-action/faithful-citizenship/church-teaching/catholics-in-political-life.

[392] "A Message from The Provost," *Friarside Chats*, September 23, 2013, https://friarsidechats.wordpress.com/2013/09/23/a-message-from-the-provost/.

[393] Cara Newlon, "Catholic College's Students Protest Canceled Gay Speaker," *USA Today*, October 1, 2013, https://www.usatoday.com/story/news/nation/2013/10/01/providence-college-cancels-gay-speaker/2903375/.

York Times, Fred K. Drogula, president of the Providence College faculty senate, said he could not find a college policy dictating that every lecture must have an equal opposing viewpoint. Further, Drogula said it was "inappropriate" to invoke the bishops' document, *Catholics in Political Life,* because it only applied to politicians. Professor Drogula is wrong about that. Provost Lena knew that providing Professor Corvino a platform without an opposing voice on Catholic teachings on same-sex "marriage" could easily be taken to suggest that Providence supports same-sex "marriage." Sadly, by then, it was clear that many on the Providence faculty really did support it.

What is even more interesting is that the *New York Times* reported on this Providence story at all.[394] The *Times* does not usually become concerned with regional stories like this. But it is likely that publishing such an incendiary story gave *Times* reporter Laurie Goodstein yet another opportunity to discuss and spin the controversial interview with Pope Francis that had been published earlier that month in the Jesuit publication *America.* In her article on the Providence situation, Goodstein suggested that it was just one more example of the divisions over moral issues in the Church. She reminded readers that Pope Francis himself had warned Catholics to refrain from "frequent condemnations of homosexuality, abortion and birth control," emphasizing instead mercy and love. This story was the perfect opportunity for Goodstein to reiterate how "obsessed" conservative Catholics supposedly are with these issues; in the incendiary and misleading title of Goodstein's previous *Times* article, readers learned

394 Laurie Goodstein, "Catholic College Rescinds Invitation to Speaker Defending Same-SexMarriage," *New York Times,* September 24, 2013, https://www.nytimes.com/2013/09/24/education/catholic-college-rescinds-invitation-to-speaker-defending-same-sex-marriage.html?_r=0.

that "Pope Says Church is Obsessed with Gays, Abortion, Birth Control."[395]

The truth is that the pope never said that at all. Rather, Pope Francis stressed mercy and forgiveness by saying that "without mercy, even the moral edifice of the Church is likely to fall like a house of cards." But this does not mean that Pope Francis was criticizing Catholic teachings on abortion or same-sex marriage. On the contrary, later that same week, Reuters reported that "Pope Francis, with little fanfare, restated the Church's opposition to abortion in a speech to Catholic doctors, speaking of those 'unjustly condemned to abortion.' "[396] It is clear that the *New York Times* is more obsessed with the Catholic Church's teachings on these issues than most Catholics are. It was courageous of Provost Lena to uphold Church teachings, even while misinformation and confusion abound in the media.

Three years after the same-sex-marriage speaker controversy on campus, a "perfect storm" was created at Providence by the combination of media pressure to secularize, an expanded commitment to diversity of race, ethnicity, and sexual orientation, and the growing faculty hostility to the original Catholic identity of the school. It became clear that there was growing faculty resistance to Catholic teachings on abortion, marriage, homosexual behavior, and other moral issues. All of this came to a head in 2016 when Professor Esolen published two articles in *Crisis* decrying Providence College's embrace of what he called the "growing narcissism of campus diversity activists"

[395] Laurie Goodstein, "Pope Says Church is Obsessed with Gays, Abortion, Birth Control," *New York Times*, September 20, 2013, https://www.nytimes.com/2013/09/20/world/europe/pope-bluntly-faults-churchs-focus-on-gays-and-abortion.html.

[396] Philip Pullella and Tom Heneghan, "Pope Message Heralds Change of Tone on Gays, Abortion," Reuters, September 20, 2013, https://www.reuters.com/article/world/pope-message-heralds-change-of-tone-on-gays-abortion-idUSBRE98I0S9/.

on campus. Esolen called upon the college to set aside divisive identity politics and unite the campus community around a holistic, Catholic view of the human person.[397] Esolen compared the college's new "Bias Response Team" to the tyrannical judgments of the "Star Chamber" proceedings of the Middle Ages under the early Stuart kings, when cases were heard without juries and most were convicted. He wrote:

> I notice also on that same Diversity page, that we are supposed to commit ourselves to welcoming the alphabet soup of cheered-on sexual proclivities.... For some reason that does not include F, for Fornicators, or S, for Swingers, or P, for pornographers. No political lobby for those? Now, we either affirm, as an institution, that the Church has a real and powerful and urgent message she must bring to the world, a message of harsh truth and genuine healing, or we do not. If we do believe it, then we cannot believe that a disordered inclination towards any sin, sexual or otherwise, can be constitutive of any human being.... We as the Church have the truth to bring to him, to set him free from that sin, whatever it may be. But there is no evidence on our Diversity page that we wish to be what God has called us to be, a committedly and forthrightly Catholic school with life-changing truths to bring to the world. It is as if deep down, we did not really believe it.[398]

Esolen was realizing that Providence was no longer a Catholic community that was committed to the truth. Particularly abhorrent to him

[397] Alexandra DeSanctis, "Anthony Esolen Faces the P. C. Onslaught," *National Review*, November 22, 2016, https://www.nationalreview.com/2016/11/anthony-esolen-providence-college-diversity-dispute/.

[398] Anthony Esolen, "My College Succumbed to the Totalitarian Diversity Cult," *Crisis*, September 26, 2016, https://www.crisismagazine.com/opinion/college-succumbed-totalitarian-diversity-cult.

was the Star Chamber of the "Bias Response Team," which had already ensnared some of Providence's faithful Catholic faculty members who were simply supporting Catholic moral teachings on marriage and the family. Esolen wrote:

> How precisely the fear of being hauled before the Star Chamber can possibly bring people together in friendship, is never revealed. . . .
>
> Is it permitted for a Catholic, at a college that advertises itself as Catholic, to affirm a Catholic view of sex and the family? And I am not talking merely about professors whose specific job it is to teach moral philosophy or moral theology. I am talking about all professors. . . .
>
> They have made life hell for more than one of my friends. All, now, in the name of an undefined and perhaps undefinable *diversity*, to which you had damned well better give honor and glory.[399]

Esolen knew that the Providence Star Chamber would begin to capture faithful Catholic students too. And only two years after Esolen resigned and left the Providence campus, faithful students did indeed begin to be caught up in the moral panic surrounding the school's undefined concept of "diversity." In an especially egregious case in March 2018, Michael Smalanskas, a resident advisor and senior level student at Providence, was harassed by students and denounced by administrators for creating a pro-traditional marriage bulletin board in the women's residence hall. Smalanskas said that he created the pro-marriage bulletin board in response to a pro-lesbian poster that had been put up there throughout the month of February. Before his board was torn down by angry students, Smalanskas's bulletin read: "Marriage: The Way God

[399] Ibid.

Intended It, One Man, One Woman." The poster was accompanied by a quote from Pope Francis and a passage from the Gospel of Mark affirming traditional marriage.[400] Threatened with physical harm by some, Smalanskas soon became the target of the ire of campus diversity advocates, and the Board of Multicultural Student Affairs made him the focus of their meeting with the executives of Providence College. At the meeting, the LGBT advocacy organization SHEPARD[401] addressed the audience saying, "LGBT students exist on this campus, we are here, we deserve the same respect and rights that every other student has on this campus.... We deserve to be supported the same way that every other student is supported."[402] Smalanskas began receiving harassing text messages from other resident assistants and fellow students who accused him of creating a hostile and unsafe environment on campus.

Worse, a threatening drawing was placed in a residence hall restroom depicting Smalanskas as the victim of homosexual rape. Students attacked him on social media, calling his bulletin board an act of homophobia. Demanding that Smalanskas be removed from his RA position and be punished, students insisted that the school create a policy governing campus bulletin boards so that what they considered harmful material could no longer be posted.

[400] Bradford Richardson, "Student Harassed at Providence College for Defending Traditional Marriage," *Washington Times,* March 20, 2018, https://www.washingtontimes.com/news/2018/mar/20/student-harassed-providence-college-defending-trad/.

[401] The name is an acronym that stands for Stopping Homophobia, Eliminating Prejudice, and Restoring Dignity. The name was also chosen in part to commemorate Matthew Shepard, a student at the University of Wyoming who was brutally murdered in 1998 in an event that remains one of the most discussed LGBT hate crimes in modern American history. See "SHEPARD," Providence College, https://dean-of-students.providence.edu/dean-of-students-shepard/.

[402] Rod Dreher, "Witch Hunt at Providence College," *American Conservative,* March 21, 2018, https://www.theamericanconservative.com/witch-hunt-providence-college-michael-smalanskas/.

A small percentage of the Providence faculty (thirteen professors) posted a letter of support for Smalanskas, but it did not seem to make a difference to most of the administrators—and the great majority of faculty members appeared to support the angry student response.[403] In fact, according to media reports, when SHEPARD planned to target Smalanskas in an anti-homophobia march across campus, Kristine Goodwin, vice president of Student Affairs, expressed her support for them. *National Review* reported that Smalanskas believed that the vice president's support for the march appeared to lend administrative credence to the idea that his bulletin board was homophobic.[404]

Seeking support for making and posting his pro-marriage poster, Smalanskas sent a letter to Thomas J. Tobin, the presiding bishop of Providence. Bishop Tobin gave support to the beleaguered student in a letter that was provided to *National Review*: "As your billboard expresses so clearly, marriage is designed by God to be a union of one man and one woman.… It is truly unfortunate that in explaining our Faith, you have received such a negative and even reprehensible response, particularly at a Catholic college, one that is publicly committed to professing Catholic and Dominican values."[405] Although this was greatly appreciated by Smalanskas, it did little to quell the campus controversy. Finally, Providence's President Father Brian Shanley, O.P., spoke out to condemn the "gay rape cartoon" that had threatened

403 "Providence College Faculty Should Support Smalanskas and Affirm Marriage," *Ocean State Current*, March 18, 2018, https://oceanstatecurrent.com/providence-college-faculty-pc-should-support-smalanskas-and-affirm-marriage/#!#.Wq5X2mXtlbk.facebook.

404 Alexandra DeSanctis, "Student at Providence College Attacked for Sharing Catholic Teachings," *National Review*, March 23, 2018, https://www.nationalreview.com/corner/student-at-providence-college-attacked-for-sharing-catholic-teaching/.

405 Ibid.

Smalanskas. He also added that Providence "always has, and always will, remain faithful to the teachings of the Catholic Church" but our "collective challenge is to find a way to be faithful to our Catholic identity and to be inclusive of the LGBTQ+ community."

The following year, President Shanley was removed from the presidency. Although some local media reports suggested that "Shanley's departure is being forced by top Dominican officials that oversee Providence College and that those officials are concerned about the liberalization of Providence College," no one could confirm that. According to one report, "Dominican officials reportedly bristled about emerging issues of homosexuality and abortion on campus and the controversy regarding the pro-man and woman bulletin board posting by Michael Smalanskas that set off demonstrations by pro-LGBTQ students and faculty."[406] It is difficult to know whether the reason for President Shanley's transfer was in fact due to campus controversies; the Dominican order does often transfers priests from one posting to another in order to give priests an opportunity for new experiences. One might argue that that is all that happened in this instance. But what we do know is that the commitment Providence College once had to its Catholic identity appears to have been lost. It will take time to determine whether that Catholic identity can be recovered. Father Shanley's concern that Providence needed to be "inclusive of the LGBTQ+ community" reveals the real challenge that faces all faithful Catholic colleges and universities; namely, how to acknowledge the dignity of all while at the same time calling everyone to lives of holiness and goodness.

[406] GoLocalProv News Team, "Shanley's Departure from PC Forced by Dominican Superior," GoLocal Prov News, April 1, 2019, https://www.golocalprov.com/news/shanleys-departure-from-pc-forced-by-dominican-superior.

In the spring of 2024, yet another controversy over the mission emerged at Providence College when two professors attempted to assess whether a potential job candidate for a faculty position in Healthcare Ethics would support Church teachings on gender ideology. This was a legitimate concern — especially since the potential colleague would be teaching ethics to students in the college's newly founded Nursing School. While the secular culture has embraced the idea that a man can become a woman and a woman can become a man — and actually give birth to a child as a man or a "birthing person" — Catholic teachings condemn such a preposterous proposition.

Yet, at Providence College, faculty in the philosophy department are explicitly barred from questioning potential faculty members about whether they personally support the Church's teachings on these contested issues. In fact, in a recent attempt to avoid violating the college's directive to refrain from asking potential faculty members about their personal views on contested issues, two faculty members asked job candidates about their professional philosophical views on the morality of gender reassignment surgery for minors. They were both formally disciplined by a senior academic administrator. In the letter to the offending faculty member, the senior administrator wrote: "Given that holding a specific set of personal beliefs is not a job requirement, direct questioning about those personal beliefs is inappropriate."[407]

From a Strong Embrace of *Ex Corde Ecclesiae* to LGBT Advocacy at DeSales

Like Providence, DeSales University, formerly known as Allentown College, had been strong in its positive response to *Ex Corde Ecclesiae*.

[407] Quoted in Anne Hendershott, "Hiring for Mission at Catholic Colleges and Universities, *Crisis*, April 3, 2024, https://crisismagazine.com/opinion/hiring-for-mission-at-catholic-colleges-and-universities.

In a laudatory article published in the *National Catholic Register* in 2003, DeSales was praised for its public embrace of the papal document and for its willingness to publicly share information on whether those who teach theology were willing to accept the mandatum, pledging to teach in communion with the Church. In the *National Catholic Register* investigation into whether Catholic institutions were publicizing their fidelity to the mandatum, DeSales was one of the faithful few highlighted. According to Bishop Edward Cullen of Allentown "the theology faculty at DeSales were seeking a kind of recognition even before it was absolutely necessary." Bishop Cullen said, "I received a letter from the faculty along with an endorsement from Larry Chapp [theology professor] and the president seeking the mandatum. If every bishop had that, I think they would find the faithful of their diocese much happier. Parents want to send their children to an orthodox school and have a right to."[408] Not only did all of the DeSales theology faculty enthusiastically embrace the mandatum in these early days after the release of *Ex Corde Ecclesiae* — as did the other *Newman Guide* schools, such as Franciscan University — but the faculty and administration were proud of that fact and were willing to speak about it publicly.

While the general requirement for the mandatum is in article 4 of *Ex Corde Ecclesiae,* the particular form it takes is left up to each institution. De Sales's mandatum states: "I hereby declare my role and responsibility as a teacher of a theological discipline within the full communion of the church. As a teacher of a theological discipline, I am committed to teach authentic Catholic doctrine and to

[408] Tim Drake, "Right to Truth, Right to Know: DeSales is Proud of the Mandatum," *National Catholic Register*, 2003, available at Catholic Education Resource Center, https://www.catholiceducation.org/en/education/catholic-contributions/right-to-truth-right-to-know-desales-is-proud-of-the-mandatum.html.

refrain from putting forth as Catholic teaching anything contrary to the Church's magisterium."[409]

Tim Drake, author of the *National Catholic Register* investigative study, recalled that when he asked for comments about the mandatum, his phone calls were not even returned by most Catholic colleges and universities — including calls he made to at least six bishops, five theology department chairs, and four university presidents. At DeSales, however, not only did the local bishop respond to Drake's query, but university president Father Bernard O'Connor, O.S.F.S., and theology faculty members Larry Chapp and Rodney Howsare all talked with him freely about the mandatum's importance to the university. Drake concluded that, for DeSales, "their transparency is in itself unusual." This is one of several reasons that DeSales was included in the *Newman Guide*. Unfortunately, just two decades later, DeSales is at the forefront of LGBT advocacy and has been deleted from the *Newman Guide.*

As at so many other once-faithful Catholic colleges and universities, this movement toward same-sex advocacy was encouraged by a small group of DeSales graduates who pressured their alma mater to create a campus LGBT support club. According to news reports, DeSales alumnus Tim Gallagher posted a petition in 2012 on Change.org encouraging DeSales to allow an LGBT student group on campus.[410] The petition, which garnered 531 signatures, not all of them from DeSales students and staff, was not initially effective in

[409] Ibid. This formulation matches the sample offered by the USCCB in their Guidelines Concerning the Academic Mandatum, June 15, 2001, https://www.usccb.org/committees/catholic-education/guidelines-concerning-academic-mandatum.

[410] Tim Gallagher, "DeSales University: Allow Each Student to "Be Who (They) Are and Be That Well!" Change.org petition, July 29,2012, https://www.change.org/p/desales-university-allow-each-student-to-be-who-they-are-and-be-that-well.

moving the DeSales administration. In fact, then-vice president of Student Life, Jerry Joyce, told the Cardinal Newman Society, "We are truly a Catholic institution, so we wouldn't formally endorse or support a group in direct contradiction to Church teachings." He pointed out that this doesn't mean that students struggling with their identities should feel as though they're not welcome: "Everyone is welcome at DeSales.... We want every student to know they're respected as human beings with dignity." The club was denied.

And so the LGBT student community on the DeSales campus, with the assistance of LGBT alumni, faculty, and staff, continued to lobby for a student club supporting same-sex-attracted students and for events geared to these students. Eventually, with changes in the leadership on campus, along with the creation of a Diversity and Inclusion initiative, the "BeYou Alliance" emerged a few years ago. This student-led organization, funded by Student Life, aims "to nurture an inclusive campus community where all individuals feel empowered to live as their full authentic selves." Claiming to be "guided by the Salesian values of hospitality and gentleness, the Be You Alliance promotes opportunities for students, faculty, and staff to come together and work to achieve a better understanding of issues facing the LGBTQ community on campus and off campus."[411] According to the DeSales University website, their librarians set up an elaborate display for LGBTQ pride month in the university lobby, "including books about activism, marriage and family, and fiction."[412] Needless to say, DeSales University is no longer included in the listing of faithful Catholic colleges and universities in the *Newman Guide*.

[411] "LGBTQ+ Resources: About," BeYou Alliance description, Trexler Library, DeSales University, last updated April 27, 2023, https://desales.libguides.com/lgbtq.

[412] Ibid., "Library Display" image.

Mount St. Mary's University Has Lost Its Way

Like Providence and DeSales, Mount St. Mary's University in Emmitsburg, Maryland, has been deleted from current listings of faithful institutions, even though the school had been included in that listing since the start of the *Newman Guide*. Just as at DeSales, LGBT promotion on campus was likely one of several reasons for the deletion. However, the problems at Mount St. Mary's go far beyond LGBT advocacy. A major scandal unfolded at Mount St. Mary's in 2015 that revolved around a new president and his conflict with the faculty over the vision for the curriculum and the culture of the school. Though the waters were muddied with accusations and counteraccusations, it seems that the conflict arose from an inherent resistance from academia to having a university run by a businessman.

Simon Newman, a successful Los Angeles private equity and strategic planning professional, was hired by the board of trustees in 2015 to handle the university's imminent solvency and sustainability problem. According to a strategy review conducted by external consultants in June 2015, Mount St. Mary's labored under a convoluted governance structure that failed to adequately or appropriately define, exercise, or implement the roles, responsibilities, and structures of authority and shared governance. For the faculty, shared governance became defined as "faculty governance." Along with the school's inefficient administration, the school had a declining retention rate, a tuition discount rate above 60 percent, and a declining matriculation rate that had dropped below 12 percent. While *U.S. News and World Report* ranked Mount St. Mary's highly among regional colleges in terms of academics, *Forbes* ranked it one of the "least financially fit schools in America" in 2013, assigning it a poor grade of D on "financial fitness." None of this was sustainable.[413]

Several colleges and universities, including Catholic colleges, have turned to business leaders to run their institutions. But it is still a very low number, and it appears to bring with it some serious threats to faculty morale. According to a 2017 study by the American Council on Education, 15 percent of U.S. college presidents came from fields outside academia, down from 20 percent in 2012.[414] As the *Atlantic* pointed out, while "proponents of the non-academic candidates say that leaders from the world of business or government or law are needed to innovate, control costs and manage a complex organization," faculty resistance is strong.[415] Some of this most likely derives from the discrepancy in pay between the corporate and academic worlds. In his book *Envy: The Seven Deadly Sins,* Joseph Epstein notes this type of faculty resentment when he writes that most college professors were people who performed well in school and were told over and over again how bright and extraordinary they are. This leads some of them to be angry that they are not well compensated in comparison with their corporate peers.[416] At Mount St. Mary's, some of these faculty members, willing to speak on condition of anonymity, complained that the new president was "arrogant" and "wore expensive suits." On private (and sometimes public) Facebook pages, others pointed to his wearing cufflinks, painting the

413 Mount St. Mary University Strategy Review, June 2015 (privately circulated).

414 American Council on Education, "Path to the Presidency," https://www.aceacps.org/summary-profile/.

415 Laura McKenna, "Why are Fewer College Presidents Academics?" *Atlantic,* December 3, 2015, https://www.theatlantic.com/education/archive/2015/12/college-president-mizzou-tim-wolfe/418599/.

416 Joseph Epstein, "Envy: The Seven Deadly Sins," New York Public Library Public Lecture Series, 2003, 81.

walls in his office, his wife's expensive haircuts, his car, his accent, and his refusal to have his family move into the presidential home, given that at the time it was structurally unsafe, until renovations were made. Newman had tremendous confidence, the kind of confidence that was interpreted by his faculty detractors as arrogance. However, to those outside the faculty, and to some within, Newman was an optimistic warrior who was genuinely committed to turning the school around so it could once again succeed.

Faculty hostility dogged Newman through his short tenure at Mount St. Mary's, even as he tried to initiate several major policies to reverse the school's decline. These decisions included cost-cutting by scaling back health benefits for retirees, reducing administrative staff, introducing a new plan to deal with retention rates, and expanding the university's curricular offerings beyond the traditional liberal arts. Some on the faculty, especially those in philosophy, did not want the competition for students. For the faculty involved in the core discipline of philosophy, students are a "captive audience" mandated to take a certain number of philosophy courses. These faculty resented any attempt to reduce the core or lessen the number of required philosophy courses. And although Newman did not attempt to reduce the core, some faculty claimed that they were "sure" he planned to do that.

Prior to his arrival, the school had a retention plan that Newman said was unjust for students. The school had a transfer-out rate of over 31 percent; every year, in late December, about thirty first-year students left with no transferable credits and a bill for the full semester's tuition and board — which ran to about $15,000. Newman set out to remedy this broken system by enlisting faculty members to help him identify struggling students early and to step in with an intervention and an invitation for those students, allowing them to withdraw without incurring tuition costs. The retention plan involved using a nationally normed survey, already adopted by many colleges and universities, to pinpoint these students, including those who were struggling with depression or mental health issues. However, it was interpreted by faculty critics as a plan that would remove students without giving them a chance to succeed, and consequently the plan was heavily criticized by those who would become involved in the campaign to oust President Newman.[417]

Newman denies claims that he ever wanted to "remove" struggling students without first offering to help them stay. In fact, Newman has said many times in media interviews and in private conversations with faculty that he was trying to remedy the past retention programs at Mount St. Mary's, which financially penalized failing students by keeping their tuition money, even though most of them had never even attended classes during the semester of their enrollment. However, such steps only contributed to the rift between Newman and his faculty. Attacks against him would reach their peak when Mount St. Mary's student newspaper accused Newman of using derogatory language about struggling students. The paper claimed that Newman said, "This is hard for you because you think of the students as cuddly bunnies, but you can't; sometimes you just have to drown the bunnies ... put a Glock to their heads." In subsequent interviews, Newman stated that the context and the sentiment were false, that his words were meant to be a light-hearted remark about helping failing students leave the school without incurring costs. He believed that the professor he was speaking to also knew it was certainly not a serious

[417] Comments by John Schwenkler on "Mount St. Mary's student survey tried to find out which students were depressed," *Feminist Philosophers* (blog), February 11, 2016, https://feministphilosophers.wordpress.com/2016/02/11/mount-st-marys-student-survey-tried-to-find-out-which-students-were-depressed/.

remark. Regardless, there was a massive uproar in response to the quote, with the headline of "bunny-murdering president" making over three hundred newspaper headlines across America. Faculty protestors shared in confidential emails and in social media posts that they were willing to try to destroy their own school by organizing several initiatives, including holding a "Blackout Friday" to depress fundraising, and contacting the attorney general of the state of Maryland to complain about the university's ethics violations related to the retention survey that had been sent to students. Newman denied any wrongdoing and took swift action in response to the attacks, holding two faculty members responsible for the uproar, one who organized a "Blackout Friday" and the other who advised the student newspaper. Newman had both of them fired.

Newman and the board obviously believed that the firings were justified, but the termination process was fatally flawed, as it denied due process for either of the faculty members and made no attempt to implement shared governance procedures, which are highly valued on all college campuses. And although confidential emails among the faculty demonstrate that the attempt to oust Newman began several months before the faculty firings, it was that violation of shared governance in faculty firing that sealed the fate of Newman's presidency. The two fired faculty members immediately became elevated, both in the media and on campus, into victims of an autocratic president.

The faculty mobilized at once, using select alumni, social media, and their own wives' homeschooling network to drum up national support for their action.[418] These disgruntled professors and their alumni enablers also enlisted organizations such as the American

[418] "Academics' Statement of Protest Regarding Faculty Firings at Mount St. Mary's, https://docs.google.com/spreadsheets/d/1ewOmme-BiUmGlDw12gi9Xi5cSkcDQ5av12jRmIIZtc0/edit#gid=0.

Association of University Professors and the American Philosophical Association, as well as the academic freedom campus advocacy group, the Foundation for Individual Rights in Education (FIRE). The Daily Nous, a blog that describes itself as "providing news for and about the philosophy profession," was also integral to organizing opposition to Newman. In the end, more than six thousand professors throughout the country, mostly from the humanities fields, joined in the mobbing action, signing a petition that denounced the faculty firings and lamenting the loss of shared governance at Mount St. Mary's.

Newman clearly made a mistake in his firing faculty and administrators who had undermined his authority and defied his direction, and this mistake was the ultimate cause of his resignation. However, as noted, there had been a clear and sustained campaign to get rid of him well before he ever fired these faculty members. When asked to comment on the story prior to publication in the student newspaper, then-chairman of the board of trustees at Mount St. Mary's, John E. Coyne III responded by calling the attack on Newman "the product of a disgruntled employee and the creative and destructive imagination of a student [editor] being spoon fed his information."[419] Coyne believed that the small group of angry faculty members had encouraged the student to publish the damaging information. One of the student editors of the newspaper allegedly admitted this to a senior administrator at the school, but since the senior administrator was hostile to Newman, this revelation was not made public until long after Newman had left the university.

[419] John E. Coyne III, "Letter to the Editor: A Message from John Coyne, Chair, On Behalf of the Board of Trustees of Mount St. Mary's University," *Mount Echo*, January 1, 2016, http://msmecho.com/2016/01/19/letter-to-the-editor-a-message-from-john-coyne-chair-on-behalf-of-the-board-of-trustees-of-mount-st-marys-university/.

Those looking to oust Newman framed the conflict in terms of preserving Catholic identity. One of the major allegations leveled against Newman was that he was not supportive of the school's Catholic identity, even though this was patently untrue. Newman, a devout convert to Catholicism, praised the Catholicity of Mount St. Mary's and consistently denied ever seeking to undermine it.

Ultimately, this is a story of the destructive power that envy can inflict even on formerly strong Catholic colleges like Mount St. Mary's. Shared governance, including on Catholic colleges and universities, refers to the structures and processes through which the administration, governing board, and faculty, and sometimes even students and staff, participate in the development of policies and in decision-making for the institution. Key to shared governance is shared responsibility and shared authority in delivering the curriculum and shaping the culture of the institution. But, for the faculty on most campuses, shared governance means that the faculty makes all decisions related to the curriculum and academic policies, while the running of the campus's day-to-day operations is the responsibility of administration and student affairs personnel. Faculty resent any infringement on their authority to create the curriculum or to shape the academic culture. The problem with this approach is that faculty have a self-interest in maintaining their own disciplinary autonomy, even when their actions are not in the best interests of the students and the institution itself.

It is clear that the faculty who constituted Mount St. Mary's College's "shared governance" did not have the school's Catholic identity in mind when they pushed Simon Newman out of his job. If they had, they would have encouraged the hiring of a new president who truly understood what it means to be a faithful Catholic college. The reality is that the current president, who replaced Newman, has presided over a complete erosion of the school's Catholic mission, eventually leading to the school's removal from the *Newman Guide*.

That slide to secularization continues unabated. A few years ago, Mount St. Mary's published the engagement announcement of a same-sex couple in the university's alumni publication. Replete with a published photo celebrating them, Mount St. Mary's certainly appears to be endorsing same-sex "marriage." LifeSiteNews reported that, in response to this, several of the graduates of the once-faithful Catholic university reached out to their alumni publication to express concern that the Catholic identity of the school was ebbing away. One member of the class of 1986 shared a letter she penned to Mount St. Mary's President Timothy Trainor with LifeSiteNews, where she said she was "saddened to see reported, alongside announcements of births and weddings and professional accomplishments, an event celebrating a lifestyle that is counter to everything that you say the Mount stands for.... In your letter at the front of the same magazine, you say the Mount wants to educate the next generation of ethical leaders in service to God and others."[420]

Mount St. Mary's director of Public Relations and Communications, Donna Klinger, replied with a strong statement of support for the inclusion of same-sex engagements in the school's alumni magazine:

> Mount St. Mary's University is a Catholic university where the Church and the world dialogue, giving students the knowledge and skill to ethically apply the Church's teachings in the modern world in service to God

[420] "Catholic University Mount St. Mary's Alumni Magazine Includes Gay Engagement Announcement," LifeSiteNews, June 17, 2019, https://www.lifesitenews.com/news/catholic-university-mount-st-marys-alumni-magazine-includes-gay-engagement-announcement/.

> and others. Our enduring 211-year commitment to our Catholic mission inspires engagement with the world and hospitality to all regarding of religious background. We are a diverse, inclusive community composed of individuals of many faiths and beliefs. Through its alumni magazine the university shares the news of all alumni. We do not make judgments about the news being shared and inclusion of an announcement does not imply the university's endorsement. Filtering news to reject anything that does not follow Catholic teaching would deprive all alumni of learning about life's milestones of not only people who are in same sex relationships but also those who are divorced and entering second marriages, or those who have children out of wedlock.[421]

This was not the first time Mount St. Mary's celebrated behavior contrary to Catholic teachings. In April 2018, Mount St. Mary's announced that its 2019 commencement speaker would be Mark Shriver, a former Maryland politician with a 100 percent pro-abortion rating from NARAL Pro-Choice Maryland. In response, the Cardinal Newman Society issued a statement saying that it was "shocked and dismayed" that an institution recommended in their *Newman Guide* for its faithful Catholic identity had chosen to invite Shriver. It also noted the possibility of scandal created by honoring pro-abortion politicians. In a statement to LifeSiteNews, Mount St. Mary's administration chose not to address concerns about the school's Catholic identity and focused instead on emphasizing the importance of "engagement with the world and hospitality to all."[422]

421 Quoted in ibid.
422 Ibid.

In deleting Mount St. Mary's from the *Newman Guide*'s list of faithful Catholic colleges and universities, Patrick Riley wrote:

> This is yet another scandal that undermines the University's mission to uphold and teach the Faith. The Mount's [public relations] statement unsuccessfully attempts to explain away the problem and lacks the integrity of an institution committed to the formation of its students. A Catholic university must make deliberate choices about what to publish and who will speak at commencement, and the Mount's leadership is making very bad choices without regard for the corrosive impact on its students and alumni."[423]

Conclusion

Leadership matters, and those Catholic colleges and universities that have lost their identity have had leaders who did not understand what it means to be a faithful Catholic institution. The loss of Catholic identity on once-faithful campuses like DeSales, Mount St. Mary's, Providence, and a long list of other Catholic colleges and universities, is part of any story which traces long-standing battles. Just as great victories can be snatched from seeming defeat, equally strong positions can be eroded and lost to cowardice and betrayal.

The stories of these now "lost" Catholic colleges and universities reveal some of the difficult and sometimes disastrous challenges these schools have had to navigate. From faculty, alumni, and student activists promoting abortion and same-sex "marriage" to faculty and administrative controversies over the curriculum, some schools appear to have succumbed to the pressures of secularity. Others, like Franciscan, appear

[423] Quoted in ibid.

to have emerged from confrontation with similar challenges but stronger than ever in their commitment to their Catholic identities.

Professor Anthony Esolen maintains that campus controversies over Catholic teachings on moral issues at Providence may simply be part of a much bigger effort by the faculty to completely revamp the curriculum by removing the core curriculum and the liberal arts. Esolen was "fighting for the Catholic worldview that values cultural diversity anchored in truth and virtue, against a politically-inspired moral diversity that he believes homogenizes culture by celebrating mediocrity to the exclusion of Christian civilization's wide patrimony of letters and learning."[424] He specifically pointed to the program he created at Providence in the Development of Western Civilization. Now, says Esolen, the faculty senate at Providence is made up of the more politically ambitious professors who will be "sympathetic to the students demands" for courses that are "more relevant" to their lives. Esolen came to the conclusion that

> It remains to be seen how far they will go toward dismantling the most culturally diverse program at Providence College, our program in the Development of Western Civilization. Outside of the professors who teach in that program and who love doing so, most (not all) the faculty are like the students in several ways. They don't care about reading Homer either. They don't know anything about Dante, nor do they care to know.[425]

Similar concerns about curricular issues also dominated the most rancorous disagreements between the faculty and the administration at Mount St. Mary's.

[424] Smith, "Anthony Esolen in His Own Words."
[425] Esolen, "Narcissism of Campus Diversity Activists."

Some readers might ask why I have spent this time highlighting the struggles of these delisted colleges, when it is clear from the previous chapter that even the schools still on the *Newman Guide* list have had their struggles. How are we to understand what distinguishes the two groups of schools? Alexander Solzhenitsyn famously said that "the line separating good and evil passes ... right through every human heart," and I believe that the same is also true of every campus. However, what separates the faithful schools — those colleges and universities which are lamps giving light in the darkness — is the standard by which they wish to be judged. The schools which remained in the *Newman Guide* may have had their struggles, yet their failings can be judged as such according to faithfulness to Christ and His Church. Schools like Providence, DeSales, and Mount St. Mary's have chosen another standard by which they wish to be judged: that is, success comparable with secular institutions, and the approval of those institutions. This success is measured by adoption of a liberalized notion of academic freedom among the faculty and by a rejection of the Church's sexual and social ethics by the school's administration. The schools still listed on the *Newman Guide* hold themselves to an authentically Catholic ideal of the university, an institution that was besieged when Pope John Paul published *Ex Corde Ecclesiae* and which remains under threat to this day. The universities that have fought long and hard to remain faithful are worthy of special recognition. It is only by obeying John Paul's call for a "continuous renewal" in every generation of the institution "both as 'Universities' and as 'Catholic,' "[426] that the vital work of these schools will continue. "You will be hated by all for my name's sake," says Christ in Matthew 10:22. "But he who endures to the end will be saved."

[426] *Ex Corde Ecclesiae*, no. 7.

In the final chapter, I will conclude by attempting to identify what endurance looks like for the future of Catholic colleges. I ask how these schools might successfully resist the endurance of mere *stasis* or persistence — and we turn our attention back to one that parallels the charism of ongoing conversion and adequately answers John Paul's call for continuous renewal.

Chapter 10

Keeping the Light of Christ at the Faithful Few

THE DIVISION IDENTIFIED IN this book, between the faithful few and the more than two hundred other so-called Catholic colleges and universities, is essentially one of how these schools approach their Catholic identity. In this final chapter, it may be helpful to take a step back and consider this institutional divide in light of a similar divide that C. S. Lewis identified in *Mere Christianity* about how individuals approach their Christian identity.

The primary metaphor of *Mere Christianity* is that of a large house with a hallway or a foyer leading to many rooms within that house. The hallway represents the most basic of Christian beliefs: a proclaimed faith in God, perhaps a shared belief in the salvific role of Jesus Christ, an acceptance of the beatitudes — especially those that stress social justice — and a respect for some of the commandments — especially the most important commandment for the merely Christian to "love your neighbor as yourself." But in the rooms, distinct from the hallway, the doctrinal expositions of those beliefs and various ways of living are available. Lewis writes:

> It is in the rooms, not in the hall, that there are fires and chairs and meals. The hall is a place to wait in, a place

> from which to try the various doors, not a place to live in.... You must regard it as waiting.... You must keep on praying for light: and, of course, even in the hall, you must begin trying to obey the rules which are common to the whole house. And above all you must be asking which door is the true one, not which pleases you best by its paint and paneling. In plain language, the question should never be: "Do I like that kind of service?" but rather, "Are these doctrines true: Is holiness here? Does my conscience move towards this? Is my reluctance to knock at this door due to my pride, or my mere taste or my personal dislike of this particular door-keeper?"[427]

Even though C. S. Lewis was not talking about the Catholic Church and her Catholic colleges and universities, his metaphor of the hallway and the rooms of the large house has resonance for us. The faithful few are the rooms in that large Catholic house. Each may have different décor and different appointments and amenities. Some are located in a more rural environment, replete with horses and mountains like Wyoming Catholic; others are located in gritty industrial cities like Steubenville; still others are in beautiful burgeoning towns like Ave Maria. But each of those rooms provide the same sustenance, C. S. Lewis's "warm fires," and the same commitment to Catholic curriculum, doctrine, and beliefs that will protect those who enter and begin to actually live in these rooms.

The formerly faithful colleges and universities are represented in this analogy by those who have stayed in the hallway of the great house. Lewis knew that the foyer or the hallway was never going to be a place where the individual could live and thrive, and the same is true for Catholic universities. The foyer of "mere Catholicism" was

[427] C. S. Lewis, *Mere Christianity* (New York: Harper Collins, 1962), xv–xvi.

never going to be enough to keep out the corruption of the secular culture. Only the rooms, with their defining walls and distinctly Catholic traditions and doctrines, could protect those living within them from the harm of a degraded culture. Most Catholic colleges and universities have succumbed to this "mere Catholicism."

Boston College, with its Jesuit commitment to "being men and women for others," is a perfect example of this "merely Catholic" status that banishes itself to the empty hallway of a nominal identity. The Jesuit colleges and universities often point to their social justice activities as a demonstration of their commitment to their Catholic identity. Social justice is a noble goal, but without a doctrine and strong belief system in the dignity of the human person, the "merely Catholic social justice hallway" is never going to be enough to keep out the corruption that seeps into that open hallway. For many Jesuit colleges and universities — including Georgetown — social justice has become so broadly defined as to include "reproductive choice" or access to same-sex "marriage" as a social justice imperative. These are the kinds of values that remain out in the hallway. They are not based on Catholic teachings or doctrine, but rather on secular values that may appear to be inclusive and kind but rather are a part of the culture of death. "Mere Catholic" institutions have rejected the opportunity to remain countercultural in their commitment to the truth of Catholic teachings on faith and morals and the dignity of each person from conception until natural death, instead embracing a secularized Catholicism that cannot stand against atheism, pro-abortion, and pro-sexual revolution cultures flourishing on campus.

In *Mere Christianity*, Lewis described this dilemma. He warned about the "merely Christian" institutions that have given in to the pressure to conform to the broader culture — adopting the values and norms of the greater culture even when they are counter to

Christianity. However, Lewis also insisted that those who live within the rooms of the house must preserve a spirit of charity to all: "When you have reached your own room, be kind to those who have chosen different doors and to those who are still in the hall. If they are wrong, they need your prayers all the more, and if they are your enemies, then you are under orders to pray for them. That is one of the rules common to the whole house."[428]

Some of us have spent a good portion of our professional lives in the hallway of that great house. Having taught for nearly fifteen years at the University of San Diego, a "mere Catholic" university that was once vibrantly alive with the Faith, I was disappointed to learn that the school was becoming a place that was actually hostile to the Faith. When it was time to leave, and again in looking back at what was once a faithful professional home, it is difficult not to feel sadness for faithful colleagues there who are still out there in the hall. But we all have to make the kinds of decisions to choose the rooms that will help to lead to our own salvation, despite how attractive or tempting it may be to stay in the hallway.

Fruits of the Faithful Few

The faithful few have borne the fruits that come from living out a full and dynamic Catholic identity. Instead of distancing themselves from ecclesial authority, these schools see themselves, in the words of Pope St. John Paul II, as an "essential" part of the Church.[429] They see themselves as collaborators in the Church's mission to form students in the Faith. These faithful few are schools that in some ways are "experiments" in Catholic education; just as an experiment is a way to determine the efficacy or likelihood of something previously

[428] Ibid., xvi.

[429] *Ex Corde Ecclesiae*, no. 11.

untried, the creation of Ave Maria and other faithful schools has helped to provide insight into demonstrating what outcome occurs when faith becomes central to a Catholic college campus.

Their creation has already produced men and women willing to serve the Church through vocations to the religious life, to family and parish life, and to the good of their communities through their chosen careers. Recently, educational leaders in the Archdiocese of Boston chose to focus their recruitment of potential teachers for its Catholic K-12 schools on graduates of faithful Catholic colleges and universities such as Ave Maria University, Franciscan University, and a handful of others. These recruiters were less concerned about accreditation issues and teacher training programs than they were about graduates who are already filled with the Faith and are willing to share that Faith with their students. In interviewing potential teachers from all majors, not just education majors, these recruiters know that teaching methods can be learned — but a commitment and a true love for the Catholic Faith cannot be easily learned without having been immersed in the kind of Catholic culture that the faithful few Catholic colleges and universities provide.

Tom Carroll, the superintendent of schools in the Boston archdiocese from 2019 to 2024, said in a 2023 interview that the biggest challenge he had faced since he began leading the Catholic K-12 schools in Boston had been a "lack of vision.... Lots of people have shown that if you have the right vision and you have people who are witnesses, parents will come and the enrollment will follow.... I think the schools that have a clear vision and that are committed to their central mission of helping children grow in virtue will be around for a long time. The tides come and go.... I'm in a mad rush to try and convince people to stay on mission." That's why, said Carroll, he had been "very deliberate about putting in a religious screen for anybody who's hired. It used to be if you identified as Catholic, whatever that means, that was kind of the bare minimum requirement. But I agree with Pope St. Paul VI that modern man listens more willingly to witnesses than to teachers, and if he listens to teachers, it's because they're witnesses."[430]

Carroll knew that the best place to find these witnesses is on the campuses of the faithful few. That is why he was "zigzagging across the country, hopping on trains, planes and automobiles in this search for graduating seniors who are faithful and smart, who are intellectually curious, have a work ethic and a lot of grit. I'll recruit 50 this year and then grow beyond that. I'm finding a tremendous amount of talent out there, finding lots of young adults with missionary zeal."

When asked why missionary spirit and the ability to evangelize was at the forefront of his vision for Catholic schools, Carroll responded, "Over time, Boston has become mission territory. That's our challenge, and as you know, as has been pointed out, we're now in an apostolic age.... But, I'm finding the most beautifully faithful young men and women across the country. I joke that I'm gonna put on a business card that I'm a fisher of men and women. But all this evangelization begins with the recognition that something is not quite right." For Carroll, the faithful few Catholic colleges and universities produce some of the most faithful Catholic graduates in the country, all committed to the same goal he has for his Boston Catholic school children. Like Tom Monaghan, Carroll said his schools exist "to draw kids closer to God, to help them grow in virtue, and set them on a path to eternal salvation."[431]

[430] Father Patrick Briscoe, "Catholic Schools' Biggest Challenge? Boston Superintendent Says It's a Lack of Vision," *Our Sunday Visitor*, February 3, 2023, https://www.oursundayvisitor.com/catholic-schools-biggest-challenge-boston-superintendent-says-its-a-lack-of-vision/.

[431] Ibid.

To create the kinds of faithful teachers that Superintendent Carroll needs for his Boston schools requires faithful Catholic college educations such as the faithful few can provide. Carroll knows that "mere Catholic" colleges are not enough, and that it is not enough to place a "merely Catholic" teacher into the classrooms of his archdiocese. A robustly Catholic K-12 school requires a robustly Catholic faculty.

The Collapse of Ecclesial Authority in Catholic Higher Education

While it is truly heartening to see Catholic educators such as Carroll recognizing and prizing the fruits of the faithful few, we must also examine one reason in particular that the formerly faithful colleges and universities have failed to produce such good fruit: the abdication of responsibility by their shepherds. For example, the University of San Diego's episcopal authority, Cardinal Robert McElroy, has been complicit in the decline of the school's Catholic identity by providing Catholic "cover" for the university for years. LifeSiteNews has pointed out that "In recent years, Cardinal McElroy has sparked outrage among faithful Catholics for celebrating LGBT Masses, and rebuking the Church's position on homosexual acts."[432] Concluding that "No bishop has defended giving Communion to pro-abortion politicians as vigorously as Cardinal McElroy," LifeSiteNews also reported that the University of San Diego currently provides health insurance coverage for employees' contraception, abortifacients, surgical abortions, and gender transitioning surgery, all with no

[432] Raymond Wolfe, "Pope Francis New Pick has a Horrifying Record on Homosexuality and Abortion," LifeSiteNews, August 27, 2022, https://www.lifesitenews.com/blogs/pope-francis-newest-us-cardinal-has-a-horrifying-record-on-homosexuality-and-abortion/.

pushback from Cardinal McElroy.[433] He has provided an opportunity for the University of San Diego to engage in the most extreme abortion and same-sex "marriage" advocacy.

Other than one courageous bishop, Bishop Thomas J. Paprocki of the Diocese of Springfield, Illinois, who was willing to publicly confront Cardinal McElroy's heretical statements, there has been little pushback from any of the other bishops. In a recent *First Things* article entitled "Imagining a Heretical Cardinal," Bishop Paprocki wrote,

> What if a cardinal of the Catholic Church were to state publicly that homosexual acts are not sinful and that same-sex unions should be blessed by the Church?
>
> Until recently it would be hard to imagine any successor of the apostles making such heterodox statements. Unfortunately, it is not uncommon today to hear Catholic leaders affirm unorthodox views that, not too long ago, would have been espoused only by heretics....
>
> It is deeply troubling to consider the possibility that prelates holding the office of diocesan bishop in the Catholic Church may be separated or not in full communion because of heresy.[434]

Cardinal McElroy is not the only bishop who has chosen to lend his support to heterodox activities on the Catholic campuses within his

433 Lela Gallery, "Catholic University of San Diego Health Plan Pays for Abortion and Sex Change Surgeries," LifeSiteNews, August 16, 2021, https://www.lifesitenews.com/news/catholic-university-of-san-diego-health-plan-pays-for-abortions-sex-change-surgeries/.

434 Bishop Thomas J. Paprocki, "Imagining a Heretical Cardinal," *First Things*, February 28, 2023. https://www.firstthings.com/web-exclusives/2023/02/imagining-a-heretical-cardinal.

diocese. Most bishops join him in being far from implementing *Ex Corde Ecclesiae,* though none will acknowledge their lack of engagement — just as they will not take a Catholic stance against heterodoxies. The United States Conference of Catholic Bishops (USCCB) was charged with drafting and implementing a regional *Application of Ex Corde Ecclesiae*. When the bishops' conference issued a one-page report on its implementation, rather extravagantly called the "Ten-Year Review," its authors claimed that "the relationship between bishops and presidents on the local level can be characterized as positive and engaged, demonstrating progress on courtesy and cooperation in the last ten years. Clarity about Catholic identity among college and university leadership has fostered substantive dialogues and cultivated greater mission-driven practices across the university."[435] Rather than giving facts about the implementation, the bishops issued a self-congratulatory, platitudinous document that praised ongoing dialogue and the spirit of collaboration but said nothing about what was really happening in Catholic higher education. Any Catholic who has been paying attention to the culture and curricula on many of these campuses could be forgiven if he felt like he had stepped into a chapter of George Orwell's *1984* when reading a headline about the Ten-Year Review in the *National Catholic Reporter,* which proclaimed "Bishops, colleges find good collaboration in 'Ex Corde' review."[436] That same

[435] USCCB Committee on Catholic Education, "Final Report for the Ten Year Review of *The Application of Ex Corde Ecclesia for the United States,*" June 11, 2012, United States Conference of Catholic Bishops, https://www.usccb.org/beliefs-and-teachings/how-we-teach/catholic-education/higher-education/upload/Final-Report-for-the-Ten-Year-Review-of-The-Application-of-Ex-Corde-Ecclesiae-for-the-United-States-2012.pdf.

[436] Catholic News Service, "Bishops, Colleges Find Good Collaboration in 'Ex Corde' Review," *National Catholic Reporter,* January 11, 2013, https://www.ncronline.org/news/theology/bishops-colleges-find-good-collaboration-ex-corde-review.

Catholic must have been even more surprised to read a headline in *Our Sunday Visitor* that claimed "Progress Seen in Boosting Catholic Identity on Campuses."[437]

None of this was true. There was no collaboration, for example, between the bishop and the president of Notre Dame when the school granted an honorary degree to President Obama. And certainly there was no collaboration between the bishop and the president of Notre Dame when the school awarded the Laetare Medal to then-Vice President Joseph Biden. But no one at the USCCB wants to acknowledge that fact. The report claimed "increased cooperation over the last decade" without any data, even anecdotal data, supporting its assertions. The report simply asserted that "Bishops report that they believe our institutions of Catholic higher education have made definite progress in advancing Catholic identity."[438]

It is unlikely that the local ordinary for the University of Notre Dame, Bishop Kevin Rhoades of the Diocese of Fort Wayne-South Bend, believes that "there is increased cooperation" with Notre Dame in recent decades. It is even more unlikely that Bishop Rhoades believes that Notre Dame has made "definite progress in advancing Catholic identity." It would be hard to view Notre Dame's recent event with abortion doula Ash Williams, mentioned in chapter 1, as anything other than an example of a declining, not an advancing, Catholic identity. Although Bishop Rhoades condemned the scandal in his own column in his diocesan newspaper, his condemnation is too little and too late to make a difference. And, we should note, this latest abortion scandal was not just a fringe event

[437] Cited in Anne Hendershott, "The Orwellian World of Catholic Higher Education," *Catholic World Report*, February 20, 2013, https://www.catholicworldreport.com/2013/02/20/the-orwellian-world-of-catholic-higher-education/.

[438] USCCB Committee on Catholic Education, "Ten Year Review."

sponsored by a renegade Gender Studies department. Rather, it was supported by the Dean's Office in the College of Arts and Letters, as well as by seven other major departments in the university. It is a sign that a school is thoroughly secularized when an event like this could be supported by so many departments at the university.[439] However, it is puzzling why Bishop Rhoades would describe the pro-abortion event as being "in opposition to Notre Dame's commitment to a culture of life." By honoring prominent pro-abortion politicians in the past, Notre Dame has shown over and over that it no longer has a commitment to a culture of life. Bishop Rhoades should know that this abortion scandal at Notre Dame is just the latest in a long list of pro-abortion scandals on that campus.

One professor we spoke to at another once-faithful Catholic university lamented the lack of leadership on his campus: "For more than thirty years I have upheld and defended Church teachings and have criticized the failure of this school's leaders to do the same, to the point of hurting my career. But when my bishop won't address the serious problems here, and the bishops at large won't do anything, I wonder, 'Why even bother?'" In fact, the USCCB has not issued a single statement on *Ex Corde Ecclesiae* since 2012. The twentieth anniversary of the *Application of Ex Corde Ecclesiae* passed without a single comment from the bishops.[440] According to Barbara

[439] Bishop Kevin C. Rhoades, "Reproductive Justice Series Promotes Injustice of Abortion and Provides Platform for Abortion Activists in Opposition to Notre Dame's Commitment to a Culture of Life," *Today's Catholic,* March 21, 2023, https://todayscatholic.org/reproductive-justice-series-promotes-injustice-of-abortion-and-provides-platform-for-abortion-activists-in-opposition-to-notre-dames-commitment-to-culture-of-life/.

[440] Anne Hendershott, "Catholic Universities and Colleges Continue to Ignore *Ex Corde Ecclesiae*," *Catholic World Report,* March 17, 2022, https://www.catholicworldreport.com/2022/03/17/catholic-universities-and-colleges-continue-to-ignore-ex-corde-ecclesiae/.

H. McCrabb, the assistant director of Higher Education at the USCCB, there are no plans for another assessment of the implementation of *Ex Corde Ecclesiae*. In an interview, she said, "The U.S. application called for a five- and ten-year assessment.... At this time, there are no plans to do an additional review."[441] This attitude suggests the bishops have stopped even pretending to care about Catholic higher education.

Echoing these concerns about the relationship between colleges and their local bishops, Providence College theology professor James F. Keating published an article in *First Things* in April 2023 entitled "Who Killed the Catholic University?" In his article, Keating blamed the bishops for the loss of the Catholic identity on most Catholic campuses. He suggested that the USCCB-drafted *Application of Ex Corde Ecclesiae*

> soft-pedaled the role of the bishops. It repeatedly asserted that a Catholic university enjoys institutional autonomy, that it possesses academic freedom as an essential component, and that its governance is and remains internal to the institution itself.... The local bishop would not be internal to the regular functioning of the university — he would not disrupt, as *Ex Corde* intended, the essential principle of the Land O'Lakes consensus.[442]

For Keating, "Any reader of the *Application* can feel the defensiveness of its authors. They sought to implement the pope's requirements without eliciting pushback from the leaders of American Catholic

[441] Ibid.

[442] James F. Keating, "Who Killed the Catholic University?" *First Things*, April 2023. https://www.firstthings.com/article/2023/04/who-killed-the-catholic-university.

higher education or unflattering stories in the *New York Times* — which meant in the end, ensuring that nothing important would change."[443] And indeed nothing did change for the better on these now-faithless campuses. If anything, things got much worse, and the passage of time has made both bishops and college administrators more comfortable with their autonomous relationship. *Ex Corde Ecclesiae* was "not received," and Keating believes that it "became a dead letter long ago."[444] It is likely that it will never be received on those campuses which seem to have given up the Faith. The bishops may continue claiming that there is "increased cooperation and dialogue," but there is no cooperation at all on most of these campuses. Status-seeking administrators, indifferent and sometimes actively hostile to Catholic teachings, now run the majority of Catholic colleges and universities. Most faculties on these campuses do not even have the ability or the desire to bring together faith and reason in their teaching. Father James Heft's open-circle Catholic campus, as described in the opening chapter of this book, has been a failure. And yet, Father Heft is viewed as an "expert" on Catholic higher education, collecting large donations and speaking fees from his perch at the Institute for Advanced Catholic Studies at the University of Southern California,[445] despite the fact that, for the past three decades, he has not been concerned with hiring Catholic faculty to lead the classrooms.[446] As Keating pithily observed, "If you aren't intentional about hiring Catholic educators, you won't have them, and if you don't have them, you can't have a Catholic university."[447]

443 Ibid.

444 Ibid.

445 "The Future of Catholic Higher Education," *Royal News*, University of Scranton, February 22, 2022. https://news.scranton.edu/articles/2022/02/fac-talk.shtml.

446 Heft, *Future of Catholic Higher Education*.

447 Keating, "Who Killed the Catholic University?"

Keating was especially critical of the "gross hypocrisy" shown by universities in refusing the teaching authority of their own bishops on matters of faith and morals on their campuses — while at the same time they are scrambling to welcome federal government interference, like the expansion of Diversity, Equity, and Inclusion in their hiring practices, student life, and non-discrimination policies. Acquiescing to federal calls for inclusivity for the transgender community, many of these Catholic campuses are now creating campus bathrooms and locker rooms that are welcoming to transgender students, opening access to sports teams for transgender athletes to play on the team of their gender choice, and creating co-ed dormitories to accommodate transgender individuals who demand them. Most once-faithful colleges and universities have rushed to comply with every federal suggestion for making their campuses inclusive — and at the same time they resist every effort by the few bishops who have tried to help them recover their Catholic identity.

Despite this sorry state of affairs, all is not lost. As I have shown throughout this book, another way is possible.

The Collapse of Academic Leadership in Catholic Higher Education

Along with the bishops, the president and the board of trustees of each school have the responsibility to provide the leadership and accountability that keep it faithful. Good leadership is essential in keeping the Faith at the center of the college's identity. This has been true from the from the days of the 1960s and 1970s when the moral fiber of these schools started deteriorating rapidly. Even a supporter of laicizing Catholic higher education like David O'Brien, professor emeritus of Holy Cross College, acknowledges that many of today's problems of secularization arose with the rapid changes following Land O'Lakes: "In an act of unprecedented trust, religious orders of men and women gave their schools to lay dominated boards of trustees. But there was little attention given to the criteria for the selection of trustees, their orientation to Catholic higher education and their continuing education on issues of importance to the Catholic mission and identity."[448] O'Brien observes that, while the presidents who first laicized their boards acknowledged that they understood the change to be a sharing of responsibility with the laity, in the spirit of Vatican II, their choices were made on the basis of the skills or experience the laypeople could bring. Lawyers, benefactors, key alumni, and businessmen could give the colleges specialized advice, such as on investments or insurance. Wealthy donors were also highly favored. Ultimately, commitment to the Catholic identity did not feature as an important qualification for these trustees. We are still paying the price for this oversight. In 2007, the survey of trustees that was commissioned by the *Chronicle of Higher Education* indicated that "status concerns" were especially salient for the trustees, who said their most important goal was improvement in their institution's *U.S. News and World Report* ranking.[449] In contrast with this practice among the majority of Catholic universities, many of the faithful few have required in their bylaws that all trustees must be practicing Catholics, with some requiring letters of recommendation from their parish priests about their Church attendance and good standing within the Church.

Another problem has been the practice — especially on Catholic campuses — of appointing former and current college presidents to the board. In fact, the percentage of current and former college presidents on Catholic college boards is much higher than at other private college boards because Catholic colleges have

[448] David J. O'Brien, *From the Heart of the Church: Catholic Higher Education and American Culture* (New York: Orbis Books, 1994), 76.

[449] Jeffrey Selingo, "The Chronicle Survey: What Trustees Think," *Chronicle of Higher Education* 53 (May 11, 2007), A11.

sought out such leaders as members for several decades. This has had tremendous influence on the decisions made by the board. The idea of appointing current college presidents to sit on another institution's governing board has raised a number of questions — including whether a president who chooses to stack the board with presidential colleagues with similar status strivings does so for the purpose of having comfortable and congenial allies on the board who will "educate" the rest of the board on the issues that are viewed as "too complex" for non-academic board members to understand. Although allegations of collusion have never been made, there has been collaboration evident in the negative response to *Ex Corde Ecclesiae* by most of the once-faithful Catholic colleges and universities.

Ideally, a board member is going to ask hard questions about mission and identity. But, too often, the board members of Catholic colleges and universities have been rubber stamps for the president. This can be a problem in any realm, as recent corporate scandals involving the 2023 bank failures in Silicon Valley and elsewhere have shown. While Catholic college boards do not have to answer to the same kinds of creditors and investors, there are indeed stakeholders in higher education — including donors, faculty members, students, administrators, alumni, and Catholic Church members who have invested their money, time, and sometimes even their careers in a college. They, too, want to know that the institution will not squander their contributions. Too often, however, the board becomes isolated and ends up being micromanaged by the president of the college rather than providing independent oversight, receiving only the information that the president wants it to hear. As any student of management and board relations knows, the trustees will only rise to the level of expectation of the chief executive.

Still, the ultimate responsibility must lie with the trustees themselves. While trustees can claim that they are not always given all the information needed to make decisions, the reality is that under American civil law, the board holds in trust the purposes for which the institution was founded. Board members have a responsibility to find evidence that the Catholic identity and mission of the university are being implemented. In his book on *The Moral Responsibilities of Trusteeship*, David H. Smith suggests that "the trustee form of governance is defined by loyalty to the purpose for which the organization was created. It inevitably leads to concern with the history of the organization which should become what Robert Bellah and his colleagues called a 'community of memory.'" Smith maintains that "the fiduciary principle establishes the organization's own particularity, slant, or vision," and then based on that mission the trustee acts on behalf of the entruster for the benefit of the beneficiary.[450] The trustee is always constrained in some way by the will of the founder or by the purpose for which the organization was created.

The founder and current leadership of Ave Maria University understand better than most the important role played by the trustee form of governance in maintaining the mission. To ensure faithfulness to the Catholic mission, Tom Monaghan asked all incoming Ave Maria University trustees to commit to *Tres Magna* — Latin for the "Big Three": attending daily Mass, praying the Rosary every day, and going to Confession at least monthly. Monaghan, who practices the Tres Magna himself, believes that such a spiritual commitment will help to keep trustees on the path to sanctity and will give them the grace to truly safeguard the mission of the university.

[450] David H. Smith, *Entrusted: The Moral Responsibilities of Trusteeship* (Bloomington, IN: University of Indiana Press, 1995), 5.

Two Roads Diverged

Smith's metaphor of "a community of memory" might quite comfortably be expanded to include the entire university. And at every stage, this community has a choice to live in faithfulness to its communal memory or to enter into a state of active forgetfulness. These two roads — the way of remembrance and the way of neglect — represent the two strands of Catholic universities moving along divergent pathways; like the roads in Frost's poem, the choice makes "all the difference." In this book, I have tried to delineate between these two types of Catholic universities, which are divided by a genuinely different vision of what it means to *be* a Catholic university in the twenty-first century. The fierce debates that are alive today — debates over the form and function of Catholic higher education which separate the faithful few schools from most other Catholic colleges and universities — are direct descendants of the debates and turmoil in the postconciliar church.

The division between the two types of Catholic colleges was identified by the late theologian and university administrator Monika Hellwig, when she described the two different reactions that Catholic universities had to the Church's canonical guidance for universities, as expressed in the 1983 Code of Canon Law and in the "Norms" of *Ex Corde Ecclesiae*, which summarized the relevant canons applicable to universities. The split, said Hellwig, was between schools with a "desire to tighten hierarchical supervision and control through canonical legislation and practical administrative arrangements" and schools that choose to "search for the basis of Catholic identity in a clearer appropriation of the Catholic intellectual tradition, a more forthright statement of the Catholic character, identity, and purpose of the institution both in words and operation values." Delivering these remarks at a 2000 Harvard conference on the "Future of Religious Colleges," Hellwig believed that the future belonged to this second camp, who built their Catholic identity with "a clearer appropriation," a "more forthright statement" and a "purpose." What they do not build their identity on, however, as her statement perfectly captures, is an adherence to magisterial authority.[451]

Hellwig had a clear repugnance for what she seemed to view as the crudeness of holding magisterial authority to be the foundation of Catholic identity. For many Catholic universities today, there is something vaguely reductionistic in describing identity in terms of obedience. Hellwig, and those who fall into her camp today, believe that the move to decouple from an institutional commitment to the hierarchical Church has allowed universities a freer "search for the basis of Catholic identity." This search has created a more vibrant Catholic identity among Catholic universities, Hellwig contended, and, since the 1960s, "Many changes and adjustments have been made in order to realize Catholic character more fully."[452]

That this has not actually been the case has been thoroughly indicated throughout this book. Hellwig was correct that the living out of a Catholic identity goes far beyond obedience to the infallible and legal authority of the Magisterium, but she is mistaken to think that the identity can exist without first a commitment to believe and obey all the Church teaches on faith and morals. It is a variation of the worn-out trope infecting secular society that there can be freedom without a good toward which that freedom is aimed. In fact, it is the faithful schools which have the true freedom to develop their Catholic identify. To return to our "Mere Christianity" analogy, each school, each "room," expresses the rich potential and diversity of a

[451] Monika K. Hellwig, "Emerging Patterns among Roman Catholic Colleges," in *The Future of Religious Colleges*, ed. Paul J. Dovre (Grand Rapids, MI: Eerdmans, 2002), 109.

[452] Ibid., 113.

faithfully lived Catholicism. But fidelity to the Church is the walls, and the floor, and the ceiling; without it, there simply isn't a room. I have argued, sometimes negatively through examples of secularized schools but mainly positively through a discussion of the missions, curricula, leadership, and worship at the faithful schools, that the recognition of ecclesial authority is a *sine qua non* of the Catholic university. Without it, universities are "in danger of developing a Gnosticized version of the 'Catholic intellectual tradition,'" rejecting the incarnational, historical Church in favor of some etherealized and abstracted intellectual heritage.[453] Faithfulness to the Church unifies all the divergent elements of the faithful schools discussed in this book. Without fidelity, there is no "Catholic identity" to live out.

The Way Ahead

The past forty years in Catholic higher education have been defined by the division between these two types of schools. In this final portion of the book, we want to turn to the future of Catholic higher education and ask: What does the path ahead look like for the faithful few? As the stories I have recounted in these pages make clear, there is nothing inevitable about institutional fidelity, just as there is nothing inevitable about a collapse into infidelity. Like the houses in Jesus' parable that are built on rock or sand, each school's flourishing or failure is the direct result of actions that provided or significantly affected the institution's structure. The winds of our secular culture will continue to blow, and the rain and floods will continue to rage, and so, if they hope to survive, the faithful few must be persistent in building upon rock: four rocks, to be precise.

[453] John Cavadini, "Open Letter to the University Community," 2006, quoted in "Dissent At Notre Dame," *Via Media* (Amy Welborn blog), Beliefnet, https://www.beliefnet.com/columnists/viamedia/2006/04/dissent-at-notre-dame.html.

Rock 1: Institutional Fidelity to the Church

As already stressed, faithfulness to the Church is the *sine qua non* distinguishing mark of a Catholic university. This must translate into a tangible commitment to the ecclesial dimension of the university's mission and identity. Such a commitment can take various forms, though the mandatum required by *Ex Corde Ecclesiae* is an obvious one. Another form of this commitment is evidenced by Don Briel. When he was starting the flagship Catholic Studies Program at Minnesota's University of St. Thomas, he initially sought a pontifical charter for the program because "the work of Catholic Studies was not merely intellectual but also apostolic."[454] This approach contrasts sharply with that represented by the Land O' Lakes statement, which prioritizes a relationship between Church and university that is strictly "asymmetrical: to the Church, the university offers 'the benefit of counsel'; *from* the Church, the university asks only to be left alone."[455]

As well as these external commitments, the university can also strengthen fidelity from within by paying attention to some key pillars of institutional fidelity. First among these pillars is a school's faculty. There are good reasons why schools should maintain a robust Catholic majority among their faculty, even if they are accused of dogmatism or mocked for preferring a Catholic teacher in a non-theological area. In his authoritative *The Dying of the Light: The Disengagement of Colleges and Universities from Their Christian Churches*, James Burtchaell, C.S.C., calls the faculty "an inertial force" within the university. As he traces the loss of Christian mission at universities of various denominations over many decades, he identifies faculty as the first group to lose interest in the ecclesial

[454] Don Briel, "A Reflection on Catholic Studies," in *Renewal of Catholic Higher Education*, ed. Matthew Gerlach (Bismarck: ND, University of Mary Press, 2017), 30.

[455] Burtchaell, *Dying of the Light*, 595.

mission of the university. They consistently "became dissociated from responsibility for [the students'] moral discipline and from partnership in their piety."[456] As specialization increased, teachers even became exclusively interested in their disciplines, to the point of ignoring the moral and intellectual integration proper to education. Burtchaell's account merely adds sociological weight to *Ex Corde Ecclesiae*'s explicit instruction that "the number of non-Catholic teachers should not be allowed to constitute a majority within the Institution, which is and must remain Catholic."[457] Every hire counts when it comes to maintaining institutional integrity; faculty ought to be committed to the Catholic educational vision. Otherwise, students will be given a fragmented education and an incoherent vision when they should be getting the formation to live their Faith in a diverse society. Burtchaell summarized the consequences of this problematic approach to college hiring practices with the quip, "The pluralism would thus be within the college instead of the college being within the pluralism."[458]

Another pillar of institutional fidelity is, unsurprisingly, leadership. Strong leadership at a school includes having a strong board of trustees, as the board is ultimately responsible for sustaining the mission of the institution. However, the reality is that it is the university president who can "make or break" the school; numerous stories throughout this book have revealed the immense directional impact of the president's leadership. Choosing the wrong president, even at one of the faithful few, can destroy the school. Choosing the right president is the *most* important task of the board of trustees. Mission fit is the most important criterion. When a president is hired who meets this criteron, the other

[456] Burtchaell, *Dying of the Light*, 828–829.

[457] *Ex Corde Ecclesiae*, General Norms, art. 4, sec. 4.

[458] Burtchaell, *Dying of the Light*, 603.

pieces — including faithfulness in the curriculum and student life, economic sustainability, commitment to hiring according to the mission for faculty and student affairs staff — all seem to fall into place. The stories of Franciscan, Ave Maria, University of Mary, Catholic University of America, Walsh, and Wyoming Catholic all reveal that a leader's commitment to faithfulness or desire for compromise will ripple throughout the entire institution. Leadership has the ability to turn a university around, whether toward or away from its Catholic identity.

Rock 2: Achieving Financial Freedom (and a Cautionary Tale)

Except for Christendom College, which has remained completely independent of the federal government by refusing all grants and loans from federal sources, all of the faithful few I have profiled have found the need to accept federal money to some degree or other in the form of student loans and grants. These funds often carry with them federal regulations and mandates that can infringe upon religious freedom. So far, the faithful few have been successful in declining to comply with those state or federal mandates that could cause them to compromise their Catholic identity.

Another school that sets itself apart in this regard is Thomas Aquinas College, though, unlike Christendom, it is not completely disentangled from federal funding. The college proclaims: "To preserve its Catholic character and religious liberty, Thomas Aquinas College does not accept any government funding that compromises its Catholic mission." Although the college acknowledges that "some students receive government-guaranteed loans, veterans benefits, and or individual tuition grants," its website makes clear that "the college carefully monitors federal and state regulations as they pertain to higher education to ensure that participation in these programs does not compromise the College's Catholic character or its educational mission in any way."[459]

It should be the goal of every faithful school to disentangle itself from federal funding, working toward full independence from government money. As an educational institution in receipt of public funding, there will be government pressures to compromise aspects of faith or morals to keep a secure line of capital. The past decade alone has thrown the precariousness of federal funding into sharp relief, and these struggles will only intensify. Universities that would fail without government money are in a constant state of Damocletian risk, with the sword of financial ruin held by a mere thread above their heads.

In 2012, Franciscan was the first — and for a while, the only — Catholic university which refused to enforce the Obama administration mandate requiring that employers provide insurance coverage that includes abortion-inducing drugs, contraceptives, and sterilization procedures. Franciscan filed a federal lawsuit against then-Health and Human Services (HHS) Secretary Kathleen Sebelius and the Obama administration, seeking to have the HHS mandate declared unconstitutional.[460]

Then, in 2023, there was yet another confrontation with the federal government — much like the contraception mandate of 2012 — over the proposed expansion by the Biden administration of Title IX mandates surrounding transgender student rights on Catholic campuses. The faithful Catholic colleges and universities that

[459] "Catholic Character and Government Funding," Thomas Aquinas College, https://www.thomasaquinas.edu/giving/catholic-character-and-government-funding.

[460] "Franciscan University Reacts to Latest HHS Mandate Ruling," Franciscan University, https://franciscan.edu/franciscan-university-reacts-to-latest-hhs-mandate-ruling/.

accept federal money in the form of loans or grants are required to follow Department of Education statutes, including Title IX, which is the federal law that mandates procedures for handling complaints of sexual discrimination, harassment, or violence. Ave Maria University has been proactive in implementing a strong and faithful Catholic response to the transgender issue on campus (see chapter 8) and others will likely follow.

The temptation to compromise over issues of funding has deep roots in the story of American Catholic universities. In fact, it was a desire for state funding that drove Fordham University, one of the then-premier Catholic institutions in America, to give up its "sectarian" religious identity in the 1960s for the sake of access to public funds.[461] In the 1960s, the state of New York had a well-endowed higher education network that included the City University of New York, the State University of New York, and state colleges. State leadership wanted to ease pressure on their schools by providing limited funding to private institutions; however, a remnant of the state's anti-Catholic Know-Nothing era, the Blaine Amendment, forbade funding going to universities that were under "sectarian," that is, religious, control.

The governor appointed McGeorge Bundy to run a blue-ribbon commission to investigate whether private schools in the state, most of which were Catholic, could get around the Blaine Amendment. Bundy's report came back with a simple solution: These schools should "simply find a way to certify they weren't under sectarian control."[462] University consultants at Fordham, Gellhorn and Greenawalt, followed up with their own commission. They drew up a long list of recommendations that would make the university "completely independent" of Church control by changing certain characteristics

[461] Burtchaell, *Dying of the Light*, 600.
[462] Burtchaell, *Dying of the Light*, 599.

while, they claimed, maintaining the school's "fundamental character." Fordham adopted almost all of Gellhorn and Greenawalt's recommendations.[463] It successfully made itself eligible to receive public money, but one immediate consequence was that the university was no longer able to discriminate on the basis of religion in the faculty hiring process. It took a little over a decade for Fordham to realize, in 1977, that it had become almost unrecognizable as a Jesuit institution.

Once a school begins compromising on characteristics such as its public identity as a Catholic institution, it is much harder than perhaps Gellhorn and Greenawalt anticipated to maintain its "fundamental character." While this outcome may appear obvious in hindsight, Jesuits in the 1960s did not anticipate that, by the late 1970s, they would have to acknowledge their loss of college ownership in any meaningful sense. What they first embraced as a choice they thought to control soon became an outcome imposed upon them with irresistible force.

This is not to say there are any easy answers when it comes to issues of funding. In these uncertain financial times, even the faithful few have struggled with financial challenges that have threatened their very existence. This is especially true of some of the smallest faithful Catholic colleges and universities whose very survival has been and continues to be precarious. Some of the most faithful Catholic colleges and universities in the country have not survived the financial challenges that brought them down. In fact, the cautionary tale of the demise of the once-faithful St. Gregory's University in Oklahoma in 2017 reveals what can happen when a university relies too heavily on federal government largesse.[464]

[463] Ibid., 600.

[464] Jennifer Palmer, "Final Stages for St. Gregory's University," *Oklahoma Watch*, April 9, 2018, https://oklahomawatch.org/2018/04/09/historic-st-gregorys-final-stages/.

Oklahoma's oldest institution of higher education was founded in 1875, when a group of Benedictine monks reached central Oklahoma and immediately laid the framework for a Catholic college designed to educate both Native Americans and settlers moving to Oklahoma. Known first as the Catholic University of Oklahoma and renamed St. Gregory's University in 1997, the school was the only Catholic college in a state where Catholics made up about 4 percent of its nearly four million residents. With a dedication to the Catholic Benedictine tradition and programs for student evangelization and orthodox theology courses, St. Gregory's was lauded by the Cardinal Newman Society as one of the recommended "faithful few" included in the first edition of the *Newman Guide to Catholic Colleges and Universities.*

However, financial struggles had long plagued St. Gregory's. With a student body of eight hundred and a staff of four hundred, the university inaugurated its sixteenth president in early 2017, who soon issued the university's strategic plan, "Vision for Our Next Century." Less than a year later, the school filed for Chapter 7 bankruptcy and closed. According to *Oklahoma Watch,* a local media outlet, "The strategic plan hinged on a $20 million loan from the U.S. Department of Agriculture, which ultimately the university failed to qualify for.... The university owes a total of at least $15 million to creditors, which include the Citizen Potawatomi Nation, the Catholic Order of Foresters, and more than one hundred eighty businesses and individuals."[465] In 2015, the Potawatomi Nation had given the university $5 million in exchange for full scholarships for tribal students. But if the university defaulted or lost accreditation, the funds would transfer from the university to the tribe within sixty days.

[465] Ibid.

Adding insult to injury, on December 11, 2019, Hobby Lobby, and the Green Family who founded and owns Hobby Lobby, formally announced their donation of the former St. Gregory's University campus to Oklahoma Baptist University (OBU). Hobby Lobby had purchased the seventy-two-acre property in 2017 following St. Gregory's bankruptcy proceedings that same year. According to the OBU website, it offered a "teach-out" agreement to current St. Gregory's University students, with many of them transferring to OBU to complete their degrees.

And in yet another sadness for those of us who support the faithful few Catholic colleges and universities, Magdalen College — a fifty-year-old faithful Catholic college in Warner, New Hampshire — held its final commencement ceremony on May 11, 2024. According to an audit report, Magdalen faced foreclosure when the school was unable to repay a ten-year, $3.1 million loan that came due in 2024.[466] The Catholic Order of the Foresters, the insurance company that called in the loan, now owns the buildings and the land.

For some of those who supported Magdalen, there was a sense of inevitability. In fact, in an interview with the *Concord Monitor*, Mike McGrath, a 1991 graduate and former chair of the board at Magdalen said that "Magdalen closed in effect because of the financial issues, but the financial issues were really a symptom of the lack of loyalty, adherence. The college always struggled more than many of its peer institutions to generate financial support from its alumni — in part because of the rigidity of its social policies."[467]

466 "Audit for Period Ending June 2022," Magadalen College, ProPublica NonProfit Explorer, https://projects.propublica.org/nonprofits/display_audit/25318420221.

467 Jeremy Margolis, "A Turbulent 50-Year History: Inside the Rise and Fall of a Tiny Catholic College in Warner," *Concord Monitor*, last modified May 5, 2024, https://www.concordmonitor.com/Magdalen-College-closing-this-year-54859354.

McGrath was referring to what some believed was a rigidity in the rules governing student behavior including a "'no steady company keeping' policy that prohibited exclusive relationships among students." Over the years, McGrath said that he encouraged the president to loosen some restrictions and eventually the college stopped discouraging dating, controlling students' study times, and mandating participation in Mass.[468]

It is likely that the inability to recruit students was really the reason for the demise of the school. The Warner campus was built for one hundred twenty-five students, but it never was able to meet its recruiting goals. Magdalen reached a high point of ninety students in 2016, but there were years when only fifty-three students enrolled. A college that small with the kind of services that are needed to support residential students is not sustainable. McGrath blamed the lack of loyalty from Magdalen's graduates: "There are other small Catholic colleges out there — not as small as Magdalen, but less than one thousand, maybe even less than five hundred students — who have very large endowments because the graduates saw their time as positive. They believed in what they got and so they made investments." Sadly, it is clear that far fewer Magdalen graduates made those investments.

Universities are obligated to be good stewards of their financial resources, as the continuation of the institution depends on sound management. While each school must prudentially evaluate its capacity to gain independence from government funding, I believe that the goal of these schools should be as much financial freedom as possible.

Rock 3: A Network of Faithful Colleges

Though each school is fighting, often valiantly, to maintain its integrity, the most sensible path forward is for these schools to create

[468] Ibid.

a formal association. It is taxing to maintain both a robust *and* open-facing community, to be both faithfully Catholic *and* active within the current academic scene. As discussed in the previous chapter, since the *Newman Guide* was created in 2007, multiple schools have abandoned this tension and consequently fallen off the list. It is an impossible situation for these schools to remain siloed, each in its own struggle.

I believe the future of the faithful schools would be more secure if they organized with each other. Compared with the more than two hundred other nominally Catholic institutions of higher learning, these schools are a true minority, and the spiritual and intellectual formation they offer under the aegis of a committed orthodoxy is increasingly rare. Since the Second World War, a creeping uniformity has neutered most education of its distinctive qualities, as Burtchaell concisely summarizes:

> All began to fill out their programs and diversify their offerings. In their competitive drive to appeal to all available students, the single-gender schools became coed, liberal arts campuses pullulated vocational training, technical schools began to offer general education, universities added on more professional schools, junior colleges began to build up baccalaureate programs, undergraduate campuses begot graduate courses, then programs, then degrees. The result was paradoxical: the competitive drive to replicate all possible diversity within each campus caused a sharp decline in diversity between them. The Carnegie Commission on Higher Education warned of "a trend towards homogenization."[469]

[469] Burtchaell, *Dying of the Light*, 832–833.

Laboring under their status aspirations, Catholic institutions have fallen in lockstep with the homogenizing trend. They began evaluating themselves based on the metrics of Protestant and secular universities. The various pro-abortion scandals at Notre Dame that we have discussed are an example of what happens when a Catholic university hosts an event that is not in line with Catholic faith or morals. When challenged for this, the school can (and in fact Notre Dame did) easily appeal to a standard *other than* fidelity, whether it be academic freedom, diversity, inclusion, or some other metric. By forming more intentional bonds along the model of the Association of Catholic Colleges and Universities or similar organizations, the faithful schools could institutionalize standards of faithfulness. Their shared vision would increase accountability and increase positive pressure in support of orthodoxy.

This collaboration could go beyond accountability to also create a more dynamic environment for the schools that would enrich those areas of intersection where each lives the Catholic vision of the university. There are many respects in which the modern world of higher education has become dysfunctional and unjust — and uncatholic systems have become baked into the institutions. We will take a look at how the faithful few could fix academia's problematic approach to women and the family, for instance, as well as what some schools are doing to solve issues around tenure. There are many other areas in which a robust anthropology, along with Catholic social teaching, could create more just educational institutions.

First, what could these schools be doing to augment a more genuinely female-friendly academic scene? Secular universities make a big deal out of diversity quotas, and yet, as Catholic scholar Angela Franks recently wrote, academic institutions fail women by evaluating them according to a male standard, instead of valuing their contributions as women.[470] A major factor here is academia's enmity toward motherhood. As Franks attests, the simple fact is that it is incredibly hard for a woman looking to bear and raise children to advance in the academy. We spoke with a Ph.D. student at a Catholic university who recently found out she was pregnant, and the overwhelming response from the department to her exciting news was sourness and negativity. The academic timeline set by the academy pressures women to choose between having children and advancing professionally, and academic programs and tenure tracks are built around this assumption. The faithful schools would provide an incredible service to their institutions, to the Church, and even to the wider academic community at large if they developed systems that were pro-femininity, instead of following the secular model with its bad anthropology. Some of these schools are already doing that. Pregnant students at the Catholic University of America have support to help them choose life and continue their education, according to several individuals associated with pro-life efforts on campus. Founded in the fall of 2022, the Guadalupe Project aids pregnant students and student mothers by giving them vital resources such as diapers, childcare, maternity and baby clothes, and other support. It is named for Our Lady of Guadalupe, a Marian apparition in Mexico and the patron saint unborn babies.[471]

Likewise, Franciscan University has established Guadalupe House near campus to provide a safe haven and source of hope for pregnant students and their children. Invoking a Christ-centered approach inspired by the examples of Blessed Mother Mary and St.

[470] Angela Franks, "Why Does Higher Ed Throw Women Under the Bus?" *Church and Life Journal*, September 15, 2022, https://churchlifejournal.nd.edu/articles/how-and-why-universities-fail-women-and-what-to-do-about-it/.

[471] Gigi De La Torre, " 'Guadalupe Project' Supports Pregnant Students at Catholic University of America," The College Fix, June 23, 2023, https://www.thecollegefix.com/guadalupe-project-supports-pregnant-students-at-catholic-university-of-america/.

Joseph, Guadalupe House helps single moms move toward a new life of hopeful, independent, and healthy living and educates the broader Franciscan University community on the importance of fostering a culture of life. Pregnant mothers attending Franciscan are welcome to stay at Guadalupe House for up to two semesters.[472]

Beyond this, the faithful schools need to address the tenure crisis undermining academia, making sure it stops at their campuses. In our many conversations with faculty members on faithful campuses, the issue of tenure often emerged. And in most of these conversations, faculty have told us that the kind of job security that tenure provides — even on the faithful campuses — is necessary for their "academic freedom." But as I have shown in chapter 5, tenure can be destructive to the mission of a university when it lacks a Catholic understanding of academic freedom.

Tenure may no longer be a viable option for a faithful Catholic campus. Faculty could be hired on renewable contracts, with two-year contracts in the beginning, and five-year contracts once they have proven themselves to be faithful to the mission. The greater flexibility provided by this system would allow these colleges to improve the quality of the education students receive. It would also benefit the faculty members. Salaries would rise for faculty teaching on these campuses, as faculty would trade higher salaries for less job security. And they would have to perform well to be retained. As Stephen Prothero, professor of religion at Boston University said, "It would be so much different if there were a free and open labor market. People wouldn't be stuck for life in all kinds of cities they don't want to live in."[473] Talented faculty would find a number of possible openings if other Catholic colleges moved to extended contracts instead of tenure. Naomi Schaeffer

[472] "Guadalupe House," Off-Campus Housing, Franciscan University, https://reslife.franciscan.edu/off-campus-housing/.

[473] Riley, *Faculty Lounges*, 144–145.

Riley suggests that it would be akin to "introducing free agency into the major leagues.... It brought more flexibility to team managers and players, but it also made things much more expensive."[474] Faithful Catholic colleges like Christendom, Ave Maria, Thomas More, and Wyoming Catholic, as well as conservative secular schools like Grove City, West Point, and Hampshire, have been successful in recruiting stellar faculty members without offering tenure. And they offer higher salaries than those schools that offer tenure.

Rock 4: Creating a Catholic Studies Program

This recommendation continues building on the previous comment that the faithful schools are offering an increasingly rare and authentically Catholic education. Catholic Studies Programs (CSPs) are one of the most recent attempts to rekindle the rich Catholic educational ideal, drawing on roots from the nineteenth and twentieth centuries. Of course, some of the smaller, liberal arts-focused colleges are by their nature already embedded in this tradition. Thomas Aquinas College, Wyoming Catholic College, Christendom College, and Thomas More College all have highly developed liberal arts programs, inspired by John Henry Newman, Christopher Dawson, John Senior, and the like.

However, larger schools have to meet the diverse educational needs of their student bodies, and CSPs, usually offered as a major within the school, provide a vibrant Catholic education that is accessible to students in non-liberal arts programs. W. Scott Cleveland, who runs the CSP at the University of Mary, told us that they deliberately structure the program to be "flexible enough that students in a variety of situations can make it work."[475] It was designed to be taken as a double major, because of how many students the university has in the

[474] Ibid., 146.

[475] Interview with W. Scott Cleveland, May 11, 2023.

program (around 10 percent of the student body, according to Cleveland). This was the vision that inspired Don Briel when he founded the first CSP at the University of St. Thomas, Minnesota. Briel's program develops the Catholic educational tradition, and it was particularly inspired by Newman's philosophical text, *The Idea of a University,* and Christopher Dawson's historical work on Christian culture in the West.[476] Briel saw that an institution which fully incarnates the integrative ideals of the Catholic tradition is only feasible at "a relatively small Catholic liberal arts college. Catholic Studies is, in effect, a creative minority, a college within the larger university."[477] All of the schools which have a fully integrated education are small, with no more than five hundred fifty students. However, as demonstrated by the CSPs at University of Mary and Ave Maria, as well as Franciscan University's Humanities and Catholic Culture undergraduate major and its master's in Catholic Studies, a larger university can host a program that provides an excellent, integrated education in Catholic studies.

An additional benefit for a school hosting a CSP is its ability to prompt innovation and exploration within the university. A CSP provides a premier place for crossover and exchange between faculty. University of Mary stresses the importance of engaged and former faculty in the guiding document for its CSP: "The integrity of the program is not secured by the curriculum but by the faculty's grasp of and living of the Catholic intellectual and spiritual tradition, and by their capacity to transmit it to the students entrusted to them."[478] A school

[476] Matthew T. Gerlach and R. Jared Staudt, "Introduction: Catholic Studies and the Renewal of Higher Education," in *Renewal of Catholic Higher Education: Essays on Catholic Studies in Honor of Don J. Briel,* ed. Matthew T. Gerlach (Bismarck, ND: University of Mary Press, 2017), 5.

[477] Briel, "Reflection on Catholic Studies," 34.

[478] "Key Aspects of the Catholic Studies Program," University of Mary, 4, https://www.umary.edu/sites/default/files/2021-10/KeyAspectsOfCatholicStudies-82119.pdf

that provides a program of this kind that unites faculty will not only benefit the students; it will also give the faculty opportunities to grow through an active engagement with adjacent disciplines. This benefit has been given the sociological label "serendipitous creativity," and it describes the overall enrichment that comes from placing intelligent people from disparate fields alongside each other.[479] In a CSP, or in any Catholic liberal arts program, the serendipitous creativity springs from the dynamic unity of truth, which scholars from varying disciplines can explore together when given the opportunity.

For example, at Franciscan, there is a new interdisciplinary course that is cross-listed in sociology and philosophy on the great Catholic novelist Walker Percy's philosophy of the human person. Bringing together one professor's expertise in sociology and her colleague's mastery of philosophy, the course will examine the texts of Walker Percy at the intersection of sociology, anthropology, and philosophy. Students will examine both Percy's philosophy of language and his dyadic science of man, reading his work within the larger intellectual contexts of the philosophy of Husserl and the psychology and sociology of Solzhenitsyn. This is the sort of class which can only be fully taught from an interdisciplinary approach; it is this sort of class which allows students to get a rich exposure to the Catholic intellectual tradition. An ideal CSP program would find ways to bring professors together for cross-sectional studies in Catholic culture, creating fruitful partnerships between, for example, theology and biology professors, between history and psychology professors, and between philosophy and sociology professors.

Franciscan University's master's in Catholic Studies does exactly that. The goal of the program is to teach students to

[479] Cal Newport, *Deep Work: Rules for Focused Success in a Distracted World* (New York: Grand Central Publishing, 2016), 91.

> See the world with Catholic eyes.... It means seeing God's hand working in human history to save us, guide us, and lead us to Him.... It means seeing a world where art and architecture, food and literature, politics and psychology, poetry and sport can all be occasions for grace because they all can teach us about God and give glory to God.... It also means seeing the true, the good and the beautiful, understanding that to know the truth is to know God, to desire the good is to desire God, and to love the beautiful is to love God.[480]

Franciscan University's Catholic studies program offers an integrated Catholic vision of the world through an interdisciplinary program of study. Building on a foundation of four core courses in topics like Ancient and Medieval Catholic Culture and the History and Theory of Catholic Arts, students can also choose from a list of ten electives, such as The Works of Dante, The Natural Law, The Crusades and the Inquisition, and Catholic Social Theory and Practice.

Professor Andrew Jones, director of Franciscan's CSP, summarized best the value of any interdisciplinary CSP: "For a couple of centuries now, education has been dividing into increasingly isolated specialties. There is some good reason for this — when people can devote themselves to a particular discipline, say physics or history, they can make far greater progress in that particular area of study. But there is a trade-off. As the branches of knowledge become increasingly isolated from each other, often the end or the objective of knowledge itself becomes obscured.... Catholic Studies provides a unifying vision that ties together all the branches of knowledge."[481]

[480] "MA in Catholic Studies Program," Franciscan University, https://spt.franciscan.edu/programs/ma-in-catholic-studies/

[481] Emily Simpson Chapman, "Through a Catholic Lens," *Franciscan Way Magazine*, Winter 2021, 24–25.

The aim of Catholic Studies at Franciscan, according to Professor Jones, is "for people to leave the program viewing the world as a Catholic in a Catholic way. Many of us can be profoundly sincere in our Catholicism, but because we've all been trained in modernity, our faith is all too often sealed off in this little compartment.... We want our graduates to look at the world and see the world seeking Christ and Christ answering that search."

Franciscan's CSP director knows that such programs do not only belong at heterodox schools, as isolated bastions of sanity, or what Keating described as "ghettos" within the larger system.[482] Rather, they should be refreshing educational fountains that overflow with the rejoicing that comes from discovering the Goodness, Truth, and Beauty in creation, cultivating a love of wisdom in the hearts of students. These programs can serve the campuses of the faithful schools by holding them accountable to their educational mission and by inspiring those on the peripheries of the programs with the joy of learning.

Conclusion: Keeping the Light of Christ

In these last pages, it is fitting to recall the symbolism that the Easter Triduum — particularly the Easter Vigil — holds for the Christian life. The hushed church, shrouded with the darkness of forty days of Lenten penance, is suddenly shattered by a chant from the narthex: "*Lumen Christi!* The light of Christ!" As the light of the Paschal candle slowly processes down the darkling aisle, beams of light begin radiating out across the pews as the faithful's candles are lit in turn. The rhythm of the ritual seems to bring to life the command of the ancient liturgical hymn, "Awake, O sleeper, and arise from the dead, and Christ shall give you light" (Eph. 5:14).

[482] Keating, "Who Killed the Catholic University?"

This book has told the stories of those few institutions that have kept the light of Jesus burning in the towers of higher education, handing it down from generation to generation. It is a story of institutions often wrapped in a Lenten darkness but punctuated by moments of great grace and light. Pope John Paul called the university a "primary and privileged place" for bringing the transcendent message of Christianity to the culture.[483] He also described his "well-founded hope for a new flowering of Christian culture," inspired by the Catholic universities he saw around him. I have written this book inspired by a similar hope. I have also written this book as a tribute to all those, some still living, many now deceased, who gave up everything to keep the flame of Catholic higher education kindled. These countless men and women believed in the intellectual and evangelical mission of Catholic universities, and they underwent immense adversity to preserve that mission in all its vitality.

One of the primary barriers preventing many Catholic universities from offering an authentic Catholic liberal arts education is the historicist view that truth cannot transcend the limitation of the time and culture in which it is communicated.[484] Many schools fell by the wayside because they faltered in their belief of the truth of Christianity's irreplaceable mission in the world. The gospel offers the unique and universal truth, and Catholic universities must teach from the stable center of this truth. The faithful schools must maintain confidence in what is their own, preserving "deference to their tradition" built upon "the ability to read their own books well."[485] Catholic universities are supposed to connect students to what Alasdair MacIntyre described as

[483] *Ex Corde Ecclesiae*, no. 43.

[484] J. Brian Benestad, "Liberal Education: Ancient and Modern Perspectives," in *Jerusalem, Athens, & Rome: Essays in Honor of James V. Schall, S.J.*, ed. Marc D. Guerra (South Bend, IN: St. Augustine's Press, 2013), 351.

[485] Benestad, "Liberal Education," 362.

the long conversation that Catholics have been conducting for millennia. In his book *God, Philosophy, Universities,* MacIntyre writes that he was inspired by the need for Catholic laity to understand the long, rich tradition of Catholic philosophical thought, "a continuing conversation through centuries, in which we turn and return to dialogue with the most important voices from our past, in order to carry forward that conversation in our own time."[486]

The faithful schools are resting points in the long corridor of history, rooms that students can enter and stay awhile. Here they can pull up deep armchairs next to roaring fires, and, supported by their nourishing mother — alma mater — listen and slowly learn to understand the Catholic conversation. Our culture suffers from mass amnesia, and if these schools fail to awaken their students to the collective memory and love of the Good, there are few else who will. There must be a fervor that sustains us, as we realize that what is being handed on through the educational tradition is precious beyond measure. It prepares students not just to live the good life, as the ancients thought, but to live it in such a way as to merit eternal life, to "not be conformed to this world but be transformed by the renewal of your mind" (Romans 12:2). Catholic education, at its heart, is a love affair, a kindling of desire for the eternal things, seen in and through the fields of study. It was St. Augustine who spoke most movingly of this passionate romance that is a renewal of the whole person:

> Think of ordinary human love; think of it as the hand of the soul. If it is holding one thing, it can't hold another. To be able to hold something it's given, it must let go of what it is

[486] Alasdair MacIntyre, *God, Philosophy, Universities: A Selective History of the Catholic Philosophical Tradition* (Lanham, MD: Rowman & Littlefield: 2009), 1.

> already holding.... God says to you, "Here, hold what I am giving you." You are reluctant to let go of what you were holding already; you cannot receive what is being offered you.... Do not remove cupidity or desire, but change it.... *Transfer your love.* Break your fetters to earthly goods; bind yourself to the creator. Change your love, change your fear. Only good and bad loves make good and bad morals.[487]

While the faithful schools continue their mission of transferring our love from things of earth to a longing and a love for the perfect happiness promised in Heaven, God will reward their faithfulness.

It is easy to feel bleak, looking at the state of modern culture and particularly at the decomposing state of higher education. It is tempting to think that all the battles have been lost—all the ones that mattered, anyway—and that the secularization of society and of our schools is a fait accompli. Indeed, it is possible that, from a sociological point of view, the battle has been lost. The faithful colleges and universities are too few and too small to make much of a difference. This bleak feeling of loss is aptly expressed by these stanzas from Chesterton's *Ballad of the White Horse*:

> But you and all the kind of Christ
> Are ignorant and brave,
> And you have wars you hardly win
> And souls you hardly save.
>
> I tell you naught for your comfort,
> Yea, naught for your desire,
> Save that the sky grows darker yet
> And the sea rises higher.

[487] Quoted in Benestad, "Liberal Education," 364.

> Night shall be thrice night over you,
> And heaven an iron cope.
> Do you have joy without a cause,
> Yea, faith without a hope?[488]

However, as I have constantly sought to illustrate, God does not see as humans see. God chose one-hundred-year-old Abraham to father a nation. He chose David, the smallest child of Jesse, to be a king. And He chose the teenage virgin Mary to bear His Son. That same God chose a lawyer to redeem Franciscan University, a pizza mogul to start Ave Maria University, and a penniless historian to found Christendom College. The pattern that unites all these figures is not their strength, wealth, or wisdom, but rather their willingness to say yes to His plan. The hope that inspired us in the writing of this book and that caused Pope John Paul to prophesy of a new flowering of Christian culture is not borne from particular signs of worldly success, but rather is founded on the person of Jesus Christ and on His promise that we would not remain in darkness. "The light shines in the darkness, and the darkness has not overcome it" (John 1:5). The same light burns in the lamp of each faithful school today, and, by God's grace, the darkness has not overcome it.

[488] G. K. Chesterton, *The Ballad of the White Horse*, bk. 1, available at Project Gutenberg, https://www.gutenberg.org/files/1719/1719-h/1719-h.htm.

Sirach 51:13–30

While I was still young, before I went on my travels,
I sought wisdom openly in my prayer.
Before the temple I asked for her,
and I will search for her to the last.
From blossom to ripening grape
my heart delighted in her;
my foot entered upon the straight path;
from my youth I followed her steps.
I inclined my ear a little and received her,
and I found for myself much instruction.
I made progress therein;
to him who gives wisdom I will give glory.
For I resolved to live according to wisdom,
and I was zealous for the good,
and I shall never be put to shame.
My soul grappled with wisdom,
and in my conduct I was strict;
I spread out my hands to the heavens
and lamented my ignorance of her.
I directed my soul to her,
and through purification I found her.
I gained understanding with her from the first,
therefore I will not be forsaken.
My heart was stirred to seek her,
therefore I have gained a good possession.
The Lord gave me a tongue as my reward,
and I will praise him with it.
Draw near to me, you who are untaught,
and lodge in my school.

Why do you say you are lacking in these things,
and why are your souls very thirsty?
I opened my mouth and said,
Get these things for yourselves without money.
Put your neck under the yoke,
and let your souls receive instruction;
it is to be found close by.
See with your own eyes that I have labored little
and found for myself much rest.
Get instruction with a large sum of silver,
and you will gain by it much gold.
May your soul rejoice in his mercy,
and may you not be put to shame when you praise him.
Do your work before the appointed time,
and in God's time he will give you your reward.

About the Author

Dr. Anne Hendershott is Professor of Sociology and Director of the Veritas Center at Franciscan University in Steubenville, Ohio, and serves on Ave Maria University's board of trustees. She is the author of *The Politics of Envy* (Sophia Institute Press), *Status Envy: The Politics of Catholic Higher Education, The Politics of Abortion,* and *The Politics of Deviance* (Encounter Books). She is also the co-author of *Renewal: How a New Generation of Priests and Bishops Are Revitalizing the Catholic Church.*

Sophia Institute

Sophia Institute is a nonprofit institution that seeks to nurture the spiritual, moral, and cultural life of souls and to spread the gospel of Christ in conformity with the authentic teachings of the Roman Catholic Church.

Sophia Institute Press fulfills this mission by offering translations, reprints, and new publications that afford readers a rich source of the enduring wisdom of mankind.

Sophia Institute also operates the popular online resource CatholicExchange.com. *Catholic Exchange* provides world news from a Catholic perspective as well as daily devotionals and articles that will help readers to grow in holiness and live a life consistent with the teachings of the Church.

In 2013, Sophia Institute launched Sophia Institute for Teachers to renew and rebuild Catholic culture through service to Catholic education. With the goal of nurturing the spiritual, moral, and cultural life of souls, and an abiding respect for the role and work of teachers, we strive to provide materials and programs that are at once enlightening to the mind and ennobling to the heart; faithful and complete, as well as useful and practical.

Sophia Institute gratefully recognizes the Solidarity Association for preserving and encouraging the growth of our apostolate over the course of many years. Without their generous and timely support, this book would not be in your hands.

www.SophiaInstitute.com
www.CatholicExchange.com
www.SophiaTeachers.org

Sophia Institute Press is a registered trademark of Sophia Institute.
Sophia Institute is a tax-exempt institution as defined by the
Internal Revenue Code, Section 501(c)(3). Tax ID 22-2548708.